Joe Tait

It's been a real ball

Stories from a Hall-of-Fame
Sports Broadcasting Career

TERRY PLUTO
& JOE TAIT

GRAY & COMPANY, PUBLISHERS

CLEVELAND

Photos are from the author's collection except where noted.

Library of Congress Cataloging-in-Publication Data
Pluto, Terry
Joe Tait, it's been a real ball : stories from a hall-of-fame sports broadcasting career / Terry Pluto and Joe Tait.—1st ed.
    p. cm.
 ISBN 978-1-59851-070-6
1. Tait, Joe, 1937- 2. Sportscasters—United States—Biography. I. Tait, Joe, 1937- II. Title.
GV742.42.T37P56 2011
070.4'49796092—dc23
[B]
2011042082

Gray & Company, Publishers
www.grayco.com

ISBN: 978-1-59851-070-6

Printed in the United States of America
10 9 8 7 6 5 4 3 2

To my wife Jean, who taught me that
there is more to life than games.
— Joe Tait

To the memory of Don Robertson: A real Cavs fan
and an author who inspired me to write.
— Terry Pluto

Contents

Introduction

[BY TERRY PLUTO]

For years, people wanted Joe Tait to write a book.

I was never one of those people.

That's because Joe has been a close friend for nearly 30 years. He always told me that he'd never do a book.

"I don't want to do one of those tell-all things where you pick up the rocks and look for toads," he said. "And I also have seen what you've been through with some of your co-authors. I'm not sure it's worth it."

Most of my co-authors have been very good, but Joe's point was that a book can be a lot of work. He didn't need the headaches or the money. And authors of sports books that have a Cleveland-area market will never have to worry about being the next John Grisham and needing an army of accountants and tax specialists to figure out where to put the royalties.

Which is why I was stunned right before the start of the 2010–11 basketball season when Joe called and said, "I'm thinking about doing a book, are you interested?"

"Of course," I said. "But I need to know if you are committed."

Joe did a line about needing to "be committed" after doing nearly 40 years of Cleveland sports, mostly on the radio.

If any Cleveland-based broadcaster should do a book, it is Joe Tait. And not just because he is in the media wing of the Naismith Basketball Hall of Fame. He came to town in 1970 when the Cavaliers were in their first season. He called Indians games on radio, and later television, from 1973 to '87. He also called some minor-league hockey games, called some indoor soccer matches and was with the Cavs for 38 of their 40 seasons. No other broadcaster in Cleveland history has called more games than Joe Tait.

"I've been around a long time, but I've had a boring life," said Joe. "Bill Fitch said when the coaches would get together and start to tell stories about their play-by-play men, I didn't give him any material. He said I pretty much lived like a monk."

Joe also started to read some books done by other broadcasters, "and most of them seemed like the Tower of Babble."

But many of Joe's friends told him that he should write a book—and that it should be with me. As we talked about it, we realized that the book should not be in Joe's first-person voice. He "hated" that idea. I also thought the third-person approach with Joe at the center of the story would lead to a more in-depth look at Cleveland sports and Joe during his 40 years.

Joe and I had spent hours casually discussing our lives and careers over the years—especially in the eight seasons when I covered the Cavs for the *Akron Beacon Journal*. That involved a lot of time in hotel coffee shops, arena press rooms and in the car. But it wasn't until Joe discussed his early life for the book did I realize the complex relationship he had with his father, who never believed Joe would have any success as a broadcaster. At one point, Joe father's sent his son to a psychologist because Joe was spending so much time alone in his bedroom, playing sports board games and doing his own play-by-play. This book also reveals that a young Joe Tait was extremely driven to rise above the small Midwestern radio jobs and make it to a major-league market. He was even fired twice by small stations before being hired to do the Cavs. He actually kept all his rejection letters in a scrapbook, and some are quoted in this book. In his early years in Cleveland, Joe took every radio job he could find—trying to make extra money and increase his exposure in the market.

One of the strange experiences was to be riding in the car, talking to Joe—and then hearing Joe do a commercial on the radio. He just ignored it and talked over himself. He did listen to tapes of games about four times per year, checking his work. His former baseball partner, Herb Score, never did. Herb once told me, "I heard that garbage going out of my mouth, why would I want to bring it back in?"

Joe said he never planned any of the phrases that became his trademarks.

"The first time I said, 'Wham with the right hand' was when Hot Rod Williams did it in a game," he said. "I never recall hearing that phrase before. It just came out. [Producer] Dave Dombrowski told me after the game that 'Wham with the right hand' sounded good, and I should use it once in a while . . . and I did."

Many fans loved it when Craig Ehlo hit a game-winning basket against Utah during the Christmas season, and Joe said, "Yes, Virginia, there is a Santa Claus, and he comes from Lubbock, Texas." Ehlo is from Lubbock.

"I still have no idea where that came from," Joe said.

Joe is like a great basketball player who has several moves—but really doesn't know when he will use them. He just reacts to the action. One of Joe's favorite calls was "THREE BALL . . . GOT IT!"

"That also is something that I never heard before," he said. "The same with 'Left to right on the radio dial.' These things just came to me."

But when it came to baseball, Joe was shocked several years ago to discover how he had been influenced by Bert Wilson, who was a Cubs broadcaster when Joe was growing up.

"I heard some tapes of him, and I realized that he sounded like me," said Joe. "For him, every night was a beautiful night for baseball. He even said, 'Up on your feet' for the seventh-inning stretch. I didn't set out to imitate him, but it turned out that in some ways, I did."

Just as many area broadcasters have used Joe's cadence and some of his phrases when they call local high school and college games. Nev Chandler once said he used some of Joe's techniques when he did the Cavs on television for a few seasons. He did it "because Joe was the best that I ever heard."

Many fans will say the same.

"I don't look at it that way," said Joe. "I always saw my job as being the guy at the game who was there in place of the guy who wanted to be at the game. I wanted to reflect the excitement and enthusiasm of the game to the fans who wanted to be there—but couldn't. Doing a good job for them is what meant the most to me."

Joe always was a sportscaster first, a fan second. He kept the game at the heart of his broadcast, preferring to be the eyes and ears of the fans—and not engaging in a lot of opinion or analysis.

"Too many broadcasters do the games to show off what they know," he said. "How about giving the score, the time and who has the ball? And recap what has happened. Never assume people have been listening to most of the broadcast. It drives me nuts when I have a game on for 5 to 10 minutes, and they don't tell me the score."

In this book, Joe gives you the final score on what it was like to call games for 40 years in Northeast Ohio.

(Almost) Working on the Railroad

Most Cleveland sports fans know Joe Tait loves railroads. He collects books and pictures of trains. He reads train magazines. He loves to take photos of trains, especially those from the small "short lines." The more obscure, the better.

"Most of my relatives were in the railroad business," said Joe. "My father went back to Edinburgh, Scotland, and researched our family. He found that one of our great-great-grandfathers was an engineer helping George Stephenson build the first locomotive (at the age of 20, called "The Blucher," In 1814). More than once, I went down to the depot in Aurora, Illinois, with my dad, and he would introduce me to a relative who was the fireman or the brakeman or had some other job on the railroad. About every 10 days, I'd hop on the train and go into Chicago to meet my dad—and we'd take the train back to Aurora."

Joe's father was J.R. Tait, and he worked for Illinois Bell Telephone. While he was born in Evanston—the home of Northwestern University, near Chicago—the family moved to Amboy, Illinois, when Joe was 5.

"My father was always a little paranoid," he said. "I really believe we moved farther away from Chicago during World War II just in case the Japanese bombed the city."

After saying that, you'd expect Joe to laugh.

He didn't.

"When my dad died and we went through his stuff, we found something like 25 rifles in the house, all loaded," he said. "A couple had armor-piercing ammunition. He was convinced that sooner or later, the black folks from Chicago were going to come out to our pastoral scene and plunder, rape and rob."

*   *   *

Yes, the relationship between Joe and his father was . . . well . . . complicated. "He ran a tight ship, a real disciplinarian," said Joe. "I was a bit afraid of him. When he administered a spanking, you remembered it. It was always on the butt, never on the head. He spanked us with willow switches on the rear end. My sister and I had to cut our own willow switches. If we brought in a branch that broke, you had to go back outside and cut down a bigger one that wouldn't break."

Joe lived next door to his uncle's farm. There was a rule that he was not allowed to venture over a hill that led away from Uncle Allen's farm. One day, he was playing soldier with his sister Mary.

"She went over the hill and up the road to Ina King's house," said Joe. "She was an old widow. And for whatever reason, my sister went up to Ina's back door and yells, 'If you don't give me something to eat, I'm going to hit you with a rock.' Ina immediately called my father."

J.R. Tait nearly ran to his car and drove up the road. Joe said he and his sister hid in a ditch near the road. His father spotted them and ordered them into the car.

"He didn't lecture us, he didn't say a word," said Joe. "We got home, and he went out and cut the willow switches, and beat the crap out of our butts. Finally, my grandmother, who was living there at the time, came out and said, 'RICHARD, THAT IS ENOUGH!' He finally stopped because the one person in the world that he'd listen to was his mother."

Joe said he was about 10 when that happened.

"I just remember my rear end being so hot and red, you could fry an egg on my butt," he said.

*   *   *

When Joe was about 13, his mother wanted J.R. Tait to give his son "the facts-of-life" speech.

Joe remembered his father telling him to go into the basement. When father and son reached the bottom of the stairs, J.R. Tait said, "Do you know the facts of life?"

Joe said, "Yes."

He said, "Good."

That was the end of the facts-of-life speech.

*   *   *

When Joe Tait was 8 years old, he received this progress report from a teacher named Olive M. Randall:

> DEAR MR. AND MRS. TAIT:
>
> Joseph undertakes difficult problems with confidence. He expresses himself with ease when reporting, or making explanations before the class. He shows the ability to work independently for long periods of time. Most of the time, he's thoughtful and considerate of others. He has made many friends since enrolling in our school. He is willing to share worthwhile experiences with others.
>
> He thoroughly enjoys reading during class periods. He discusses what has been read independently, thus showing keen interest in the content. He has reported the reading of two books during his spare time. He has spelled correctly all the Friday spelling test and shows interest in arithmetic. He makes his figures and spaces his problems well.

When Joe was in the first grade, a teacher named J.D. Vay Bellows reported that he missed two days of school in the first system, seven in the second. He was never tardy. That was in 1943–44.

On April 27, 1945, Joe received an award for perfect attendance signed by S. H. Claire Flach Walker.

How do we know this?

Joe keeps these reports in his scrapbooks.

"I can be a bit anal retentive," he admitted.

*   *   *

Joe's grade school teachers gave him good
reports. (He can prove it—he still has those
reports in one of his many scrapbooks.)
Soon his young mind would begin to wan-
der toward sports and trains.

Joe has extremely neat handwriting, and he is like a human
spell-check. He always could spell but nearly flunked penman-
ship in the first grade.

"My mother made me practice my handwriting all that summer," he said. "It's been good ever since."

Laura Tait took her son to church every Sunday. Joe remembers a time when the pastor said he was going on vacation for a
few weeks, and there would be no services.

She stood up and delivered a stirring speech about "taking no
vacations from God," said Joe. "She said, 'Let's get someone in
here to fill in or have someone from the congregation do it. We're
not closing the doors of this place just because you're not here.'
They found someone to do the services."

Joe added, "My mother's religion helped her keep her sanity, especially being married to my dad. He never hit her, but it was a difficult marriage."

Joe also has a certificate that he "received a Christian Baptism on the 8th day of May in the Year of our Lord 1938 in the Oakton United Church of Evanston." He also has that in a scrapbook.

*   *   *

"Back when I worked on the family farm," Joe said, "one of my chores was to take the 'honey buckets' out from under the beds in the morning and dump them in a two-holer in the back."

It wasn't exactly honey; it was just that color. Hold your nose.

"During World War II, my grandmother sometimes would hand me a fishing pole and say, 'Breakfast is on the other end,'" said Joe. "Then I'd go down to the pond and catch fish. She'd cook them, and we'd eat breakfast."

*   *   *

"I loved sports, and I loved railroads," said Joe. "I used to wear railroad overalls, a railroad cap and have a pocket watch. I dressed like a railroad engineer when I went to high school. I'm sure some people there thought I was a little touched in the head."

Joe laughed as he talked about that.

He recalled his 50th high school reunion, sitting with Barbara Conway—and how she remembered him walking her home from school.

"Barb, after 50 years, I guess I can confess," he said. "I didn't walk you home for any reason other than the fact that the Elgin, Joliet and Eastern Railroad had a freight yard right across the street from your house. Once I deposited you there, I walked across the street and watched the trains."

She laughed and said, "You think I didn't know that? My mother and I would look out the window and watch you staring at the trains."

At Least He Could Talk a Good Game

Here's the good news.

Joe Tait scored a touchdown.

Once.

Despite himself.

Joe was rarely on the field, at least not when the verdict was in doubt.

"I got into a game when the score was 32-6," Joe said. "We had the lead and had been chasing the quarterback all over the field. On this one play, the kid went back to pass and threw a pass . . . it was really a desperation heave down the field."

Meanwhile, Joe had been knocked down, and just as he was getting up . . . well . . . here came the ball . . .

"I HAD to catch it," said Joe. "It was almost self-defense."

Joe paused, then added, "I could have dropped it. I thought about dropping it."

But the ball was somehow in his hands.

Suddenly, Joe heard his coach yell, "Run, Tait, RUN!"

"If ever there is a contradiction in terms, it's Joe Tait and the word . . . run," said Joe, laughing.

He caught the ball on his own 35-yard line, and huffed and puffed and wheezed and staggered and stumbled and rumbled . . . and somehow, stayed on his feet.

And somehow, no one caught him.

"You know when they say that someone was closing in for the kill?" said Joe. "I got to about the 15-yard line, looked back and it was like *everybody* on both teams was closing in on me . . . for

On the farm in Amboy, Illinois. "Obviously, the next Bob Feller,"
Joe said.

the *kill*. The guy with the best shot at me was the quarterback. I
guess the indignity of throwing an interception to me in a blowout inspired him to chase me. But then he took one look at my
blood-red face and my tongue hanging out . . . and he laughed . . .
and fell down. I mean, he just went down . . . and I staggered into
the end zone."

This was in junior high football.

It's not exactly like Irwin Shaw's classic short story, "The 80-

Yard Run," which actually took place in a practice. But the general truth lingers . . . so many of us who love sports have so few good athletic memories.

*   *   *

Most of Joe's football memories are like this one from junior high.

"I loved the game, I really did," Joe said. "But the coach was always on my butt because I didn't have the eye of the tiger. I just didn't enjoy hitting people, which is not a good trait for a defensive lineman. We were scrimmaging Elgin High, and the offensive tackle came up to the line of scrimmage and said, 'They're coming right at you.'"

Joe was confused for a moment, especially when the tackle didn't block him—rather, he stepped out of the way.

"Here came the fullback," said Joe. "And it was . . . BAM! He ran right into me. I was hanging on his legs for dear life and eventually brought him down. I came off the field, spitting dirt. I had grass in my helmet. I was a mess. The coach slapped me on the butt and said, 'Now that's what I expect on EVERY play, so get back in there.'"

Joe returned to the line, and the same tackle said the same thing, "It's going to happen again."

And the same thing happened . . . somehow, Joe brought the guy down.

"The coach again slapped me on the butt and said, 'Now you're playing football,'" recalled Joe.

Back to the line again . . . and the offensive tackle looked at Joe and said, "One more time."

"The guy with the ball hit me as hard as I ever had been hit in my life," Joe said. "I thought I was dead."

*   *   *

Another football story, this one from grade school. This one has to do with his mother and a clothesline. Joe was the defensive tackle. His belt on his football pants broke. As he went down in his football stance, he had one hand on the ground, another holding up his pants.

"After the play, we were in the huddle," said Joe. "My mother came on to the field, right into the defensive huddle. She had a clothesline and tied it around my pants to hold them up."

In the fifth grade, Joe was the biggest kid on the team at 5-foot-10, 185 pounds. When quarterback Eddie Mitchell dropped back to pass, he complained he couldn't see down the field because Joe was so big, he blocked his view.

"My parents thought there was something wrong with me because I grew so much, so fast," he said. "I had a doctor giving me shots to try to control my pituitary gland."

Joe said he played football through much of high school until his senior year.

"That's when I hurt my knee," he said. "The doctor told my mother that he could stabilize the knee and avoid major surgery."

Joe said his mother and the doctor went into another room, but he heard his mother say, "Doctor, fix him so he can walk, but don't fix him so he can play football again."

And that was the end of his football career.

*   *   *

"I was on our school's slow-pitch softball team," said Joe. "The bases were loaded. The score was tied. It was the last inning. The pitcher was wild and had walked some guys."

Before Joe stepped into the batter's box, the coach told him, "If you swing at one pitch, even one, I'll take you right out of the game. Just stand there and let him hit you."

Remember, this was SLOW-PITCH softball.

But the pitch did indeed hit Joe. And the winning run scored.

"That was in the fifth grade," he said.

*   *   *

Not long after Joe announced his retirement, he received a package from a childhood friend named Bill Nicholson. It was a baseball jersey. On the front were the words: OAK AVENUE

OWLS. On the back, it was TAIT . . . with his number 9. Joe looked at it and thought about when there were four neighborhood teams . . . the Owls, the Yellow Jackets, the Pirates and Giants.

"It was a Wiffle-ball league," he said. "The ball was really just a rolled-up ball of tape. We played in the backyard and had the whole field laid out."

It was a league without coaches, without umpires, without adults. It was just kids playing ball . . . in the backyard.

Pure as it can be when it comes to sports.

*   *   *

The backyard Wiffle-ball league once had a championship game. Joe asked his father to be the umpire.

"He called me out on strikes to end the game," Joe said.

Then he told the story of how he had to umpire his daughter's softball game. The real umpires didn't show. The coaches pressed Joe into duty.

"I was just there to watch the game, and they put me in," he said. "In the last inning, my daughter Karen came up with the winning run on base. I called her out on strikes, and she turned around and said, 'You only did that because your father did it to you!'"

*   *   *

So did the man who'd eventually be enshrined in the media wing of the Basketball Hall of Fame ever play basketball?

"I was on a high school team called the freshman/sophomore reserves," he said. "We played Saturday mornings at 9:30. The custodian used to leave the key by the door so we could let ourselves in. He didn't even want to watch us play."

Joe said there were 11 players. They played 5-on-5, meaning one guy was left out.

"That was me," he said. "I was uncoordinated, but then again, I also was slow. I had nothing to commend me to basketball. While they played, I'd go over to the next court and practice. Sometimes, I'd stand at half-court and shoot a long hook shot. Once in a while, it went in. Now, I'd win a million bucks if I did that at halftime of an NBA game."

Joe said that one day, the coach said, "I saw what you were doing over there. If you ever get into a game and try one of those, you'll never play again."

Joe thought, "So what? He's never put me in the game."

But the day came.

"We were losing, 74-28," he said. "The coach said, 'Tait, get in there.' I went in for Jerry Stroud. I sort of gravitated to the center circle, and the ball rolled to me. I picked it up. I heard the coach screaming. I didn't care. I heaved my hook shot and headed straight to the bench—never dreaming what would happen."

SWISH!

"It really was nothing but net," he said. "It really was from half-court. And the coach did take me out. And I never did play again. That was in my sophomore year at Elgin High."

Notice the details . . . Joe remembered the score. He remembered the player whom he replaced on the court. He could close his eyes and see a play from 60 years ago, the ball rolling his way, him picking it up and letting go with the hook shot that he had practiced for hours.

And the SWISH.

Joe admits to recalling very few details from Cavs games of the last 20 years . . . but he could remember that game. Just as he could name all four teams from his Wiffle-ball league . . . he also could remember the name of the quarterback who complained that he was "too big" to see around, and the name of the fullback who ran him over.

*   *   *

The best games Joe played were in his imagination.

"I had this baseball game with a spinner—Jim Prentice Baseball," said Joe. "I used to sit in my bedroom with that game and make up lineups, keep stats and announce the game as it was being played. I did lots of play-by-play. I also made up one-man football games to play by myself in the backyard, and I'd announce those. I had my own set of rules. If you stepped on a certain leaf—you were tackled. Sounds ridiculous now, especially as I was doing play-by-play of my own games."

Joe's father was worried about his son.

"My dad thought my doing play-by-play of my imaginary games was a sign that I was unbalanced," said Joe. "He sent me to a child psychologist at a place called Mooseheart, which was a home for orphans run by the Moose club. They also had a child psychology department. My father paid to have me examined. They talked to me twice."

And?

"My father would never tell me what the psychologist said," said Joe. "But my mother finally did: 'The psychologist told your father that your only problem was that you obviously have a vivid imagination, and it centers on sports. There is nothing wrong with your son at all.'"

Joe was in high school when that happened.

"My father backed off after that," he said.

*   *   *

Joe doesn't talk much about the impact of all this. Consider that sports had to be frustrating for him. He was the kid bigger than anyone else, yet he couldn't really play. He had to know that other more physically gifted kids wished they had his size. His coaches didn't understand his lack of fire on the football field. His father had no interest in comprehending why his son would spend hours in his room, playing a baseball game and announcing it.

In fact, as Joe said, "My father thought I was a little deranged."

He laughed as he said it, but it had to hurt a gawky teenager who longed to please his dad, his coaches, his teammates—but found it so hard to do so. Joe was creating his own world, an escape from the harsh reality of some unmerciful coaches, an unfeeling father and a world of athletics that he so loved—but where he didn't quite fit.

Left photo: Joe (center) the high school reserve team. "Student athlete? That's putting it in the most generous terms," said Joe. "I was tall, but height didn't mean a thing." Right photo: At Monmouth College. "It was frustrating not to be good at any sport," said Joe. "I loved sports. I'd have loved to have had the talent to play them well. Sports broadcasting gave me the outlet that I never would have had as a player."

"When I was in high school, a friend and I would go to watch the Elgin baseball team in the Tri-State semipro league," said Joe. "There weren't many people in the bleachers, but we'd go into the far corner—as far away as we could get from anyone else. Then we'd do a play-by-play. On the way home, we'd critique each other. It was at a place called Wing Park."

*   *   *

"It was frustrating not to be good at any sport," said Joe. "I loved sports. I'd have loved to have had the talent to play them well. When I blew out my knee, I didn't quit the football team. I became the manager for the football and basketball teams in high school. I did the same at Monmouth College until I started broadcasting the games. First sportswriting and then sports broadcasting gave me the outlet that I never would have had as a player. Broadcasting became something that I knew I could do well, and that was important to me."

Catchphrases

My best friend and I listened to Joe's broadcasts since we can remember. We are now 24, and although Joe deservedly moved on, he's still a part of our everyday life. Our favorite phrase to still use? "Three balllllllllll . . . GOT IT." Whether we're watching a game on TV or playing in the driveway, there usually isn't a day that goes by that we aren't imitating Joe's 3-ball call in our homegrown Cleveland accents.

—*Ryan Mirabedini, Cincinnati, Ohio*

In my house, we would turn off the TV and go to the radio just to listen to Joe. "From right to left on your radio dial." (Back when there was a radio dial!)

—*Elia Freedman, Portland, Oregon*

I've been the public address announcer at Norton High School for the past seven years. From the first game I ever announced, I have given my favorite Joe Tait line at the end of each game, "Have a good night, everybody!" I don't do this to copy him but to honor him and the professional he is.

—*Phil Seenes, Norton, Ohio*

When I think of Tait, I always think of the Cavs, in their heyday in the 1980s, and Larry Nance or Ron Harper dunking while Tait excitedly proclaimed: "Line, to the lane, and WHAM, with the right hand!"

—*Joe Donatelli, Los Angeles, California*

From the early years: "Lenny upcourt with the left-hand dribble." And always: "Whistle . . . and what?" He had some directional shortcuts that I hadn't heard from other broadcasters before like, "Between the circles," which took me some time to figure out.

—*Ed Cohen, South Bend, Indiana*

During his brief description of a particularly lurid halftime show during a Cavs game, Joe wistfully fell into a light soliloquy about mid-game entertainment and ended it with a gentle reverie: "Kids and dogs. . . . You just can't lose with kids and dogs."

—*Robert F. Whitmer, Akron, Ohio*

As a kid growing up in Brunswick, me and my brothers and the other fellas in the neighborhood played "driveway basketball" almost every single evening after supper. We loved being Austin Carr or World B. Free or Walt Wesley. But no matter what, whenever any of us took a shot from the corner, the automatic line that was always said was: "Bingo Smith from the corner . . . (pause long enough for the ball to go in) . . . BINGO!!!" A classic Joe Tait line, repeated a dozen times a night, night after night after night. These days while living in Savannah, Georgia, and playing driveway basketball with my son, Alex, he loves hitting the jumper from the corner and shouting "BINGO!" Brings a smile from dad every time.

—*Joe Marinelli, Savannah, Georgia*

Even when we listeners can sense something annoyed Joe, he used his humor to turn it into radio material. . . . During a Cavs road game in 2008, he was given the usual "hard as a rock" folding chair. Maybe this was intentional for the visiting team press. So every now and then, the subject of Joe's numb behind would come up. He's so fluid in his delivery, he's calling plays in this crummy chair without missing a beat! "Mo brings it up to the halfcourt logo . . . passes to Delonte behind the 3-point

line . . . got it! 43–37, Cavs, and my butt is officially numb from this chair . . ."

—*Mike Krebs, Uniontown, Ohio*

I'm in my 50s now, but when we were younger, we always would turn on the game on the radio and try to determine if we were winning or losing by Joe's voice. To this day, I only buy DiGiorno pizza. My little tribute to Joe.

—*Bill Webb, South Euclid, Ohio*

As a kid, I loved to hear Joe Tait call Cavs games. I would mute the television and turn on the radio to listen to Joe Tait. During halftime of the games, my little brother and I would go outside, and we'd shoot hoops while announcing the moves just as Joe Tait would. My family could hear us yell things like "To the line, to the lane . . ." or, "Three ball . . . GOT IT!" This was a weekly occurrence for my brother and I, which I'm sure I'll remember years from now.

—*Paul Kebker, Holly Springs, North Carolina*

As I went to college to be a sports broadcaster, I would always begin my game broadcasts the same way Joe did: "It's basketball time at (fill in the venue here)!" It was the only way to start a game. And of course I would always sign off the way he did, too. I'll always remember his final broadcast words, and they are my wish to him as well, "Have a good life, everybody!" Joe was caring, class, honest and fun.

—*Josh Hooper, Mansfield, Ohio*

I don't think this is necessarily a catchphrase, but I loved when Joe Tait once said, at the tail end of a LONG road trip, "It's 43-35, and the Cavs have been on the road since Naismith invented the game."

—*Mike Fitzpatrick, Cape Girardeau, Missouri*

Growing up in the Youngstown area in the 1970s (well within earshot of WWWE), my brothers and I listened to Indians and Cavaliers broadcasts on a small transistor radio as Joe Tait brought us the action. We recorded some of those radio broadcasts on an old cassette recorder. Just snippets of key moments or random games. For years, we would replay those recordings to relive the excitement.

Here are my favorites:

After Campy Russell drained a rainbow from way out, Joe emphatically added above the crowd roar: "They picked that one up on radar at Hopkins [airport]!"

Starting every Indians broadcast with "It's a BEEEAAAU-UUTTTIFUL DAY for baseball!"

This one was recorded during a rather ordinary Indians game. Buddy Bell hits one "deep to right-center field, ball going all the way to the wall. . . . Buddy hustling around second, heading for third. . . . Here comes the throw . . . the slide . . . ball gets away, but Buddy won't go anywhere, he's flat on his back at third and safe, with a triple!"

—Don Sebastian, Columbus, Ohio

Working for Free

Once upon a time, Joe Tait had a dream. A big dream.

He wanted to be a sportswriter.

That's right, a sportswriter, not a sports broadcaster. Even though he broadcasted all those imaginary games to himself in his bedroom and backyard, this was the 1950s. The real source of news was the newspaper.

"I read it in the paper" means you learned it there first . . . and you could trust it. After all, it was in the paper.

Yes, there were radio reports, but the paper counted the most. It made the news official.

Television?

It was still in its infancy with a few channels in black and white. On the screen, everything seemed gray. Television was a strange-looking aerial on the roof which looked like a very inviting place for birds to land. Or it was a pair of wire rabbit ears on top of the TV. The connections could waver; the picture could turn wavy and fuzzy.

"My father never allowed a TV in his house when I was growing up," said Joe. "He didn't buy one because he thought they were too expensive . . . and after a while, they'd make them better, and they wouldn't cost so much."

Joe saw his first television when he was 12.

"I hid in the bushes," he said. "There were three other kids with me. We looked through the window of Tommy Dunkell's house. He had a round TV with the rabbit ears on top. I remember watching *Kukla, Fran and Ollie.*"

*   *   *

Joe does not own a computer. He has never even turned on a computer to find anything online. He had a cell phone . . . for a while. He only turned it on to make a call and then turned it off. He never checked messages on it.

Yes, he does have a television, and yes, it's a color TV with cable . . . not rabbit ears. He has a landline telephone. That's about as high tech as it ever will get for Joe.

Joe was a strong high school student, and he had scholarship offers to schools such as Northern Illinois. But none of them had journalism or writing programs. He went to Monmouth College in Illinois because they had a program with the University of Missouri, which had one of the top journalism departments in the country. The idea was Joe would spend three years at Monmouth and then do two years at Missouri's writing department.

At Monmouth, Joe wrote for the school paper and the yearbook. He volunteered in the Sports Information Department and wrote press releases that sometimes found their way into small local newspapers.

"I tell kids to do jobs not for money, but the experience," he said. "I wasn't paid anything by the SID department. Three papers used my stories—the *Monmouth Review Atlas*, the *Galesburg Register Mail* and the *Rock Island Argus*. None of them paid me, either. I didn't care, I was happy to get my work out there. Too many kids worry about what a job will pay rather than what the job can do for them in terms of experience."

Joe is often annoyed when students tell him they want to be a sportswriter or sportscaster but don't consider the idea of working for nothing. Or working long hours in a small town for a smaller paycheck. Or they have a sense of entitlement that because they had good grades in college and worked on the school paper or at the school radio station, the best stations and papers should throw open the doors and bow down as they enter.

Many students miss a good opportunity to make contacts working in the SID office, which puts you in close contact with media members covering events and stories. If you are aggressive and creative, you can make your own job.

Yes, some jobs are based on Who You Know. But you can work hard at getting to know the right people.

That's something Joe Tait did at Monmouth.

*   *   *

Joe said he liked to write. But he also loved to talk.

There was one radio station in Monmouth, WRAM.

"We were called 'The Pride of Prime Beef Country,'" Joe said. "It was a daytime station only. They gave me a 15-minute sports show at 5:45 p.m. We signed off at 6 p.m. My show—it had no name—was sponsored by Adelman Green Motors."

Joe was the manager for the Monmouth basketball team, and he'd also do play-by-play of the games into a tape recorder. The next day, Joe offered the tapes to the student center—which played his account over the loudspeaker.

"Not a lot of people listened," he said. "Most were members of the basketball team. I'd watch them listening to it . . . sometimes they laughed."

But what struck Joe was that those athletes cared about what he was saying . . . they were listening to the towel guy do the games on tape in the student center. He was worthy of their attention.

Joe approached the WRAM station manager about doing the Monmouth College football games. But Joe didn't ask to be paid for it. Rather, he said, "If we sell enough commercials, will you put the games on?"

Joe was making his own job.

The station manager agreed, "But make sure we make a profit." He meant that Joe must find a way to bring in more money for the commercials than it cost to put the games on the air.

"I found plenty of businesses around town who were willing to buy time on the games," he said. "The station manager got into it big time. He owned a single-engine Tri-pacer airplane, which would land in fields that were nothing more than cow pastures to do the games on the road."

Joe also was doing high school games. And the sports news show. And the commercials.

"I'd do a Friday night high school game into a tape recorder and play it back at 7 a.m. on Saturday," said Joe. "I also was the engineer, so I had to set it up at the station to get the tape on the air. Then I'd go down to the restaurant for breakfast or to get my hair cut. And people would talk to me about the game . . . and also tell me what they thought of the broadcast."

*   *   *

Joe had other jobs, the kinds of jobs that were a lesson about what he wanted out of life.

"I worked in a steel mill one summer, and that was tough," he said. "I worked at a plastic factory—no bargain there, either. The hardest one was when I had a job stirring those big metal corn bins. I stood on top of them and used a long pole to stir the corn so it wouldn't rot. It was hotter than hell."

His best summer job other than radio?

"I loaded trucks at a place where I could watch the trains go by," he said.

Joe paused.

"I disliked that work, that manual labor," he said. "I didn't want to just work 9-to-5, punching a clock, going home. I wanted more, but doing those jobs was good. It made me determined to do something else and also to appreciate the radio jobs that I did have."

*   *   *

"My parents were divorced when I was a junior in college," Joe said. "The incident that probably ended it was when my mother drove the car right through the back wall of the garage. They really got into it. Nothing physical, but my father could really lay into you with all the verbiage. I called a fraternity brother and asked him to come get me—I had to get out of there. I said, 'I'll pay you, I don't care how much. Bring your station wagon, empty it out, because I'm putting everything I own into it and going back to Monmouth.'"

Joe paused again.

Joe got started at the only radio station in Monmouth: WRAM—"The Pride of Prime Beef Country." For one promotion, a lucky listener won breakfast with the mayor. "We cooked the breakfast and broadcast right from the kitchen," said Joe.

"I didn't see either parent for a while," he said. "My dad did start to come to some Monmouth football games when I was a senior."

*   *   *

Doing those Monmouth games would change Joe's life, but it would take about 10 years for him to realize that.

The year was 1957.

Joe Tait was 20 years old.

Coe College had just hired a new basketball coach, a 23-year-old named Bill Fitch.

"I was still doing that daily 15-minute sports show, and I called up Bill Fitch," Joe said. "[Coe College was] in the same Midwest Conference as Monmouth. I don't remember why I had Fitch's home phone, but I did. I just called cold. I never had met Fitch.

His wife answered, she brought Bill to the phone and I taped an interview for the show."

Their next connection came in the fall when Fitch showed up at a Monmouth football game. Fitch had played football at Coe, and he was doing some scouting for the Coe football team. Joe interviewed Fitch again.

"Monmouth was horrible in football," said Joe. "Fitch would sit by me in the press box when I did the games on radio and Fitch was scouting. He used to kid me how I could make Monmouth 'the worst team I ever saw sound like Notre Dame.' I was very enthusiastic back then."

Fitch always said Joe could make a 66-0 blowout sound like a 6-6 tie.

Think about all of this for a moment.

Joe arrived at Monmouth with no media connections. He got to know people at the radio station, and talked them into giving him a 15-minute show . . . for which he was not paid.

Then he sold commercial time to put the football games on the radio.

Then he made a contact in Bill Fitch, a basketball coach who was scouting for the football team.

"I didn't know he was going to be a great coach," said Joe. "But the first time I interviewed him, I knew he was a great guest. I'd just ask him two, three questions, and he'd fill the time. Then I saw that he was a tremendous basketball coach."

And Fitch saw something in young Joe Tait, the broadcaster.

Oh, it's not true that Joe worked at the station completely for free.

"I was paid a dollar an hour to be the janitor," he said. "It was two hours a night, five nights a week—10 bucks."

But wait, his pay was cut.

"Once I got on the air a lot, the station manager said it was like going to school, and I should pay him," Joe said. "So he cut my janitorial pay from a dollar to 50 cents an hour—five bucks a week."

Trains

Joe never learned to drive until he went to college.

Think about that. Think about how most males can't wait to turn 16 so they can drive. Think about how driving represents freedom for many people.

"My father did try to teach me to drive when I was 16," he said. "As we pulled into the driveway, I hit the gas instead of the brake. I nearly hit the water pump. . . . My father grabbed the emergency brake and stopped the car just short of it."

Joe laughed.

"That experience was like being taught how to drive a tank by General George Patton," he said. "Not a lot of patience."

Joe thought he'd just forget driving for a while—it was not something he longed to do.

"As a little boy, I'd stand in the barnyard in Amboy [Illinois] and stare at the tracks," said Joe.

He meant train tracks. He meant a time when trains were powered by steam locomotives.

"From that spot on our farm, I could see the Illinois Central," said Joe. "The fireman would kick open the fire door and put in the coal. . . . You could see the flash at night. You'd hear the steam whistle."

Joe paused.

"For me, it really was the romance of the rails," he said. "The steam engine was like a beast, it was alive to me. The diesel engines today are not like that. But the steam locomotive . . . the steam pouring out, the whistle as he roared down the track . . ."

To Joe, that was freedom as much as hopping into a souped-up Chevy was to many of his friends.

If he wanted to drive anything, it was a locomotive, not a car.

"My father worked at the phone company, but many of my relatives worked on the railroad," he said. "In high school, I wore a railroad cap, railroad overalls, a red bandana and had a railroad watch. I was the only kid dressed like that, and despite my clothes, I was still voted vice president of my high school class."

Joe laughed at the memory.

"When I was real young, I liked the idea of Casey Jones," said Joe.

Joe then launched into "The Ballad of Casey Jones," a popular song when he was young:

> Come all you rounders if you want to hear
> A story 'bout a brave engineer,
> Casey Jones was the rounder's name
> 'Twas on the Illinois Central that he won his fame . . .

Joe knew all the words but had sung enough.

"Later, I learned that Casey was a bit reckless," said Joe. "He was running about eight hours late, and when he tried to make up time, he exceeded the speed limit."

As he roared into a town, he saw there was a train on the same track.

"He told his fireman, Sim Webb . . . 'Jump, Sim, Jump!'" said Joe. "Sim jumped and lived. Casey didn't and died in the crash."

According to Wikipedia:

> On April 30, 1900, [Casey Jones] alone was killed when his passenger train, the 'Cannonball Express,' collided with a stalled freight train at Vaughan, Mississippi, on a foggy and rainy night. His dramatic death, trying to stop his train and save lives, made him a hero. He was immortalized in a popular ballad sung by his friend Wallace Saunders, an African American engine wiper for the IC.

The "IC" is the Illinois Central, the line that ran by Joe's home in Amboy, Ill.

"My favorite railroad lines are short lines," said Joe. "They are feeder lines that go from a main line to various businesses." He has about 300 train books and subscriptions to four train magazines.

"When I was growing up, I never wanted a job on the railroad because I knew they were in trouble," said Joe. "They were laying off a lot of people. Railroads themselves were changing. They came back, but that took years."

Joe said his love of trains has never left, although he misses steams engines, which have been replaced by diesels.

"And the caboose," said Joe. "I used to ride in a caboose from Amboy to the defense plant, then switch at the defense plant, taking the caboose back to Amboy. It was a 10-mile trip."

Joe loves to prowl old railroad yards and once in a while, "You find some decrepit caboose . . . I miss them!"

During the 1930s and the Depression, men looking for work slipped into freight cars going . . . well, they weren't sure . . . but they were going somewhere, and maybe it would be better there. The same with some kids running from home, they would jump a train and just go.

It was an early version of the Bruce Springsteen songs such as "Thunder Road," where people just drive off into the night . . . somewhere.

Joe loves Harry Chapin's music, especially the song "A Better Place to Be" about a night watchman at a place called "Miller's Tool and Die" where he "watches the metal rusting and the time go by." For Joe, he could imagine the guy being a night watchman at an old railroad yard with the old steam locomotives and cabooses just sitting there, forgotten relics of another age.

"My favorite railroad lines are short lines," said Joe. "They are feeder lines that go from a main line to various businesses. For example, there is the Ohio Central out of Sugar Creek that goes to Clinton and hooks up with the main CSX. They haul grain and mixed freight."

Joe collects pictures of short line locomotives. The smaller and more obscure, the better. He has about 300 train books, has subscriptions to four train magazines—he says the best is simply called *The Shortline*. He loves to read the history of trains . . . it takes him back to those days when he was a boy staring at the Illinois Central . . . going somewhere into the night. Or the boy, hopping onto the caboose, pretending he was heading farther than the defense plant—and then back home. Or the teenager in the Casey Jones outfit who found his own way of being different in school.

"My wife [Jeannie] and I took a train trip from Cleveland to Chicago, and then on to Las Vegas," he said. "I enjoyed sitting in the room at night, looking out the window at all the little towns going by—places like Benkelman, Nebraska. That was the home of Ward Bond, a classic character actor. He was in most of the John Wayne movies."

So why did Joe learn to drive?

"I dated a girl in college who had a Buick," he said. "She taught me. She thought it would look better if I drove when we went out."

What did his dad think of that?

"He was glad I learned," Joe said. "He gave me one of his old cars when he decided to buy a new one. He used to tell people that he never had to worry about me getting hit by a train because I'd come to a crossing and sit there for an hour, waiting for one to come by."

Influenced by Joe Tait

[FANS WRITE IN]

One of the greatest nights of my life was sharing the Cavs' first-ever trip to the NBA Finals with Joe in 2007. Saturday night, June 2nd, at The Q. I was working for the opposition, the Pistons, as their radio pregame and postgame host. I got the chance to sit in "The Perch," just two seats away from Joe.

As a native Clevelander and longtime Cavs fan, I had to admit I was torn. The Pistons are my employer, and the more they win, the more I get to work and enjoy a run to the NBA Finals again. But I wanted to see history, and I wanted to see Joe finally get to the biggest stage.

Fast forward to the fourth quarter and the Cavs clinging to a one-point lead. Daniel "Boobie" Gibson hit back-to-back 3-pointers, and the crowd at The Q went crazy!

The Cavs were ahead by six points, and the Pistons called a timeout. I leaned back in my chair, and I looked at Joe. He looked at me.

I said, "Joe, this is it, brother! Are you going nuts?"

In classic Joe Tait fashion, he takes off his headset and answers back, "Matthew, win or lose, I get to go home in 10 minutes and 45 seconds, and this is just another ballgame."

He then resumed his spot at his table next to his mini lamp and continued to call the action. The Cavs were not going to be denied. Gibson hit another triple, and then the Cavs were up, 83-71. The dagger 3-pointer had the crowd in a frenzy.

Timeout, Pistons.

I could not help myself. I leaned back in my seat again, looked to the right and made eye contact with my idol. We smiled at each other, and I said, "Come on, man, admit it—this is awesome! You are going to the Finals, Joe!"

I didn't know what Joe would say. Would he acknowledge the moment? He looked to his right and then his left, almost to make sure that nobody was creeping in on our conversation. I waited for a response.

Joe then nodded his head in approval and says, "OK, you got me. This is pretty neat!"

That was all I needed to hear. It was so special. I was so happy for him, and I felt so lucky and honored to be able to share that moment with him. The Cavs won, and after the game, Joe even donned an Eastern Conference Champions hat.

—*Matt Dery, Royal Oak, Michigan*

In 1966–67, Joe gave his protégés at Ohio University assignments to cover various team sports for the Bobcats. I remember being assigned the Ohio U. wrestling team with coach Harry Houska, a Cleveland native. I didn't know anything about wrestling but sure learned in a hurry. He also assigned me to the 6 a.m. sportscast on a daily basis. That was nice—waking up at 5 a.m. Joe would listen to tapes and make his critique. With FM radio still a passing thought in those days, Joe gave us the OU freshman football and basketball games to broadcast as well as plenty of high school action in both football and basketball.

Joe was also able to experiment covering lots of sports that you would never hear on radio back then. We covered the track meets, lacrosse games and created opportunities for great learning experiences that helped us all in our broadcast careers. I do remember Joe creating a post-football scoreboard show that I anchored. We were able to put our own twist into the show.

Joe gave me great advice when I became the sports anchor on WFMJ TV in Youngstown. Work hard, meet and greet as many people and coaches, and get involved in the community. I did just that. He also said when people criticize you, make sure they spell your name right. I use that philosophy today in my radio career.

—*Art Greenberg, Akron, Ohio*

Over the past few years, my mother has baked her famous chocolate chip cookies for Joe. I delivered them to him at his perch personally before Cavs games. The cookies are actually really fantastic and, during the broadcast, Joe made it a point to sing my mother's praises. A few weeks after this tradition began, my girlfriend wanted to get into the act, so she baked peanut butter squares. As always, I delivered them to Joe pregame, but noticed that he didn't mention her or her squares the entire night. About a week later, Joe was approaching in the hallway near the Cavaliers locker room. As he got closer, I asked, "Joe, what did you think of my girlfriend's peanut butter squares?"

Without breaking stride, Joe smiled and said, "I hope she's good-looking."

—*Joe Gabriele, writer for Cavs.com, Rocky River, Ohio*

I first met Joe Tait as a high school student-athlete in the early 1990s, when he was the emcee at the Medina County Sports Hall of Fame/Awards ceremony—which he continues to do to this day. Later on, early on in my career in sports public relations, I worked for the Cavs and got to work with Joe on a regular basis. I loved his honesty, sense of humor, approach and work ethic, even in the midst of one of the worst seasons of all time (2002–03). Most of all, I loved how he made me feel welcome and asked how I was doing—be it during a home game or on a Cavs road trip. I'll never forget the conversations we had regarding his interests in trains, history and the best places to eat in NBA cities. He went out of his way to take me to breakfast before shootaround, and was simply a class act in his own way.

—*Karen Kase, Medina, Ohio*

I had the pleasure of working with Joe for many years as one of his radio engineers. I now live in Chicago, and when Joe would come to town for the Bulls-Cavs game, we would usually get together for a bite to eat. One evening, I picked up Joe, and we went back to his hometown of Aurora, Illinois. As we drove down the streets of the town, I only wish I had a tape recorder with me.

Joe showed me where his old house was. He showed me where the old fish market was where his mother use to have him pick up fish for his family fish fry on Friday nights. We came to a street corner, and he said this was where he broke his foot and had one of his worst summers as a kid because he had to wear a cast and couldn't play in ballgames.

Since it was so long ago, I asked Joe if he had a job lighting the candles in the street lights, too. We had a good laugh. On the way back, Joe said he knew a short cut, soooo, I took his advice and ended up in a huge housing development big enough to look like a city itself!

Joe said, "Well, it USED to be all cornfields here. I guess it was longer than I thought since I came this way."

—*Steve Foltin, Darien, Illinois*

I was working in radio in Bellevue, Ohio, back in 1975 when we hired a kid part time who had graduated from high school in Streetsboro. He had told me time and time again he knew Joe Tait, which, of course, I didn't believe. We went to a Tribe game together. My friend said, "C'mon let's go meet Joe—I'll introduce you." He then headed up to the booth. I thought for sure we were going to get bounced from the stadium. We got up there, and I'll be damned, he did know Joe Tait, who I found to be very genuine and friendly during that short meeting that I've never forgotten.

By the way, our part-timer was Vince Koza, who graduated from Ohio University and was sports director at a TV station in Lima, Ohio, for some time.

—*Tom Goodsite, Kirksville, Missouri*

I am the radio voice of the D-League's Erie Bayhawks. Back in the summer of 1977, I was a 10-year-old Indians fan living here in Erie. I listened to every game on the radio, as telecasts were only occasional in those days. In June or July, the Tribe sent Ron Pruitt down to AAA. I was incensed because, for some reason, I thought he was a valuable piece. So I wrote a letter to Joe in search of an explanation.

A few weeks later, I received a detailed, handwritten letter from Joe that was written on stationery from the Anaheim Hilton. He explained the "option process" and pointed out that Pruitt still had options remaining while other candidates did not.

Recently, I met Joe before a Cavs game and related the story to him, asking him if he recalled it.

He told me he didn't remember what he had for lunch that day.

Good guy.

—Chris Hughes, Erie, Pennsylvania

I was working at WSWR Radio in Shelby, Ohio, as the sports director. We were a small-time station, trying to be a big boy in the Mansfield market. The station was a member of the Cleveland Cavaliers Basketball Radio Network. The time frame was 1989 to 1992. What always impressed me was that when Joe Tait and Dave Dombrowski made their yearly visit to Shelby, Ohio, Joe always treated us like we were the most important radio station on the network. He didn't show up with an attitude that "Joe Tait has entered the building." Joe and Dave gave us respect and showed us true appreciation for the work we did to promote the Cavaliers. It was a great lesson for me!

—Michael Reinhart, New Riegel, Ohio

I had the privilege of broadcasting two high school basketball games with Joe in the 1990s for WLKR FM 95.3. We would talk by phone before the season, to see when he would be available to come to Norwalk, Ohio, for a broadcast. It was simply amazing. He would show up, sit in the broadcast chair and rattle off two quarters of play-by-play and two quarters of color commentary.

And of course, Joe being Joe, it sounded like he knew each of the players and coaches personally.

I'd like to note this—Joe would make the hour-long drive on his night off, in not-so-great weather, and wouldn't accept a dime. Not even for gas.

—*Scott Truxell, Sports Director, WLKR FM 95.3, Norwalk,*
Ohio

Spying on the Russians

OK, Joe Tait wasn't a real spy, but he did some sneaking around in Turkey.

"If I told you what we really did over there, I'd have to kill you!" said Joe. "I always wanted to say that!"

Joe laughed.

"I was in army intelligence," he said. "We listened to the Russians, and they listened to us. They had a submarine right off the coast near our base."

So they were spying on each other.

"I don't think either side found out much of anything that was useful," Joe said. "We heard them doing some military exercises, maybe moving some tanks around—nothing exciting."

Joe graduated from Monmouth College in 1959, and he joined the army in 1960.

"Back then, you either were drafted and lugged a weapon around for two years or you could enlist and supposedly get a better assignment if you did three years," he said. "I wanted to be in Armed Forces Radio."

This was 1960, when the U.S. and Soviet Union were in a duel for world domination. It was Democracy vs. Communism. It was the USSR engaging in a major European land grab. It was the Berlin Wall. It was two super powers with nuclear weapons. It was school kids hearing sirens and heading to the basement—drills in case the Russians dropped the bomb. It was a time when no one was sure who'd eventually win this struggle.

It also was when every male over the age of 18 knew at some point, he'd have to join the military or secure a deferment. But Uncle Sam wanted you, either after high school or college.

"I joined to get it over with," said Joe. "I wanted to go into

"Talk about a lean, mean fightin' machine," said Joe.
"When I got to basic training, I weighed about 200
pounds. The sergeant tapped me in the tummy and
said, 'Tait you've got a problem and I'm here to solve
it for you.'"

broadcasting, and I had a lot of experience from what I did at
Monmouth. I figured the army would give me more experience."

The army had other ideas.

"They had a two-year wait for Armed Forces Radio," said Joe.
"When the recruiter told me that, he suggested I check out the
guys 'on the third floor.' He said he didn't know what they were
doing on the third floor, but they were interested in college gradu-
ates with foreign language experience. So I went up to the third
floor."

He talked to different people, and they discovered Joe had four
years of Spanish.

An officer told Joe that he'd be a good candidate for the Army
Language School in Monterey, California. But the one language
that he certainly would not study was Spanish.

"We'll give you another language because we teach it differently," the officer told Joe.

Joe said he was in a barracks where there was a street with a
white line. The moment you stepped across that line, you only
spoke one language—Russian.

"All the instructors were Russian, some had escaped from
Russia," said Joe. "The head of the Russian department was a guy
whose uncle was a czar who had been machine-gunned during
the Russian Revolution. These guys all had great stories to tell, but
they'd only tell them in Russian. They immersed you in the language. You really learned it."

*   *   *

Joe was shipped to Sinop, Turkey, on the Black Sea.

"The military had to get permission to blow holes in the walls
surrounding the city because the entries were so small—army
trucks wouldn't fit through," he said. "It was an old city on top of a
hill that was a dormant volcano. There were ruins from a building,
a Roman fortress that went back to when Apostle Paul was there."

An old fortress had been converted into a prison.

"The families of the inmates had to bring them food and
clothes or else they didn't get any," said Joe. "The problem pris-
oners were put in the lower part of the building, right on the Black
Sea. Twice a day, the tide came in, and the guys had to climb the
walls to stay dry."

Anything else?

"They cooked with olive oil," he said. "The first two weeks, it
really cleaned you out."

*   *   *

"We had a guy in our unit named Steve," said Joe. "He was
Jewish. That was a real novelty for the Turks in that town. They'd
stare at him when he went to town. He was one of three guys who
ended up playing on the town soccer team."

*   *   *

That reminded Joe of this story of sitting next to a colonel when flying from Germany to Turkey to begin his assignment.

Colonel: "Where are you headed?"

Joe: "Sinop."

Colonel: "Ah, Sinop."

Joe: "Have you been there before?"

Colonel: "I was there once."

Joe: "How far is it from Ankara [the Turkish capital, where they were first landing]?"

Colonel: "About a thousand years."

*   *   *

"While we were playing softball and basketball in the army compound, they had Turkish soldiers there to guard us," said Joe. "They'd get bored and have bayonet fights. It was a grand old time for them, lots of cheering. The first guy to cut the other guy won."

Joe said they usually took the Turkish soldiers from southern Turkey (where St. Paul was born in Tarsus) and sent them to serve in northern Turkey. The soldiers from the north were sent south.

"In case there was an uprising or revolution, they didn't want the soldiers in a spot where they had to shoot an uncle or some relative," Joe said. "This way, if there was shooting, the hope was you'd have to shoot someone you didn't know."

*   *   *

"Most of the people there didn't like their pictures taken," said Joe. "They thought you were capturing their souls. But if they wore an amulet [a lucky charm], then it was OK to take their pictures."

*   *   *

What was the best part of his 13 months in Sinop?

"I started a one-watt radio station that could be heard all over the base," Joe said. "I rounded up some guys who'd had professional radio experience in the U.S., and we got the station going. After six months, I was no longer listening to the Russians, I was running the station full time."

Even while serving in the army in Turkey, Joe (left) couldn't get away from sports. Here, the Armed Forces Softball Association presides over the Black Sea Softball Championship. "I was manager and did play-by-play for the little one-watt radio station we had back on the base," Joe said.

Joe has some old tapes of softball games on the base . . . including one where he babbles for what seems like an eternity because a softball got lost in the weeds during a game, and it took them forever to find it. They'd forgotten to bring another ball.

"My news director was Charles Bierbauer, who later worked at ABC and CNN," Joe said. "His mother had connections with a print shop in Philadelphia, and she printed up a bunch of stationery for us—'KBOK, VOICE OF THE HILL.'"

*   *   *

"I really think young people should be required to do something after high school or college," said Joe. "Either the military or civil service. I know that after my three years in the army, I was really serious about settling down and getting a career going."

Joe Is the Morning Mayor...
Twice and Gets Fired... Twice

When Joe finished his three years in the army, he needed a job. He had a friend who remembered him from his days in Monmouth. That was Steve Bellinger, who had become the station manager in Decatur, Illinois.

Bellinger had been the owner and general manager in Monmouth, and he was willing to apply for a military deferment, claiming Joe was "necessary for his business operation."

But as the army recruiter told Joe: "You take that, and you are going to be with him for a long, long time. You are necessary for his operation."

Joe said: "I didn't want to be with him for a long time. I didn't want to stay in Monmouth for years."

He wanted to work in a major market, especially Chicago. He grew up listening to WGN, WLS and other Chicago stations.

"The farm where I spent some time was about 100 miles from Chicago," he said. "I grew up a Cubs fan, which I later realized was great preparation for being a broadcaster in Cleveland."

Joe sometimes acts as if he's a small-town radio guy who made it in the big time, but in his own way, he was very driven and ambitious. Consider how he created opportunities to broadcast games, everywhere from Illinois to Turkey . . . and now he was back in Illinois.

*　　*　　*

Bellinger had a job for Joe in Decatur.

He was "Jolly Joe Tait," the morning voice of WDZ. "Dee Zee Does It!" was the station's motto.

"SPORTSMAN CORNER"

– JOE TAIT –

On WJRL *1150 on your dial*
Thursday – 5:05 to 5:15 P.M.
Sponsored by
ACE PREMIUM & NOVELTY WHOLESALERS
March 1st, 1966

But there was nothing "easy does it"—working long hours for little pay—especially for a young man just out of the army with big radio dreams. Joe applied for an opening in Rockford at WJRL. The last three letters of the station were JRL for the man who owned it: John Rogers Livingston. Rockford was a larger market and closer to Chicago. When Bellinger heard Joe was looking for another job, he was very unhappy with "Jolly Joe Tait."

"He called me in and fired me," said Joe.

Bellinger believed Joe should have been more loyal because of their experience together in Monmouth, along with Bellinger hiring Joe when his tour in the army was over. Of course, Joe did most of the work for free in Monmouth and was paid a fistful of nickels and dimes in Decatur.

Joe recalled Bellinger also telling him: "Everyone should be fired twice. The first is for shock value. The second time is to make you realize that it may be your fault."

Joe sat there for a moment, just staring at him.

"Then I called John Rogers Livingston and told him that I had been fired," said Joe. "He said that he had a place for me."

One of a series of early jobs, at WBOW in Terre Haute, Indiana. "I'd cover anything," Joe said. "Believe it or not, here I am broadcasting an arm wrestling contest. I'm actually doing the play-by-play."

Joe became the "Morning Mayor of Rockford."

"I played music in the morning and did sports at night," he said. "I said things like, 'Here's Joe Tait . . . turning the tables on you.' Then I'd put on a record."

Joe paused.

"I did two terms as Morning Mayor of Rockford," said Joe. "I worked there twice."

*   *   *

Joe loves the Harry Chapin song "WOLD," about an aging disc jockey and talk show host who bounces from town to town.

"It's the theme song for those in small-town radio," he said.

He spent less than a year in Decatur.

He spent about a year in Rockford.

He went to WILO in Frankfort, Indiana . . . "Home of the Hot Dogs!"

"I was fired there on Christmas Eve," said Joe. "The owner

called me in and said there had been 42 people come and go in the six months that I was there."

Joe wasn't sure where this conversation was headed, but he didn't feel good about it.

The owner then said: "Only you and [news director] Dick Partridge are still here. I've got to believe it's your fault. You're fired."

This was firing number two, and Joe discovered himself leaning over the desk, his right hand on the station manager's throat.

"There was one of those old radiators on the wall, and I was so close to pounding his head into that radiator," Joe said. "I finally pulled back and asked him to give me my third-class license—you needed one of those to work at a station back then—and let me get out of there before I did something that would make both of us sorry."

That was in 1964, and Joe had been fired twice in less than two years since leaving the army.

But Rockford was willing to take him back, and he also did a television sports show in addition to the second term as Morning Mayor.

*　　*　　*

Joe later did three years at WOUB in Athens, Ohio, where he also taught broadcasting classes at Ohio University. He lasted there for three years.

"I couldn't handle the eggheads anymore," he said. "The academic types drove me nuts. This was the late 1960s, with Vietnam and all the student protests. I left in 1968. As I drove out of town, the National Guard showed up in full combat gear because the students had tried to burn down the bookstore. They also had set fire to the porch of the president's house."

His next stop was WIOK: "Serving the Twin Cities."

Not Minneapolis-St. Paul . . . it was Bloomington-Normal, Illinois.

He broadcasted Illinois State football and basketball games, and the Bloomington Bobcats of the Illinois Collegiate Baseball League. A local newspaper story reported: "Besides Bobcats baseball, Joe has lined up a 22-game football schedule, including all Illinois State games, home and road, live and direct. For roundball games, he has arranged to broadcast over 70 basketball games, including all ISU games, live and direct. . . . One weekend in September, he will have four football games in 40 hours . . . two college, two high school games."

Notice how nearly everywhere Joe went, he created opportunities for himself to broadcast games. He didn't wait for someone to ask—he found ways to make it happen.

*   *   *

He also was applying for jobs and being rejected.

Joe kept the letters in his scrapbooks.

One is from Darrel Jones, operations manager of Peoria's WMBD, "First in the Heartland."

"Your excellent tape background and tape are most impressive. However, it arrived about two weeks late as we hired a new sports director about one week ago."

This was from WLW in Cincinnati: "Thank you for your application for the position of Programming Director . . . we have had over 60 applicants and we finally have found the right man in Cliff Hunter of New York."

Rex Davis of KMOX in St Louis wrote: "Your tape was given a careful hearing by our entire Sports Department and the consensus was that it's 'pretty good.' But there is no sports opening here, and I do not see that possibility in the near future. . . . One complaint was that there was not enough variety in your delivery—especially in the basketball and football sequences. As they put it, you were 'always up' instead of a lower pitch, at times, which would increase the opportunity of a dramatic 'rise' when such is necessary. . . . It might interest you to know that Jack Buck thought your baseball was quite good."

This letter meant a lot to Joe, because Buck did the Cardinals on KMOX, and a major-market station did take him seriously.

"I came very close to getting a job in Chicago doing the Major Soccer League," he said. "It was at WGN in Chicago, and Jack

"I interviewed the oldest living harness race driver, at county fair in Indiana," said Joe. "He was 90 years old and still driving. I broadcast the race out of the back of a convertible."

Brickhouse was doing the games. He admitted knowing nothing about soccer. I had done soccer at Ohio U, and I sent them a tape. They invited me to Chicago."

He sat in the radio booth for a Cubs game with Vince Lloyd and Lou Boudreau. He went to dinner with Brickhouse, who said, "As far as I'm concerned, you've got the job."

Here it was . . . the big break . . . WGN . . . Chicago.

"As I was driving back to Ohio U, there was a sports report on the radio that the Chicago soccer franchise had been sold and moved to Kansas City," he said. "A few days later, I got a nice letter from Brickhouse saying he was sorry things didn't work out, and they didn't have any other openings."

Joe thought he had a job as a sports director at WCFL, a 50,000-watt Chicago station that billed itself as "The Voice of Labor."

"I was going to be hired to do 60- to 90-second blurbs on high school sports," Joe said. "Three days later, they were no longer 'The Voice of Labor.' They'd changed formats, and my job disappeared."

*   *   *

Between rejections and after a year in Bloomington-Normal, Joe took a job in Terre Haute, Indiana. It was at WBOW: "On the banks of the Wabash."

Joe did some high school and college games. He was interim station manager and was doing some pregame and postgame shows for the Indiana Pacers of the old American Basketball Association.

At this point, Joe was 33 and had a sense that he'd never make it to a major market. He had done everything from being a morning disc jockey to selling and reading advertisements to being a program director to being an engineer to broadcasting nearly every sport.

He had started at the bottom and worked his way up to the middle of the radio markets in the Midwest.

One day, he was reading the Terre Haute paper and noticed Bill Fitch had been named coach of the Cleveland Cavaliers, an NBA expansion team. Joe decided to write him a note, congratulating him on the new position.

"I always knew you'd make it in the big time," wrote Joe. "By the way, if you ever need anyone to do for the Cleveland Cavaliers what I did for those Monmouth Fighting Scots (66-0), let me know. Ha! Ha! Ha!"

Then Joe said, "I mailed it and forgot about it."

He had not seen or talked to Fitch since 1960. It was 10 years later. He wasn't even sure if Fitch would remember him.

Sitting Behind Joe

[BY ANDRE KNOTT]

My friends and I all tried our best to do our best Joe Tait impersonation anytime we played hoops in the backyard. As I finished up
school and dreamed of being a media member in my hometown,
the first thing I wanted to do was meet Joe Tait. I wanted to ask
him, "How do you 'make it' in this business?"

I was working part-time at WKNR right out of school, and as
thrilled as I was to be "in" the business, I was broke and still deliv-
ering pizzas so I could actually pay rent. A friend, Joe Frietchen,
worked next to Joe for more than 12 years. He told me the Cavs
were in the process of looking for an in-house music coordinator—
a DJ. I didn't go to school to be a DJ. I didn't want to be a DJ. But I
knew I needed the money. The biggest plus was that I'd get to sit
behind Joe Tait for every home game.

So taking the job was a no-brainer for me, more so because of
the opportunity to be so close to Joe Tait.

What I didn't realize is that Mr. Tait absolutely hated the job I
was hired to do by the Cavs. I'd sit up in the little perch directly behind Joe, and I'd be preparing and excited for the game that night.
Then Joe would walk up. I'd sit there nervously, trying to think of
the right thing to say to Joe.

Joe would snarl at me, "I see they let the circus back into the
gym."

He absolutely *hated* my role in game-day presentation. I went
from sheer excitement for getting to work so close to this legend,
to scared out of my mind of what he would say to me next. My
only saving grace was Joe Frietchen, who explained to Mr. Tait that

I was in radio and that he thought I was pretty talented. Mr. Tait then turned around and looked at me. He wished me good luck but added, "I still don't listen to sports talk yahoos!"

So, strike two, in my mind.

I was realizing that my relationship with the one guy I always wanted to learn from was not going very well.

I watched Joe closely, in how he prepared and how he treated fans, even as he was trying to work. He respected the other teams' announcers. If he thought the person that sang the national anthem took too long, he'd give a thumbs-down. If he liked it, then he'd give the thumbs-up.

One day, he walked in to prepare for that night's game. He looked at me and said: "Hey, I heard you on the air the other day. You're pretty good. Now don't tell anyone I listen to that trash!"

This became one of the best nights of my career. I gained the No. 1 fan who meant the most to me, other than my father. As time went along, Joe would tell me what he liked about one of my shows or sideline reports. He also still told me to turn the sound effects/music down during games.

I moved on from the job of doing the sound, and I handed the job off to a close friend. But I continued sitting right behind Joe.

What Joe doesn't know is that his approval has done wonders for my career. Not only did I learn from watching how this veteran handled his business, but his honest approach to me and his honest appraisal of my work gave me the confidence to continue to grow.

If I interviewed Joe on the air and asked a dumb question, he'd look at me and tell me it was a dumb question. I appreciated his honesty. I've been so blessed to have this Hall of Famer just accept me. I'll probably never reach the heights that Joe has reached, but his mentoring/friendship to me has enriched my life.

The best interview I ever had with Joe was on a summer night during the off-season. I called him and told him I had a surprise for him. I won't repeat what he said about a surprise from me, but he wasn't expecting something good. The surprise was having on the line former Mount Union quarterback Jim Ballard, who was going into the NCAA Hall of Fame. Joe was in heaven that night recalling Ballard's games. At the end, he thanked me for allowing him to be a part of the interview. I had chills afterwards that he actually thanked me, of all people.

Andre Knott is a sportscaster on WTAM radio and STO television.

Joe Teams Up With Bill Fitch

Bill Fitch doesn't remember the note, just The Voice.

"The first time I was in the Monmouth press box, I heard Joe," said Fitch. "I didn't know his name, just The Voice. And it was The Voice of an announcer. You could just tell that he was going to be good."

Fitch was the basketball coach at Coe College in the late 1950s, but he also helped coach the school's freshman football team. And he also scouted the next opponent for the Coe varsity football team. So he showed up a few times a year in Monmouth's press box, where he heard The Voice.

"Joe interviewed me a few times, and I could tell that he was prepared," said Fitch. "His teams were terrible, but he made them sound so good. I just knew that one day, he was going somewhere special."

As if Fitch didn't have enough jobs, he also was the head baseball coach at Creighton from 1956 to '58, where his star was future Hall of Fame pitcher Bob Gibson. And Fitch scouted for the Milwaukee Braves. To Fitch, The Voice of Joe Tait was like the sound of a line drive off the bat of a pure hitter. Or the pop of a Bob Gibson fastball into the catcher's glove.

There was something pure and true about it.

"I never forgot that voice," said Fitch.

And Joe never forgot Fitch as he watched Bill climb the coaching ladder.

In the summer of 1967, Fitch was hired to be the men's basketball coach at Bowling Green University. Joe was at Ohio University, teaching broadcasting and also broadcasting the school's football and basketball games. In the Mid-American Conference preseason basketball poll, Bowling Green received one first-place vote.

It belonged to Joe.

"Fitch had taken over a bad team, but he knew I was at Ohio—and right away, he knew who voted for his team," said Joe. "He said, 'It's that crazy guy down in Athens [Ohio].' But I knew Bill was a great coach and that he would surprise the MAC."

Bowling Green did win the 1967–68 MAC title in Fitch's only season at the school.

"When Bill took over at BG, he brought the players together and asked who was the toughest S.O.B. on the team," said Joe. "A player stepped forward—and bang, Bill popped the guy."

Joe laughed as he recalled the story.

"Then Bill asked the players, 'Now who is the toughest S.O.B. on the team?'" said Joe. "Bill was still young, 33, and he was a former Marine. He was the toughest S.O.B. on that team."

By 1970, Fitch was running the Cavaliers.

That's when Joe sent him the note reading: "I knew you'd always make it in the big time. . . . By the way, if you ever need anyone to do for the Cleveland Cavaliers what I did for those Monmouth Fighting Scots (66-0), let me know. Ha! Ha! Ha!"

When Joe mailed the note, he was "Morning Mayor" of a station in Terre Haute, Indiana . . . WBOW: ON THE BANKS OF THE WABASH!

"I also was the station manager, because the general manager had died and someone had to do it," said Joe.

*   *   *

Fitch was hired as the Cavs' coach and general manager on March 18, 1970. Six months later, the team that started without a player or even a basketball was set to open the season. The Cavaliers didn't get around to hiring a broadcaster until after the season opened. Public relations director Bob Brown did the first seven games in team history. All on the road. They played at Buffalo, at Portland, at San Francisco, at Portland (again), at San Diego, at Phoenix and at Los Angeles.

They returned to Cleveland with an 0-7 record, losing by an average of 17.3 points.

The Cavs had no money in the early days, but Brown discovered he couldn't help owner Nick Mileti run the front office and do the games on the radio. They needed to hire a broadcaster.

Mileti, Fitch and Brown talked about who should be the voice of the Cavs.

Joe said Mileti later told him that he said: "We need a guy who will come in and be so excited about being in a big city that he won't think about the fact that I'm not paying him that much."

So the Cavs wanted someone cheap. They also wanted someone who would be glad to have a job, and that would temper any criticism of the team.

At this point, they all knew the Cavs were going to be a bad team. A very, very bad team. Hiring a Cleveland broadcaster or even someone from another major market meant running the risk of having their own radio voice being perhaps a bit too candid.

"I know just the guy," said Fitch. "He used to make the worst football team that I ever saw sound good."

Fitch said the name . . . Joe Tait.

It meant nothing to Mileti and Brown.

Here is where the story takes two different roads.

According to Joe, Fitch had kept the letter on his desk. He used it to call and say, "Joe, are you interested in doing the Cavs' games?"

"Absolutely," said Joe.

"Can you drive to Cleveland and do a tryout for us?" Fitch asked.

"I'll drive right over," he said.

More than 40 years later, Fitch doesn't remember anything about the letter from Joe. He said he "had four guys in mind" from his days as a college coach, four broadcasters he had heard and met over the years.

"But Joe was the best, and I always kept track of him," said Fitch.

Note or no note . . . Joe received his chance. He was 33 years old. He had spent 10 years bouncing from one small town to another . . . from one station to another . . . from one rejection to another.

"I was making $10,000 a year," said Joe. "I figured I didn't have much to lose."

*　　*　　*

The Cavs brought Joe to town without anyone hearing even a tape. Mileti and Brown just took Fitch's word, and then asked Joe to take a tape player and climb all the way to the top of the old Cleveland Arena.

The Cavs were having their home opener against San Diego. It was October 28, 1970. The attendance was 6,144 for the first NBA game in Cleveland.

"Nick Mileti ordered miniature wineglasses with the Cavs logo on them to be given to the fans," said Joe. "His idea was to hand everyone a glass, pass out some wine—and have the fans toast the new team before the game. But there was a problem: They couldn't get a liquor license from the state of Ohio. So they toasted the team with empty wineglasses, which was perfect fodder for the newspapers. Here was a team that had lost all its games, playing in a half-empty arena with empty wineglasses."

Bob Brown did the game on the radio. Joe was in the hockey press box. It was right under the roof, behind one of the baskets. It was a horrible place from which to watch a game. From that spot, Joe talked into the tape recorder, pretending to be on the radio.

"I was really nervous," Joe said. "I knew this was my chance."

After the game, he handed the tape to Bob Brown. Joe was staying at the Midtown Sheraton on Euclid Avenue, right across from the old arena.

"I'll give the tape to Nick, and we'll call you in the morning," said Brown. "We'll let you know what's going on."

Joe spent a long night trying with little success to sleep. This was the closest he had ever been to a job in a major market. Having been turned down so many times before, it was easy for him to imagine it would happen again.

"At 8:30 that morning, Bob Brown called and said to come across the street and meet with Nick in 30 minutes," said Joe. "His office was on the second floor of the old Arena. He shook my hand and said: 'Joe, I like your work. I've gotta tell you, I don't have any money. I can't pay you very much. In fact, all I can pay you is $100 a game. But if you are willing to work for $100 a game, it's yours. And someday, I will make it up to you."

Joe did some quick math—the Cavs had 74 games left, meaning he'd be paid $7,400. He had to leave the $10,000 job in Terre Haute and move his family. It was a 25 percent pay cut.

Mileti put out his hand.

Joe shook it.

Welcome to the NBA.

Did Fitch ever listen to the tape that convinced Mileti to hire Joe?

"Never," said Fitch. "I didn't need to hear Joe's tape. I knew he was good."

As for the game Joe called from the hockey press box, the Cavs lost, 110-99. At the end of the first quarter, San Diego had a 38-17 lead, and it was 59-45 at the half. Elvin Hayes scored 40 points. Rookie John Johnson led the Cavs with 19, Bobby Smith had 18. Fans left in the middle of the fourth quarter.

"It was a perfect introduction to what was coming next," said Joe, who still has the homemade scorecard from the game that he drew on a long, yellow legal pad.

The loss dropped the Cavs' record to 0-8 as Joe drove home to tell his family that they were moving to Cleveland.

*   *   *

Joe becoming the voice of the Cavs is something that probably wouldn't happen today.

Think about it:

The coach picks him after not hearing him do a game for 10 years . . .

The owner is looking for someone young and really, really cheap . . .

The team didn't even consider hiring a radio voice until two weeks into the regular season . . .

But the hiring of Fitch as coach would seem to be just as improbable in the modern NBA.

Mileti was a Bowling Green graduate. Fitch was the coach there for only one season, 1967–68.

"I got to know Nick when he wanted to promote a game at the Arena between Bowling Green and Niagara," said Fitch. "Niagara had Calvin Murphy, and we upset them. That had something to do with him hiring me."

Mileti was thrilled when the game drew nearly 11,000 fans— and his alma mater knocked off Murphy. Several months later, Mileti put together a group of investors and purchased the Arena and the Cleveland Barons minor-league hockey team.

His goal was to bring the NBA to Cleveland. That happened in the spring of 1970, when the NBA added three teams—Portland, Buffalo and Cleveland.

The league didn't spend a lot of time checking Mileti's finances. He already owned an arena and a hockey team. The upstart American Basketball Association kept expanding and was looking to add Cleveland. The NBA wanted Cleveland, Portland and Buffalo in their league—so in came three teams. The NBA of today would never bring in three expansion teams in the same year. It also would be very alarmed about how Mileti was paying for the team with several investors, very little of his own money and not much cash in reserve.

But in 1970, Mileti looked good as an NBA owner.

And he needed a coach. He was proud of what Fitch had done in his one season at Bowling Green. He remembered the electricity in the old Arena when Fitch coached Bowling Green to that victory. While Mileti told reporters that he had "more than 100 applicants" to be coach, he had only one name in capital letters on his list—BILL FITCH.

After leaving Bowling Green, Fitch had coached at Minnesota for two years. He was scouting a junior college tournament when Mileti called him.

"I was in Hutchinson, Kansas, and Nick called me at 5:30 in the morning," said Fitch. "At 8, we were still talking."

Mileti had several gifts, but his best was the power of persuasion. He not only made Fitch the coach but also the general manager.

"I wasn't taking it unless I could pick my own players," Fitch said.

And his own announcer, too.

*   *   *

Along with tracing their roots to small colleges in the Midwest, Fitch (Coe) and Joe (Monmouth) also were very determined and ambitious young men. Just as Joe went from small market to small market, never staying anywhere longer than three years, Fitch kept chasing his dream.

He coached freshman basketball and varsity baseball at Creighton (1956–58).

He was the head basketball coach and freshman football coach at Coe (1958–62).

He was the basketball coach at North Dakota (1962–67).

He was the basketball coach at Bowling Green (1967–68), his first Division I college basketball job.

He was the basketball coach at Minnesota (1968–70). That gave him three total seasons as a major-level head coach when he was hired by the Cavs at age 36. His record at Minnesota was 25-23 in two years.

"I don't think it was that strange," said Fitch, about his hiring.

Of course, he was speaking 41 years after it happened. He was speaking after a career of coaching 2,050 games with five NBA teams. But today, some in the media would ask: "Why are you turning over the entire franchise to a guy with zero background in the NBA? You are going to let him draft the players, make trades and coach?"

But that question wasn't raised in 1970.

The Cavs were new, and Cleveland was not familiar with the ways of the NBA. This also was when the NBA was looking to the colleges for coaches. Dick Motta (Weber State) and Jack Ramsay (St. Joseph's) were hired before Fitch. There was a theory that the NBA had little coaching because it was mostly former players who rolled out the balls and watched the guys scrimmage. It was the college guys who really knew the X's and O's.

In Cleveland, Fitch was warmly received because he did win the MAC at Bowling Green. He did coach in the Big Ten at Minnesota.

How did he prepare for the NBA expansion draft?

They had done no scouting because everyone was hired so late. There was no Internet. There were no private scouting services. But there were basketball cards, which had names, records and basics statistics on the back.

Fitch's assistant was Jim Lessig, whose son had the cards. As they talked about preparing for the NBA, Lessig said his son had just bought five packs for a quarter, and they did have some information about the players. Fitch sent Lessig back to the store to buy all he could. Twenty bucks and lots of doubles later, they had about 100 different player cards. And from there, they began picking their team.

Joe just laughs thinking about when he joined the Cavs, who were playing like a bunch of rejects from a card collection. He did two more home games after the audition tape . . . a 125-110 loss to Cincinnati in front of 3,199 fans and a 131-107 loss to Atlanta watched by 3,533 fans . . . making the Cavs 0-10.

"After I was hired, I called my wife and could tell she wasn't thrilled about having to move our two kids—and me taking a pay cut—from $10,000 to $7,400," said Joe. "I drove back to Terre Haute to pack some clothes. At home, I listened to the Cavs' radio broadcast from Philadelphia. The Cavs lost, 141-87. The game was on WCAU out of Philadelphia, and the broadcasters were saying things like: 'This is the worst basketball team that I've ever seen in my life. Why would anyone pay to see this atrocity?' Sonny Hill [the analyst] said he doubted the team would even last past the All-Star break before it folded."

Joe's first wife also was listening to the game.

"Edith was slam-dunking my socks in the suitcase, and she was really upset," said Joe. "I was wondering, 'What have I done?'"

But he was committed to Cleveland, and he drove back to join those 0-11 Cavaliers.

"Had I stayed in Terre Haute, I'd have been fired," Joe said. "Right after that, the station was sold, and they wiped out everyone."

Joe was just glad Edith didn't ask him what the Cleveland Arena was like.

"I remember walking into it and thinking: 'This is the NBA?' It was dark. It was cold. It was a dump," Joe said. "And it was usually empty."

"That was true," said Fitch, 41 years later. "But it was a great place to shoot rats."

What?

"After the game, they'd throw out the old hot dogs and food in the dumpsters behind the Arena," said Fitch. "I'd go back there with another guy, and we'd shoot rats with a pistol. Those things were huge!"

The First Year

Joe Tait had one enormous advantage that no Cavaliers broadcaster will ever have again.

He was the first radio voice of the Cavaliers, who were in their first NBA season. In Cleveland, it was impossible to compare Joe Tait to anyone doing the Cavs, because there were no Cavs. He was setting the standard, teaching the public how pro basketball should sound on the radio.

Broadcaster Casey Coleman was placed in the no-win situation of replacing Nev Chandler as the voice of the Browns in 1994 and 1995. Chandler was wildly popular, extremely charismatic on and off the air. He also was blessed to take over as the Browns' radio voice in the middle 1980s, just as Bernie Kosar was reviving the franchise and the team went to four consecutive playoff appearances. Chandler was associated with those good times.

He died at age 47 from cancer.

Coleman took over. The Browns were in decline. He was a very solid broadcaster, but Coleman was not Chandler. His Browns were not Chandler's Browns. At the end of Coleman's second season, the team moved to Baltimore. Some fans tied Coleman to Bill Belichick, the extremely unpopular coach during that era.

"I would have been better off being the guy who replaced the guy who took over for Nev," Coleman said more than once. "No one could really replace Nev."

When the team returned in 1999 as an expansion franchise, Coleman was hired as the radio sideline reporter—and fans liked him in that role. Jim Donovan was named the radio voice, and he was accepted. Browns fans were just happy to have a team back once again.

When Joe arrived in Cleveland, Gib Shanley was the respected radio voice of the Browns. Bob Neal and Herb Score did the Tribe games on the radio. Neal was a "professional" broadcaster, who had also done some national network college football games. But he also made the listener feel as if the game was a bit beneath him. He rarely became excited. He could be extremely sarcastic. He got the facts right and kept up with the action. But there was a sense when listening to Neal that he'd rather be doing something else. This was especially true by the time Joe arrived in town.

So Cleveland's sports broadcasting landscape was ready for a new voice.

Joe didn't realize it at the time.

"I was just happy to have the job," he said. "When Nick Mileti said I was hired, I was relieved, especially after just missing those two jobs in Chicago. And then I found that everyone at my old station in Terre Haute was being fired . . . I was overjoyed to be employed."

Mileti and Fitch knew this—Joe was what they wanted: a young broadcaster who was thrilled to be in a major market doing a major-league sport.

"Nick never told me what to say," said Joe. "On the first day, he just said: 'Remember to have fun. Describe the game. Remember, it's family entertainment.' That was it, and he never said anything else in all the years that I worked for him."

It didn't matter to Joe that the Cavs opened the season with 15 consecutive losses.

Think about that: a new team being 0-15.

But think about being Joe Tait . . . age 33. Other than being in the military, his only other plane ride was to New York and Washington D.C. when he traveled there as part of a senior high trip. He had never been to most of the NBA cities.

"I had been to only one NBA game in my life before getting the Cavs job," said Joe. "It was a game at Purdue, with Fort Wayne being the home team. They played Baltimore. It was hand-to-hand combat. Terry Dischinger of Fort Wayne got two teeth knocked out. I remember telling the person who came with me: 'If that's NBA basketball, I don't want any part of it. It's like football.' "

The next game Joe saw in person was his tryout at the Cleveland Arena, when the Cavs faced San Diego. By then, he was ready to fall in love with NBA basketball.

"When I listen to tapes from that first year, I realize that I was really over the top," said Joe. "I was yelling, screaming, very excited. I remember when we were playing the Knicks, I was upset that the officials wouldn't call a foul on [New York forward] Dave DeBusschere. I'm screaming, '[Darell] Garretson wouldn't give a foul to DeBusschere if he pulled out a machine gun!' But I also can tell you that none of this was fake. It was genuine. It was how I felt. I didn't create it; the enthusiasm came from inside me."

That's because in 1970, Joe felt like part of the team. He was not much older than the players. Most of them, like Joe, were just glad to be in the NBA. They had a few veterans near the end of their careers, such as Johnny Egan, who had played with the Lakers in the 1960s. He was appalled at Fitch's training camp. The rookie coach had the Cavs practicing for two hours in the morning, two more in the afternoon and film sessions at night. No NBA team would dare do that today, because of the risk of injury and fatigue that it creates. This wasn't college with two games per week and players between the ages of 18 and 22. It was the NBA of 1970, when everyone flew commercial and took the first flight out, according to NBA rules. That meant a lot of 5 a.m. wakeup calls. It also was when the league allowed something it has since banned—playing three games in three days.

Fitch often said, "War is bad, but expansion is worse."

Fitch's players thought he was preparing them for the Navy Seals rather than the NBA.

The NBA did give the Cavs only eight home games by Thanksgiving . . . compared to 16 on the road.

The Cavs were 0-14 when they went to San Francisco for a game with the Warriors.

Joe walked into the arena with Fitch and assistant coach Jim Lessig.

Lessig and Joe had their game passes, Fitch did not. The security guard didn't want to allow Fitch into the arena.

"I left my pass back at the hotel," Fitch said. "I'm the coach of the Cavaliers."

"I've got to see some credentials," said guard said. "How do I know that you're the coach?"

"Do you know the Cavs' record?" asked Fitch.

"Yes," said the guard. "Zero-and-14."

"Do you think I'd say I'm the coach of the Cavs unless I was the coach of the Cavaliers?" Fitch asked.

"Go right on in," said the guard.

The Cavs lost that night, 109-74. They were 0-15 and set to play two days later in Portland. Walking around town, Fitch spotted a skull in the window of a Portland magic shop. He bought it for $1.95.

"I was there," said Joe. "We had just finished eating at the Mustang. It was a Chinese restaurant where you could eat a lot, and it didn't cost much. Meal money was only $20 a day, and I was trying to save some of that."

At 0-15, the Cavs had tied Denver for the worst start in NBA history. Before the Portland game, Fitch showed the skull to his players and said that was "all that's left of the Denver coach."

The players all touched the skull. They brought it on to the court and beat Portland, 105-103.

The game was over, but the horn failed to sound—the Portland timekeeper probably was in shock.

On the air, Joe was asking: "Did we win? Did we win? Is it over?" He kept looking at the clock, which was down to 0:00. But no horn. Finally, the officials indicated the game was over.

After the sloppy game, Fitch told reporters, "It looked like the gamblers got to both teams."

The skull worked for only one game, as the Cavs lost their next 12—including another game at Portland.

"We brought the skull out again and put it under Fitch's chair," said Joe. "A Portland player came by and dropped a towel over the skull. And we got beat."

On December 4, 1970, they were 1-27.

*   *   *

Players were coming and going.

They had a center named Gary Suiter. He was cut when trainer Ron Culp discovered him in line at a concession stand . . . in his Cavs uniform . . . an hour before the game, wanting to buy a hot dog. He also had been nabbed going through teammates' luggage. And the Cavs received a strange call from a funeral parlor that said Suiter asked to use the phone to call a relative and set up funeral arrangements. The funeral parlor manager left him alone for privacy's sake. Suiter was gone when the manager returned. A month later, a $700 phone bill arrived at the funeral parlor. Suiter had been calling every NBA team, looking for a tryout.

While some of Suiter's stories are funny in a twisted way, Wichita Falls, Texas, writer Nick Gholston did a story on Suiter in 2010. Part of it reads:

I hung around smoky old pool halls in my younger days, and that is where I met Suiter, who spent more time practicing spot shots than he did jump shots. He also had this bad habit of not paying off when he lost. That came natural to a guy who also never paid for his food at restaurants, stole more record albums than the Beatles ever recorded and had a strange habit of driving off and not paying for gasoline.

In other words, in the three years he lived here, Suiter had a reputation of being a hustler, a thief, a liar and a cheat. But he was a nice hustler, thief, liar and cheat. . . . It is true that Suiter never saw a jump shot he wouldn't take, but in 2½ seasons at Midwestern [University], he averaged right at 21 points and 14 rebounds a game. . . .

All I really remember is he left town owing me money. The last time I saw Suiter, he and his girlfriend were leaving town in her car. That was 40 years ago. . . .

Gary Suiter was murdered on Oct. 23, 1982, near Rio Rancho, N.M. He was only 37. According to court records, two men found him at a restaurant. The three left the restaurant in a pickup and drove to a remote wooded area near the Rio Grande River. One of the men got into a heated argument with Suiter over a $275 gambling debt. He shot Suiter in the hand, chest and head at close range with a .357 Magnum. His jewelry was removed and his body was dragged 30 feet away into a brushy area near the river.

A more uplifting story from that era is Bobby Washington, who was signed during the middle of the season.

"I was sitting with Fitch at the Cincinnati airport," said Joe. "We were waiting for a flight. He said that a player was coming in from Grand Rapids [of the Continental Basketball Association]. He told me to keep my eyes open. I didn't see anyone who looked liked a basketball player. Then this little stocky guy showed up wearing a cabby hat and a long coat that ran all the down to the floor. I don't know why, but I just KNEW that was our new point guard."

Joe pointed him out to Fitch, who sighed and said, "Oh, boy."

Fitch had not seen Washington play, he just heard he was a good point guard in basketball's bush leagues.

"Bobby ended up being a terrific player for us," said Joe. "He was a natural point guard, a real leader. He was not great by NBA standards, but the fans and players loved his hustle and enthusiasm. I remember how I went to Disneyland with Bobby and Ron Culp that first season during an off-day. We were on this ride called 'Pirates of the Caribbean.' Bobby got so scared, he jumped right into my lap."

The 5-11, 175-pound Washington played only two seasons. His career ended prematurely because of a severely broken leg.

"Bobby became a legendary high school coach in Kentucky," said Joe. "Just a great guy."

Tait gave the players nicknames. Washington was "The Little General." John Johnson was "J.J."

"Bobby Smith told me that he wanted to be called 'Bingo,'" said Joe. "That was his nickname in college. He could really shoot from the outside, so it fit—and I was glad to use it."

Early in that season, Joe stayed at the Sheraton Hotel, right across from the Arena. To save money, they had Joe share a room with a player—remember, this was for home games!

"My first roommate was Joe Cooke," he said. "I remember us being together on Thanksgiving. We had no families, not much was open. We went to eat at some beanery in Lakewood. Had a couple of sandwiches. That was our Thanksgiving."

When Cooke found a place to stay, Larry Mikan moved in with Joe at the Sheraton.

"He was the son of [NBA great] George Mikan," said Joe. "A really nice guy, but I never sensed that he liked basketball that much. I can understand why. Everyone figured that he was George Mikan's son, so he should be great. But he was only 6-foot-7 (his father was 6-foot-10), and it was like he played basketball because he was expected to do it."

Larry Mikan lasted only a year in the NBA.

Finally, Joe moved out of the Sheraton and found a place in Parma Heights for his family to live.

*   *   *

Joe had fun with the games and the team.

"I remember a game where we were losing, 96-66," recalled Joe. "In the huddle, J.J. [John Johnson] was telling the guys, 'Come on, we're only down by 10. We can get back into this thing.' Fitch heard that and just shook his head."

In another game, Joe screamed, "Bobby Lewis . . . 15-footer . . . GOOD!" These were the days when Joe was sitting at the press table on the floor, right near the team bench.

Fitch heard that call, turned to Joe and said: "Are you kidding? A 15-footer? That wasn't even 10 feet! You're worse than J.J."

The most famous—or infamous—play of that first season came when the Cavs were playing Portland on December 9. They had a 2-27 record. They trailed by three points at the half. The Cavs' Walt Wesley won the opening jump ball, tipping it to guard Bobby Lewis. Fellow guard John Warren bolted to the basket, as Portland's Leroy Ellis chased Warren, trying for the blocked shot.

No problem.

Warren eluded Ellis and made the layup.

Only it was the wrong basket.

Two points for Portland.

Fitch said he thought Ellis could have been called for a foul on the play, which would have confused matters even more.

Later in that same game, Portland left a timeout with six players on the court.

Joe was the first to spot it. He was screaming on the air, "Portland has six guys out there!"

Fitch heard Joe, counted the players, came up with six and complained to the officials.

They called Portland for a technical foul for too many men on the court.

No matter, the Cavs still lost, 109-102.

The "crowd" at the old Arena was 2,002.

*   *   *

There were only five games on television that season, done by Browns broadcaster Gib Shanley and *Plain Dealer* sports editor Hal Lebovitz. The Cavs were on WERE radio, which had a very limited signal.

Whatever voice of the Cavs could be heard, it belonged to Joe Tait.

"The first time that I really felt as if I were in the NBA was when we played at Boston," said Joe. "Growing up, the only time that I saw pro basketball on TV was on Sunday, and about 80 percent of the time, the game was from Boston. It was the parquet floor. When I walked out there and saw that floor, I thought, 'I really have made it.' Even though Boston Garden was a dump back then, it was still Boston Garden with all the championship banners and that parquet floor."

The Cavs had one of those three-games-in-three-days stretches from December 25 to 27. That's right, they played on Christmas Day and lost, 117-100, at Cincinnati. The next night, they were at home and beat expansion Buffalo, 120-107. The following night,

it was another home victory—a 114-101 stunner over Philadelphia. Yes, that was the same Sixers team that beat the Cavs, 141-
87, when Joe was listening to the game and wondering if he had
made the right decision about coming to Cleveland.

"[Broadcaster] Andy Musser told me that he was sitting in
his hotel room in Minneapolis after doing a Vikings game, and
the score of our win over Philadelphia came on the TV, and he
dropped the glass of beer on his lap," said Joe. "He kept saying
that he couldn't believe the Cavs beat the Sixers. He did that first
Cavs-Sixers game on the radio."

In another game, the Cavs were tied with New York at the end
of the first quarter. Joe said on the air, "The Cavs have played the
Knicks on even terms so far."

Fitch heard that, turned and asked Joe, "Good, can we go
home now?"

They lost that game, 102-94.

*   *   *

That was the Cavs' first two-game winning streak, watched by
a small circle of friends. They drew 2,332 for the victory over Buffalo. You'd think more people would show up the next night? It
was 2,022 for the Sixers game.

The 1970 calendar year ended with the Cavs at 5-39. They had
drawn only two crowds of more than 4,000. Most nights, it was in
the 2,300 range. No one was talking about this publicly, but everyone with the Cavs (including Joe) knew that Mileti had bought the
team with other people's money, and that cash was tight. They
had about 1,500 season-ticket holders.

The Plain Dealer's Raymond Hart wrote his first of several
complimentary stories about Joe in those early Cavs seasons.
Hart quoted Joe talking about the 108-106 victory over Buffalo,
the first home victory of the season.

"It's all over, the Cavaliers have won their first home game,"
Hart quoted Joe as saying on the air, and then the Plain Dealer
writer said "that was his spiel as the 2,001 fans sounded like
20,002 in their roar of approval after seeing history made."

The story had a very light tone, with Joe saying how losing didn't bother him—his Monmouth College football team won only six games in five years. Joe said, "Other announcers say they feel sorry for me. . . . Heck, this is only the second time in my life that I've worked with an engineer. I've done high school games from a stepladder in a gym. . . . I'm having a ball because it's part of being in the NBA."

The first major media endorsement for Joe came from Don Robertson, a *Cleveland Press* columnist. He also was a well-known novelist and did television commentaries on the news along with some movie reviews. He was not a sportswriter, but he loved Joe and the expansion Cavaliers.

On January 4, 1971, he wrote a rave about Joe. He sat next to the Cavs broadcaster during a game: "If you listen to him describe the games, you know he has remarkable glottal dexterity in what must be the most difficult sports broadcasting job—describing the furious pace of an NBA game.

Robertson quoted this part of Joe's broadcast: "McLemore in traffic, can't drive . . . passes off to J.J. at baseline right, into Wesley . . . 6-foot hook. No . . . rebound, McLemore . . . No . . . rebound, Wesley. No . . . cut to Warren, who is 2-timed, into Sorenson, 4-footer . . . No . . . ball off Alcindor's wrist . . . out to Joe Cooke, who shoots from 20 feet . . . GOOD! Score: Milwaukee 45, Cleveland 22."

Robertson noted that Joe was "absolutely accurate" in his machine-gun account.

"Once you learn the terminology, a Joe Tait broadcast is a joy," wrote Robertson. "He is still young (33), and his enthusiasm has not been worn away by a lot of foolish cynicism."

Joe received very little criticism that first season, other than *Plain Dealer* columnist Hal Lebovitz insisting Joe was "too tough on officials." Looking back, Joe agrees with that assessment. But at the time, he was a rookie broadcaster making $100 per game with two kids and a third on the way—and the team was terrible with an average attendance of 3,518—lowest in the NBA.

"Joe was a great announcer, you knew it from the beginning,"

Joe put in a lot of hours preparing for the broadcast.
"There I am laboring away at the old Arena," said Joe. "This
is before a game, but back in those days, the stands could
have looked like that at halftime. I would arrive at least two
hours before the game."

recalled Fitch. "He could broadcast anything, from baseball to a
cow-milking contest. He just had it."

After the 15-67 season, *The Plain Dealer*'s Raymond Hart
wrote: "Tait, like the team he was describing, was a rookie in basketball's big league. But he wound up in the All-Star category. . . .
He is unquestionably the best sportscaster to hit town since Gib
Shanley blew in from Toledo in 1961."

Joe said the team's losing combined with WERE's weak signal meant that not a lot of people were listening.

"I got only five fan letters all year," he recalled. "I got 10 the year I was Morning Mayor of Monmouth, Illinois. I swear, at night, I don't think WERE's signal carried past the Greyhound station that was only a mile from the arena. Some fans say that they were there that first year for all the games—I say, 'You and two others.' That was it. No one was there."

The NBA's approach to expansion in 1970 was horrible, admitting three teams at once. That diluted the available talent—both players and coaches. The teams played 24 of the 82 games against each other.

"We were 2-10 against Portland and 7-5 against Buffalo," recalled Joe, 40 years after the end of that season.

That also means they were 6-52 against established NBA teams.

"The league was such a mess that the NBA playoffs began, but we still had one regular-season game left with Portland," said Joe. "We lost."

On January 4, 1971, Joe received a letter from the Chicago White Sox. He had applied to do their games on radio. A manager, wrote Joe: "There was one man who could help us bring more people back to the park and more stations on the air."

The man wasn't named. But Joe knew it wasn't him, especially as the letter concluded: "All tapes presented to us will be returned as soon as possible."

Hard to argue with their selection—it was the great Harry Caray.

So Joe had to make Cleveland work, because he needed the work.

"We knew that the team could fold after the first year. Mileti told us that he had no money," Joe said. "No one was showing up. Fitch kept hoping we could get the first draft pick and end up with a good player who could create some interest. We knew something had to happen."

Joe Tait's Favorites

Five Favorite Broadcasts In Cleveland

1. Dick Bosman's no-hitter against the Oakland A's in 1974. Great to see a journeyman pitcher do that.
2. Len Barker's 1981 perfect game . . . happened on my birthday!
3. Dick Snyder's game-winning basket in Game 7 of the 1976 series with Washington. . . . It was a Miracle to Cavs fans!
4. Cavs defeated the L.A. Lakers, 154-153, in four overtimes in 1980. At the end of the game, Bill Willoughby was guarding Kareem Abdul-Jabbar.
5. Dennis Eckersley's no-hitter against the California Angels.

My Five Forgotten Sports Favorites (In No Special Order)

- Cavs guard Bobby "The General" Washington: Later became a great high school coach.
- Tribe infielder Tommy Ragland: Always smiling, made you feel good to be around him.
- Tribe outfielder Horace Speed: Had an unforgettable at-bat against Al Hrabosky—even if he did strike out.
- Tribe shortstop Jerry Dybzinski: If your hotel room TV broke, the kid from Collinwood High could fix it!
- Winston Bennett and Mike Sanders: The two forgotten small forwards on the Cavs teams with Brad Daugherty, Larry Nance and Mark Price.

My Five Forgotten Sports Heroes (In No Special Order):

- World B. Free: The Cavs guard was exactly what the team needed, scored big, loved the fans and may have saved the franchise. His No. 21 should be retired.
- Cavs center Rick Roberson: He could rebound with anyone in the NBA.
- Wayne Garland: Pitched through more pain than Tribe fans will ever know.
- Randy Smith: He was a classy veteran, an outstanding scorer who deserved better than his last season here under Bill Musselman.
- Danny Ferry: The Cavs forward could have just cashed the checks, but he worked so hard to make himself a respectable NBA player.

Five Best Places To Broadcast A Game

1. Madison Square Garden: Midcourt, about halfway up the stands.
2. Quicken Loans Arena: Joe Tait Perch. It's much better to be above the court rather than on it—because coaches, players and officials stand in front of you when you are courtside—and you can't see the game.
3. Old Tigers Stadium: Right behind home plate, about 75 feet up—right on top of the screen.
4. Cleveland Municipal Stadium: On top of the screen behind home plate, slightly to the third base side.
5. Old County Stadium in Milwaukee: On top of the screen, behind home plate.

Five Best NBA Officials: All Were So Good, They Could Work A Game By Themselves

1. Mendy Rudolph
2. Earl Strom
3. Richie Powers
4. Joe Crawford
5. Bob Delaney

Five Best Cavs Players In Terms Of Pure Talent

1. LeBron James
2. Larry Nance
3. Mark Price
4. Brad Daugherty
5. Mike Mitchell

Five Favorite Railroads

1. Lee County Central Electric: Sometimes rode the locomotive to school
2. Chicago Burlington and Quincy
3. Chicago and Northwestern
4. Nevada Northern Railway
5. Cleveland Commercial Railroad

Five Best Train Trips

1. Cleveland/Chicago/Las Vegas on Amtrak
2. Aurora, Ill., to Chicago and return on Chicago, Burlington and Quincy
3. Medina/Hartville/Canton/Brewster/Spencer/Medina

4. Heber City to Provo Valley in Utah
5. Washington, D.C./New York/Boston . . . N.E. Corridor

Five Favorite Railroad Museums

1. California State Railroad Museum—Sacramento, California
2. Colorado Railroad Museum—Golden, Colorado
3. Illinois Railway Museum—Union, Illinois
4. Duluth Railroad Museum—Duluth, Minnesota
5. Baltimore & Ohio Railroad Museum—Baltimore, Maryland

Five Favorite Ohio Eateries

1. Samosky's in Valley City
2. Lighthouse Café in Lodi
3. Bob Evans
4. Denny's
5. Skyway Drive-in, Medina

Five Railroad Publications Worth Reading

1. *Trains Magazine*
2. *Railfan & Railroad*
3. *Classic Trains*
4. *Railroads Illustrated*
5. *Model Railroader*

The Cavs' Early Years

Year Two of the Cavs' franchise, they had the No. 1 pick in the NBA Draft.

They chose Austin Carr.

Many Cavaliers fans know Carr once played for the team, and that he was good enough to have his number retired by the franchise. But they mostly know him as the team's television commentator since 1997.

But when the Cavs drafted Carr, he was supposed to change the direction of the franchise. He averaged 38 points per game in his final two years at Notre Dame. He grabbed 7.8 rebounds. He shot 53 percent from the field, 82 percent from the foul line.

He was one of the greatest scorers in college basketball history, and he was coming to Cleveland.

"That's all true," said Joe. "But there wasn't all this hype like today over the draft. Austin was in class at Notre Dame when he was drafted. The professor got word, told Austin that he was a first-round pick. Austin asked the professor what team, and the professor didn't know. There was no draft on TV, no acting like these guys were the saviors of the league."

But Bill Fitch knew what he had in Carr: "I thought he could be the next Oscar [Robertson] or [John] Havlicek. Just go back and look at his films from college. He was destined to be one of the great ones."

Fitch knew that he wanted Carr, but he acted is if he was very interested in selecting UCLA's Sidney Wicks.

"We did that because we knew that Portland wanted him," said Fitch. "They were drafting right behind us. Nick Mileti and I talked to them and cut a deal—we'd pass on Wicks, and they'd pay us $250,000."

As the Cavs headed into their second season after a 15-67 record and average of 3,518 fans, they needed every penny. So $250,000 to skip a player they didn't want to draft anyway was a major heist.

"We thought Austin would draw some fans," said Fitch. "There were a lot of Notre Dame fans in Cleveland. And he also was a very exciting player."

Only the fans never saw that player.

"I first broke my foot as a sophomore," said Carr. "Then I broke it again [in training camp] my rookie year. I'm not sure what happened, if I stepped on someone's foot or what. But I was demoralized. I knew it was bad."

Rest was suggested, and Carr sat out the first month of the season.

"I came back, played for a while and got hurt again," he said. "This time, I knew it was really bad. I came back too fast, but I wanted to play. They had to do surgery where they took a bone out of my hip and put it into my foot. They didn't have pins backs then for that kind of surgery. I did come back at the end of the year, but I was really still bothered by it. And I never got my quickness or full balance back."

Fitch said Carr had a stress fracture. This was before MRIs and other means of detailing and measuring the full extent of this type of injury. Carr averaged 21.2 points and shot 43 percent. He played 43 of 82 games that season and had another foot operation in the summer of 1972.

"He came back pretty well," said Fitch. "Except for one thing: He lost his speed. He could still score, but he wasn't explosive going to the basket."

The Cavs' average attendance jumped from 3,518 to 5,222 in Carr's rookie season. It was partly because fans had watched him on television average 50 points in seven NCAA Tournament games—that's right 50 POINTS PER GAME in the NCAA Tournament—and wanted to see him in person.

But Carr came back as good, but not great. The Cavs had only a 23-59 record. It seemed the only break the franchise could get was a compound fracture. In the 1972–73 season, the Cavs' average attendance dropped to 4,548, even though their record rose to 32-50.

"Those were just hard years," said Burt Graeff, who covered the Cavs for the *Cleveland Press*. "Fitch had a lot of one-liners and tried to create a smoke screen to cover up how bad things were, but when you got him alone—you could see that he was really suffering."

While Fitch said he never feared the team would fold, money was tight. Carr being injured and not becoming the star they had hoped made it even more of a financial challenge.

"One thing I didn't fear was getting fired," said Joe. "Not with what they were paying me."

*   *   *

Joe's salary rose $25 from his base of $100 as a rookie. So it was $125 per game in Carr's rookie season, $150 the following year.

"Along with doing all the fill-in radio work that I could find," said Joe, "I became the public address announcer at Cloverleaf Speedway, which was a short dirt track. I had never done racing before, and I knew very little about it."

Joe said that one day a man named John Lemmo was at the track and heard Joe.

"It sounds like you've never done this before," said Lemmo.

"Absolutely not," said Joe.

"I'll come next week and help you out," said Lemmo.

Who was John Lemmo? One of the best racing announcers ever. He did the Daytona 500 and other major events.

"I was doing Cloverleaf on Saturday nights," Joe said. "The next week, he sat next to me and let me do the first half of the scheduled races," said Joe. "Then Lemmo said, 'Now just listen to me. This is how you do it.' He gave me a real lesson, and I learned from the master. I picked up enough to get through that season."

Joe also began to call races at Painesville Speedway.

"I think I got $25 a night at both places," he said. "I was driving a seven-year-old Pontiac."

Joe also did some of those commercials where you'd hear a broadcaster scream: "Saturday . . . *Saturday* . . . SATURDAY!!! at Cloverleaf Speedway . . ."

It would echo.

"That started in Rockford [Illinois], when the drag racing legend 'Big Daddy' Don Garlits was racing there on Sunday," said Joe. "I did some radio spots where I yelled, 'SUNDAY!!!' It would then be over-modulated. Soon, they were using that technique all over the country to do racing commercials. As far as I know, it started at WJRL in Rockford, and I was the first one to do it."

*   *   *

Carr signed a five-year, $1.5 million deal with the Cavs. He had the same offer from the Virginia Squires of the old American Basketball Association.

"My agent told me that NBA money was better than ABA money," he said. "I also wanted to play in the NBA. But in Cleveland, I heard they had money problems. When I got my check, I rushed to the bank to cash it. A teller there told me that was a smart idea—that sometimes, some of the checks took a little while to clear."

Joe said that in certain cities, he found himself being used by Fitch in a different way.

"In our second season [1971–72], to save money on the road, the team rented three station wagons to transport the players instead of a bus," he said. "I drove one. [Assistant coach] Jimmy Rodgers drove one, and Bill Fitch drove the third with the rookies. We had just gotten blown out in Cincinnati, and I was driving Bingo Smith and a few other guys back to the hotel."

Joe paused.

"Suddenly, Bingo starts crying," Joe said. "I asked him what was wrong. He said, 'Joe, are we ever going to win another game? How come we can't win?'"

"I felt so bad for him," said Joe. "I finally told him that we weren't good enough to win then—but one day, we would be."

Or at least Joe hoped so because all of them were paying some serious dues to try and establish themselves in the NBA.

"We once flew from Seattle to Baltimore, and I had the middle seat," said Joe. "We had two 7-footers on the team—Walt Wesley and Luther Rackley. They were on either side of me, their legs folded up."

Carr said the players called the old Cleveland Arena "the smokehouse." It was because fans were allowed to smoke during games, and the smoke hung over the court.

"The floor was old with loose screws," he said. "We'd practice there some mornings, and you'd hear the screeching as the cats and rats were battling in some corner. You didn't complain about it, you just knew you should be glad to be in the NBA."

Joe said he once had a fan dump a cup of beer on him.

"It was after a game in Philadelphia," said Joe. "A game we lost."

After a victory against New York during the second season, the CBS national radio sports report played the last 30 seconds of the victory.

"I was screaming like crazy," said Joe. "Then the broadcaster, Win Elliot, said, 'Folks, you have to understand—this [winning] just doesn't happen much in Cleveland."

*   *   *

While Carr came to the Cavs in only their second season, he said he "knew Joe Tait was the man."

Meaning what?

"He was around a lot," Carr said. "You could see that Fitch and the players respected him. I made friends in Cleveland, and they loved him as a broadcaster. I thought he was a big deal, even back then."

Joe said the first time he interviewed Carr, it was nearly the last time.

"He just gave one-word answers," he said. "I used to tape seven minutes with a player to be used at halftime. I ended up talking for 6 minutes and 30 seconds. Austin was lucky to fill 30 seconds."

Carr said part of it was being somewhat intimidated by Joe, the other was, "I was basically a shy guy."

He didn't want to spend any meal money, "I ate a lot of Chee-

"In those days, the broadcaster was considered part
of the team," said Joe. Here, he dresses the part. "Rick
Roberson let me use his uniform for Halloween in 1973.
He complained that I stretched it out."

tos and orange pop," Carr said. "They didn't have nutritionists
back then."

Fitch said: "Talk about two cheap guys. You could sit down at
a lunch with Austin and Joe and grow old waiting for one of them
to pick up a check."

Carr said, "If Joe and I ever went out, we split the check."

In Carr's second season, he averaged 20.5 points and played
all 82 games.

"Early in the year, I figured I had to interview Austin again,"
said Joe. "He was playing great. He was always very friendly before the interview, then he'd have nothing to say. But this time,
I simply said, 'You should be pleased with how you played last
night'—and he went on for more than five minutes. I asked another question, and I wondered if he'd ever shut up."

After the interview, Joe asked, "What happened to you?"

"I don't know," said Austin. "I really don't know."

About 40 years later, Carr does know.

"I just felt comfortable with Joe and being in the NBA," he said. "You knew you should help him out."

The Cavs had a player named Greg "Stretch" Howard, who joined the team in Carr's rookie season. Joe went to interview Howard, and was turned down by the 6-foot-9 forward.

"Stretch was one of those guys who looked mean and tried to intimidate you," said Joe. "He didn't want to talk, that was fine with me. His exact words were, 'Man, I don't talk to anybody.' I just walked away."

Watching that exchange was Rick Roberson, a veteran forward. Howard had averaged 3.3 points as a rookie the prior season. Trainer Ron Culp later told Joe that Roberson was outraged at Howard's action.

"Hey, man," said Roberson. "That guy is with us every step of the way, home and road. If he wants to talk to you, you talk to him Got that? We all talk to Joe."

Howard came out on the court, found Joe and said, "Hey, hey . . . fella . . . I'm here if you need me."

Joe did the interview. Howard played 48 games for the Cavs that season, averaging 2.4 points. He never played in the NBA again.

*   *   *

"People were closer back then because we had a sense that we were in this together," said Joe. "Most guys weren't making much money—they were just trying to survive in the league. They didn't have an entourage. I had players over to my house."

Joe told the story of Bob Rule, who averaged 23 points per game in his first three pro seasons, then severely ripped his Achilles tendon. By the time he joined the Cavs in 1972, he had lost his jumping ability and overall mobility because of the injury.

"He became a friend of the family," said Joe. "Our dogs didn't like anybody, but they loved Bob Rule. He used to pick up my son Joey and carry him around the yard, putting Joey up on his shoulders. He visited us several times, and we went to his place on [Cleveland's] East Side a few times."

Rule played only 75 games over two seasons for the Cavs, averaging 4.3 points.

"It's a shame that he got hurt," said Joe. "He was a great player before the injury. Of course, the reason we got him was that he had been hurt—or else he never would have been traded to us."

Then Joe told the story of Rule's final game with the Cavs. It was in New York, and Rule suddenly was fighting a Knicks player. Rule was ejected. Fitch came roaring off the bench, screaming at official Richie Powers: "Come on, Richie, my wife and I have better fights than that!"

That's when Fitch was ejected.

Knicks coach Red Holzman was on his way to join the discussion but saw what happened to Fitch, quickly turned and headed back to the bench.

"We put Rule on waivers after that game," said Joe. "But he was at the airport with us the next morning. We ran into Richie Powers, and Rule said, 'Richie, you not only threw me out of game, you threw me out of the league!'"

Rule played only one NBA game after that—11 minutes with the Milwaukee Bucks.

*   *   *

During holidays, Joe and the coaches would invite players to their homes when they seemed to need some company.

"It was different back then," he said. "These guys were often alone in a strange city. We had so many players coming and going back then. It meant a lot for them to have a home-cooked meal with a family."

In the Cavs' third season, Joe invited two players to his house for Thanksgiving—forwards Dwight Davis and Cornell Warner. Davis arrived in Tait's driveway and stepped out of the car. Right behind him was Warner, who had brought his mother along.

"Suddenly, our two German shepherds saw Dwight, and they

ran right at him," Joe said. "Poor Dwight. He got so scared, he jumped right on top of the roof of his car. The dogs were barking. He was shaking up there when my wife Edith came out of the house."

Keep in mind that Davis was 6-foot-8, 220 pounds.

"The best part was Cornell Warner," Joe said. "He didn't speak three words all year, but he was laughing so hard, tears were coming down his face. His mother was behind him, telling Cornell to quit making fun of Dwight. But Cornell couldn't stop laughing."

Fitch often had dinner with Joe, whose favorite dessert was the "Hyatt Riot" sundae at the Hyatt hotels. It was big enough to feed the Navy Seals.

As Joe ate, Fitch was staring at his watch. When Joe was done, Fitch said, "Pretty good, you ate all that in one minute and 20 seconds."

"In those days, the broadcaster was considered part of the team," said Joe. "No one had to tell me to be upbeat about the team. I felt close to those guys—so yes, I wanted them to win. I wanted us to get the [officials'] calls. I watched game tape with Fitch and knew the plays better than some of the players. We had a feeling that we all had to stick together."

20 Years With Tait

[BY BOB PRICE]

I had the good fortune to work closely with Joe Tait for 20 years, as I worked in the public relations department for the Cleveland Cavaliers. My last position was senior director of communications and public relations.

I started listening to Cavs games in their inaugural campaign, when I was an eighth grader at Woodbury Junior High School in Shaker Heights. I fell in love with the team, mainly through Joe's play-by-play. The wins and losses didn't matter. It was my team.

During my freshman year at Denison, one of my Kappa Sigma fraternity brothers, Jay Ferguson, gave me the nickname "Bingo," when I hit a couple of jumpers when we were playing intramural basketball. Never did I imagine that this "Bingo" would be called "Bingo" so many times by my idol, Joe Tait. I would always enjoy seeing Joe and saying, "Tait, Tait, Tait," in my best Bruce Drennan impersonation. To my delight, Joe would always return my welcome with, "Bingo, Bingo, Bingo."

I'm not sure how many listeners noted Joe's allusion to "WAC observers" on his final broadcast. I happened to be present on the road trip to Denver when Joe was displaced from his normal radio broadcast location by "WAC observers" [representatives from the Western Athletic Conference]. It was Tommy Sheppard, the Nuggets' PR director, who bore the brunt of Joe's ire. In my 20 years with the Cavs, that was the only time that I saw Joe lose his temper, and he "blowed up good." During his last broadcast, Joe made mention to Tom Farmer from Fox Sports Ohio about WAC observers, and I nearly fell off my couch.

Before we had our team plane, Joe would prefer to drive to road games for short trips to places such as Detroit. Whenever possible, I would go along for the ride. The highlight of the trip home was during our stop for dessert. Joe put on an eating clinic as he downed a hot fudge sundae in record time. I swear that his spoon never came to rest until he triumphantly flung the spoon into his empty bowl.

Mealtime with Joe was always a highlight of any road trip. A couple of Joe's favorite stops were Flo's Diner in Toronto and Edie's Diner in Los Angeles. He loved visiting the retro diners with the '50s decor and menu. They were five-star diners whenever they served their chocolate milkshakes with the metal container, so as not to miss a sip! Edie's was a classic diner in Marina del Rey, California, just a short walk from our team hotel. Joe's favorite was "Big Al's" breakfast, which featured eggs, pancakes, hash browns and toast. The best part was getting a piece of Bazooka bubblegum when leaving!

Another favorite restaurant was St. Elmo Steak House in Indianapolis. They are a top-notch steak house, and their specialty is shrimp cocktail. They have jumbo-sized shrimp with an amazing cocktail sauce. Joe is allergic to shellfish, so he couldn't enjoy the shrimp cocktail. However, he would get a side order of the cocktail sauce, which Joe used for dipping his rolls. If one ever had any sinus issues before entering St. Elmo's, the sauce would take care of that problem!

Joe would love to go on side trips while the team was on the road, often to an old train station or to a casino. During a trip to Washington at the end of the 2000–01 season, I led Joe and assistant coach Bob Ociepka on a walking tour of D.C. Joe loved taking pictures (before the digital age), and my scrapbook is filled with his pictures of Ford's Theatre, the Vietnam Memorial, the Jefferson Memorial, the White House, the Washington Monument and the U.S. Capitol. The highlights were walking into Ford's Theatre—mistakenly through the exit—just at the conclusion of a re-enactment of the shooting of Abraham Lincoln.

On plane trips, I enjoyed watching Joe attack crossword puzzles. From time to time, I would help with an answer. Joe meticulously cut out all of the crossword puzzles from USA Today, and he would tape them into a notebook for future use. He would plow through several puzzles on a West Coast trip.

Joe loved broadcasting Mount Union College football games, as well as local high school basketball games. Joe had a great relationship with Mount Union, and he was even on their staff for a few years as a teacher in broadcasting. What better instructor could one find? I had the opportunity to be a guest speaker in his class on a couple of occasions, once joined by sportswriter and author Terry Pluto. Joe always promised a meal for helping out, and Grinders restaurant in Alliance was usually the choice, where we enjoyed super sub sandwiches and, of course, dessert. Mount Union sent many interns to the Cavs, including Jeff Shreve, who interned with me in the Cavs' PR office. Jeff became the PA announcer for Cavs games when Howie Chizek retired from the courtside microphone, and Jeff is still the PA announcer at Cleveland Browns games.

Prior to the 1986–87 season, I helped initiate the Cavs Press Tour, which allowed us to align with our radio affiliates around the area. We would visit cities such as Youngstown, Lorain, Norwalk, Canton, Dover/New Philadelphia, and Erie, Pa. I was still amazed at how popular Joe was at each of the press stops. It didn't matter if we had Hall of Fame coach Lenny Wilkens in attendance, or any of our players—it was always Joe that everyone wanted to talk to. Not only did we have media interview sessions during the press tour, but we would sell tickets to the general public for a lunch or dinner. We also conducted an auction after dinner in order to raise money for one of the local charities. Joe would always serve as the master of ceremonies and auctioneer. One time, we were auctioning off a pair of Craig Ehlo's autographed shoes. The bidding was going a little bit slow, but the shoes finally sold for $100, with the high bidder being none other than Craig Ehlo himself! Joe got the biggest kick out of that, and he would often kid Craig. Craig ended up giving a check to the charity, and then he gave his pair of shoes to one of the young men who were helping serve the meals.

Joe preferred broadcasting games above the floor at midcourt.

Most broadcasters liked to announce from the floor to be closer to the action. However, Joe felt that he could describe the action better from the perspective of his perch. When Joe broadcast the games from the floor, after a win, the PR staff was responsible for getting the Player of the Game out onto the court to visit with Joe. When Joe's broadcast location was moved upstairs, it brought a new wrinkle, as it would be difficult to get players to go into the upper section at the Coliseum. Director of Broadcast Services Dave Dombrowski hooked up a remote interview location in the radio room, adjacent to our locker room. After one of our victories, Ehlo was chosen as the Player of the Game, so I escorted him into the radio room. He donned a headset so he could converse with Joe. In a classic moment, Craig asked, "Where are you, Joe?" It was one of the few times that Joe was temporarily speechless. Craig had that ability to make all of us chuckle and shake our heads!

In general, it was difficult getting postgame guests for the home and visiting broadcasts, but once I mentioned to our players that the interview was with Joe, I got very few who said no. Opposing players were a little more difficult to come by. In the 1980s, most PR directors did not travel with their teams, so the home PR person was responsible for obtaining players for the postgame shows. Players such as Doc Rivers, Scott Brooks and Joe Kleine were some of the "go-to" guys. Eventually Joe had interviewed Kleine after Celtics wins a few too many times, so we eventually did away with getting the opposing players on the postgame show.

Joe always did a great job keeping wins and losses in perspective. After a loss, Joe would look at the box score and notice that his name was not on the stat sheet. No turnovers, no missed shots, no fouls, no need to be overly concerned about a loss.

If you think about it, social media started with Joe. It was amazing to witness all of the visitors that Joe would entertain at road games. There were always native Clevelanders on the road ready to cheer on the Cavs, often stopping courtside to drop off cookies or notes for Joe to read during road games. Joe always would take the time to relay the messages back home for family and friends. Joe may be the last person to utilize social media, but I do have a picture of him working on a computer with our TV producer, Pat Murray, during a shootaround on the road. Pat must have been showing Joe pictures of old railroads on the Internet.

One side of Joe that most people aren't privy to is his thoughtfulness. As one gets older, it's harder to remember various birthday, holiday or wedding presents. However, I'll never forget Joe's wedding present to my wife Kelly and me. He gave us money with specific instructions to have a special dinner on our honeymoon. Yes, we adhered to the directives and enjoyed a wonderful dinner on the lanai of our honeymoon suite in Maui. Joe would have been proud that I topped it off with an ice cream sundae!

Officials

Many years later, Joe knows why he was so tough on NBA officials early in his career.

"I saw the game through the eyes of Bill Fitch," he said. "He carried on a battle with a lot of officials. Not all of them, but some. Some guys like Mark Mano and Bob Rakel, Fitch just hated them—I mean professionally. He just didn't think they were very good."

Joe had seen only one NBA game in his life before he was hired by the Cavs in 1970. He came to an expansion franchise in a league that seemed to have very little interest in helping the new teams. Little talent was made available in the expansion draft. Nor was there any attempt to give the new teams an advantage in the draft.

"Some nights, you could see that the officials just didn't work very hard," said Joe. "It's like they knew we were an expansion team, and we were not supposed to win. Some of these guys walked on the court figuring we were going to get blown out. You can say what you want, but when those guys had a Boston-Lakers game and a game between Portland and the Cavs, there were certain officials who didn't work as hard in our games."

That certainly was the opinion of Fitch, and it didn't take long for Joe to buy into that view.

Not only did the Cavs' players receive little respect from officials, the same was true of Fitch. He had never played or coached in the NBA before being hired by the Cavs. The veteran officials didn't know him, and many of those officials were not very interested in the opinions and complaints of a young coach from college.

Former *Plain Dealer* sports editor Hal Lebovitz once wrote that he thought "Joe Tait would get an official killed one day." His point was that Joe's criticism would inspire a fan to harm an official—or something like that.

Lebovitz also wrote: "I think Joe is one of the finest basketball play-by-play men anywhere. I would place him at the very top if he weren't so critical of officials. His constant second-guessing always interfered with the flow of the descriptions for me. He would be describing a play, and in the midst of it, he'd say, 'Oh, Manny, blew another one.' It had to disturb the concentration of the listeners."

Most listeners probably enjoyed Joe ripping the officials, because they believed he was sticking up for their team—especially in the early years.

Remember that Fitch had hired Joe. And that he was one of the lowest-paid broadcasters in the NBA. And the franchise was in constant financial peril. And Joe was close to the players. And some of the officials gave the impression they'd rather be cutting their toenails than working a Cavs game.

Add it all up, and Joe was not about to grant some of the officials the benefit of the doubt.

"I didn't need Fitch to tell me what to think," said Joe. "I could sense what was happening in the game."

Lebovitz had another opinion as he wrote: "I don't think it's possible to do play-by-play and officiate it at the same time, to say nothing of the fact that I might question Joe's qualifications to be an official. . . . Many times, I have heard Joe scream about a call that was right in front of me, and [the call] was absolutely correct in my judgment. If the official hadn't called it, he would have been remiss. Yet Joe would be telling the world, 'He blew it.' Just as Joe didn't think the official was right, it's highly possible Joe wasn't right."

It's worth remembering that Lebovitz was a high school official in several sports and even had a column titled "Ask Hal, The Referee" in which he answered fans' questions.

*   *   *

The only time Fitch challenged Joe about something said on the air involved an official.

"Manny Sokol made a great call at the end of game that cost the Cavs a game," Joe recalled. "The next night, Fitch called me into his office. It was before we did the coach's show. He had a snippet of tape of the play, and he played it for me."

Fitch asked, "Did you really feel that he made the right call?"

Joe said, "Yes."

Fitch then ripped into Joe, saying it was an awful call, absolutely terrible. He ended the tirade by saying, "Joe, if you can't see the game better than that, I don't know what you are doing in this league."

Joe said, "I just called it the way I saw it."

Fitch said, "Well, try not to see it that way in the future."

Joe let it drop. But thinking back on the confrontation, Joe said, "I don't think it changed anything I said on the air. Bill liked to try to intimidate people, but he couldn't do that to me."

"That's very true," said Burt Graeff, a *Cleveland Press* writer who covered the Cavs in the 1970s. "Joe and Fitch went back so far, I don't think Joe was ever afraid of him—and Fitch knew it. Fitch may have hired him, but Joe was very popular. He didn't have to do things to please Fitch."

*   *   *

When an official had a very bad night, Joe sometimes waited until the official was standing near him—and Joe would begin to tell his audience what a lousy job someone such as Mark Mano was doing.

"To his credit, I know he heard me . . . but he ignored it," said Joe. "He'd stand in front of me staring at the court—his back to me. He didn't turn around or anything, but yes, he heard me, all right."

One official, not Mano, told Joe that his wife was listening to the game. The Cavs were on a 50,000-watt station that could be heard in "over 38 states and half of Canada," according to Pete

Franklin. Maybe it wasn't that far, but it was a long way. The official's wife supposedly was writing down all of Joe's critical remarks. Joe really didn't care. In fact, he mentioned it to his audience that he was being monitored by the official's wife.

*   *   *

On February 11, 1973, Fitch stunned Joe and everyone else with 1:46 left in the first quarter of a game against Atlanta at old Cleveland Arena. A ball appeared to bounce off the foot of the Hawks' Lou Hudson and rolled out of bounds. Official Bob Rakel awarded the ball to Atlanta.

Fitch stood up and pointed to his foot, indicating the ball bounced off Hudson.

"Then I walked back to the bench," Fitch said 38 years later. "I never said a word to the guy, and he teed me up."

After Fitch was given a technical foul, he glared at Rakel for a moment. Then he grabbed a folding chair that served as part of the Cavs' bench.

In the *Cleveland Press* game story the following day, Graeff wrote: "Fitch last night established an Arena record for chair-putting—22 feet, 9 inches. He got his Irish up and let fly with a piece of Nick Mileti's furniture in the direction of referee Bob Rakel. . . . Luckily, he missed."

Joe recalled being "stunned" when he saw it, "and to this day, I don't remember what I said on the air."

In Graeff's story, he reported, "Fitch has been thrown out of three Arena games in three years, and it was Rakel who did the tossing on each occasion. . . . Fitch's exit was accompanied by a standing ovation from the wild-eyed gang of 6,872 fans. It was Fitch's first such ovation in three years here."

This was before Bob Knight threw a chair during a game while coaching at Indiana University.

"That was more of a sliding toss," said Joe. "Bill really threw that chair—overhand."

He was fined $5,000 by the NBA—the largest fine ever given a coach at that point. It later was reduced to $2,000.

"I don't regret doing it at all," Fitch said in 2011. "I didn't deserve the technical. Everything just boiled over."

Did he want to hit Rakel with the chair?

"I didn't think about it at the time," he said. "I'm glad I didn't hurt him. But it also doesn't bother me that I did it."

Lenny Wilkens was a member of that team. He saw Fitch rush on the court toward Rakel and grabbed him from behind.

"I didn't know if Bill was going to hit him," said Wilkens. "But I didn't want to find out."

Graeff wrote: "It took the combined efforts of Lenny Wilkens, trainer Ron Culp, assistant coach Jimmy Rodgers and [forward] Dwight Davis to keep Fitch from turning Rakel into a punching bag."

"That was Fitch back in those days," said Joe. "He wasn't afraid to fight anyone. He was a very tough guy, and he wouldn't back down."

In case you were wondering, the Cavs lost the game, 115-107.

* * *

Over the years, Joe became less critical of officials.

As he traveled the NBA, he began to run into them in airports and hotel coffee shops. He became friends with Earl Strom, one of the greatest officials ever. Talking to them, he also began to see the game through their eyes and to appreciate the challenges of their jobs.

"After I left the Cavs and spent two seasons away [in Chicago and New Jersey], I wasn't as connected to the teams," said Joe. "That also helped me with officials. I became more objective. I realized these poor devils were on the road all the time; they never had a place to call home. They fly commercial, while the teams charter jets. I gained more respect for them. The older officials just loved the game. As I got to know them, I realized that."

It didn't stop him from criticizing the men with whistles.

One of his favorite lines when a dubious call was made: "There's a whistle and a . . . WHAT?"

He never backed away from saying certain officials gave stars the benefit of the doubt. He also said that LeBron James was given the star treatment by some officials when he played for the Cavs.

"I loved how Earl Strom didn't want to slow the game down," said Joe. "He'd tell a player, 'Do that again, and I'll call it. Now, just back off, and I'll let it go.' That was smart officiating."

Joe became friendly with Bob Delaney and gained a new respect for the NBA official when he learned that Delaney worked undercover to arrest some mob members in his early career—before the NBA.

As he talked to different officials, he began to see them as people—not guys determined to make life miserable for his team, which often seemed to be the view of Fitch.

"When I was in the hospital, Joe Crawford called me," said Joe.

Crawford is considered a great NBA official, but he has incredible explosions. One night at the old Coliseum, he threw out Cavs coach Lenny Wilkens and five Cavs players. There was no fight. He was just in a bad mood. Joe's radio account along with some newspaper stories earned Crawford a fine from the league. At least, that's what Crawford told a reporter.

"I'm in the hospital, and Crawford called and said, 'I know you hate me!'" said Joe. "I told Joe that I didn't hate him. I said he was one of the best officials ever when he kept his temper under control. We had a good talk after that, and it was great of him to call me."

*   *   *

Joe was not a big fan of Darell Garretson, who was the NBA supervisor of officials for many years. He also still called games for much of that time. It was Garretson's idea to add a third official, which Joe believes often made the situation worse. Sometimes three officials are so concerned with "covering their area of the court," they refuse to make a call because it was in the other official's turf.

"I also thought he could be very pompous," said Joe.

Veteran officials such as Earl Strom had little use for Garretson, and that also influenced Joe's opinion.

"But I do have two good stories about Darell," he said.

The first was a night when the Cavs were crushing Washington, which was coached by Gene Shue.

"The game was so bad, Shue wanted to get thrown out," said Joe. "He kept yelling and complaining to Garretson. Finally, Darell walked over to Shue and said, 'If I gotta stand out here and watch your team, then you gotta sit there and watch them, too. I'm not throwing you out, no matter what you do.'"

Joe paused, "I really liked that."

The better story was a game where Joe had his son—Joey—sitting at courtside as Joe called the game. Garretson noticed the father and young son together. Joey had little interest in basketball but loved to draw, and he later became an artist and a high school art teacher.

"Joey would take the stat sheet, turn them over to the blank side and draw dinosaurs and whatnot," said Joe. "Garretson came by a couple of times, looked down at Joey's drawings."

During a timeout, Garretson said, "Is that your son?"

Joe introduced Joey to the official.

Garretson said: "He's really good. He's got talent."

Joe said: "I thanked him. I always thought that was a nice thing to say."

The Tribe

The year was 1972. Joe was making about $12,000 per year doing the Cavaliers' radio broadcasts. He also filled in at various stations to do sports reports, even a Saturday morning swap-and-shop show, where people called in trying to sell old washing machines and baby cribs.

"I did a show called *Ask Your Neighbor*," said Joe. "At one point, I was doing news on two different stations at the same time—WERE and WJW. I did a Sunday morning show with middle-of-the-road music on WJW. Most of it was hit-and-miss as I would substitute for the regular hosts. It didn't matter, I needed the work."

And the money.

"I had three kids," he said.

The Indians' radio voices in 1972 were Bob Neal and Herb Score.

"Herb absolutely loved Bob Neal," recalled Nancy Score, his widow. "Bob was Herb's first partner, and Herb said that Bob not only treated him well—he taught Herb so much about broadcasting. He always felt grateful to Bob."

No doubt that Nancy Score was accurately portraying the relationship between Neal and Score. Neal and Score first worked together in 1964, right after Score retired from baseball. They did television games together.

In 1965, Neal moved to radio, where he was teamed with Jimmy Dudley.

Remember, this was the 1960s. About 20 games were televised each season—compared to every game broadcast on the radio. The prime job was baseball on the radio. The most popular voice of the Tribe was Dudley, who was blessed to have his first season with the Tribe being 1948. Yes, that was a year the Indians won the World Series.

Dudley and Neal first worked together on radio from 1957 to '61. Actually, they didn't work together at all. They barely spoke to each other. They shared the same booth and split up the innings. Dudley was the lead announcer, doing the first two innings and the final three. Neal believed he was a better broadcaster than Dudley. As you can imagine, Dudley had a different opinion.

"Bob never got over the fact that I was the No. 1 broadcaster," said Dudley in an interview for *The Curse of Rocky Colavito.* "I told him that it may not be fair, but it was reality."

Entering the 1962 season, Neal was moved to television. Dudley paired up with Harry Jones, a former baseball writer who later was the team's traveling secretary and then became a broadcaster. Jones got along with almost anyone.

Just as Joe developed favorite catches phrases over the years, Dudley had several.

Tribe home games were always played "on the beautiful shores of Lake Erie." When the count was full, Dudley said, "It's 3-and-2, the string is out." He opened games with "Hello, baseball fans everywhere, this is Jimmy Dudley." He also did a popular aluminum siding commercial in which he said the number rapidly, "GARFIELD-1, 2323 . . . GARFIELD 1, 2323." You didn't just have a hot dog, you ate a "Kahn's, the wiener the world awaited!"

Fans loved it.

But in 1965, Tribe President Gabe Paul—who had always liked Neal's work—put Neal back on radio with Dudley. They lasted until the end of the 1967 season, when Paul fired Dudley. Paul also helped Dudley find a job doing the games for the expansion Seattle Pilots—but that lasted only one year.

Pete Franklin loved to talk about how he first came to Cleveland in 1967 to do sports talk. He went to a game, sat in the radio booth between Neal and Dudley. It took about six innings, but he noticed that while they did speak to him, they never spoke to each other. In fact, one guy would abruptly leave the booth when the other was on the air.

"You could tell they hated each other," said Franklin. "They absolutely loathed each other. You got a chill after awhile, just being in the same booth with them."

It's a safe guess Neal was jealous of Dudley, who was very popular with fans and most other members of the media. He was a nice guy, a very enthusiastic broadcaster. When Dudley was fired and replaced by Score, Neal believed it vindicated him as the superior broadcaster. He also didn't have to worry about Score being better on the air. Herb was so new to the business, and still very raw. He never was a polished broadcaster, just a sincere one. He also had almost zero ego when it came to his role as a broadcaster. He was just content to be in the booth and have a job that kept him around baseball.

This was especially true in the 1960s when Score was first starting out. Neal also knew that Gabe Paul loved Herb Score and wanted Herb to become a solid broadcaster.

Joe Tait was a different story.

"The first time I met Bob Neal was not long after I was hired to do the Cavs' games," said Joe. "Public relations director Bob Brown introduced us. We shook hands. Neal never even said hello."

What did Neal say?

"He said, 'Joe, I hope you realize that there are a lot more people in Cleveland who'd rather hear me do minor-league hockey tonight than you do basketball,'" said Joe.

It was not said with a smile.

Joe said Neal used to do sports reports on some afternoon drive shows on WERE radio. Joe occasionally filled in for vacationing broadcasters at the station.

"For several weeks, we got along well," said Joe. "But Neal would just bitch and moan about having to do baseball. He hated it, it was a drag. He went on and on."

One day, Joe had heard enough and said, 'Hey, Bob, anytime you want to give it up, let me know. I'll be glad to take it off your hands.'"

Neal's response?

"He never spoke to me again," said Joe. "I mean, never. Not a word."

It was like Jimmy Dudley, all over again.

*   *   *

Nick Mileti put together a group to buy the Indians in March 1972. He outbid . . . or at least out-talked . . . a group headed by Al Rosen and George Steinbrenner to buy the Tribe.

Mileti often says he saved the Indians from moving to New Orleans.

That is partly true because former owner Vernon Stouffer had a tentative deal in place to play 30 games in 1972 in New Orleans—setting up the franchise to eventually move there. So, yes, Mileti did save the Indians for Cleveland. Of course, Rosen and Steinbrenner (who later bought the Yankees after being rejected by Stouffer) would have done the same thing.

But for Joe, it was a huge break that Mileti and his 54 partners ended up with the Tribe. That's because Joe was a Mileti guy—along with being a talented broadcaster.

In 1972, Neal's wife died, and Joe filled in with Herb Score for three games on the radio.

The first game done by Joe was July 10, 1972. The Indians were 31-42. The game was in Cleveland, where Gaylord Perry started for the Tribe and beat the White Sox, 2-1. That raised his record to 14-7 with an ERA of 1.87. Joe still has a copy of his handwritten scorecard in one of his scrapbooks.

Longtime hard-core Tribe fans will find this game's lineup interesting: Buddy Bell (CF), Jack Brohamer (2B), Alex Johnson (LF), Graig Nettles (3B), Ray Fosse (C), Ron Lolich (RF), Chris Chambliss (1B), Eddie Leon (SS) and Perry (P).

Nettles drove in the first run with a sacrifice fly. Lolich hit a homer. He had only four in his brief career—228 major-league at-bats. Yes, Buddy Bell was a rookie who played center. He later became a Gold Glove third baseman. The Indians still had Nettles and Chambliss, who were later traded to the Yankees—and that group headed by Rosen and Steinbrenner.

"I got raves from everyone in the media," said Joe. "Doug Clarke [of *The Cleveland Press*] acted as if I should go straight into the broadcasting Hall of Fame. It took awhile for me to realize that it wasn't that everyone liked my work that much, but they despised Neal."

Joe got a call from Ray Hart, the *Plain Dealer* media critic who had been so positive about Joe's early work with the Cavs.

"Did you enjoy all the stuff in the paper?" asked Hart.

"It's a little over-the-top," said Joe. "I'm surprised."

"Don't worry," Hart said. "You'll pay for it."

Hart did not mean that he was out to get Joe—but Hart knew how other media people were thrilled to stick it to Neal by praising Joe's work. Neal made enemies not only because of his general arrogance, but because he'd often rip sportswriters in some of his sports commentaries.

"Bob was supposed to be out for more than a week because of his wife's funeral," said Joe. "But he came back in three days."

Neal would probably say that it was because he wanted to do the games and put his mind on something besides his wife's death. But Joe and others heard whispers that Neal wanted to get back on the air as quickly as possible—and get Joe off the air. He felt threatened by the young broadcaster.

"Right after that, Harry Jones [who did Tribe TV games] had a heart attack," said Joe. "So I filled in for him. I was teamed up with Rocky Colavito. He was the big name, I was just there to fill in for Harry Jones. I had never met Rocky before. He was pleasant but not overly friendly. The Indians had a game in Baltimore. In the first inning, some yahoo in right field winds up to make a throw to the plate . . . and it ends up about 10 rows behind the dugout."

For a moment, Rocky and Joe stared at the plate.

Then Joe said, "Hey, Rock, I've been told that when you played, some of your throws from the outfield went even 10 rows deeper than that one."

Colavito just started laughing, and so did Joe.

The former Tribe star seemed to appreciate that Joe wasn't intimidated by being in the same booth with him—that they were

In the radio booth at Cleveland Municipal Stadium with Herb Score, in the mid-1970s. "I learned more baseball from Herb Score than anyone else," Joe said. "He could have been a general manager and done a great job running a team."

going to be two guys having some fun while doing the games together.

"I loved working with Joe," said Colavito. "He was easy to get along with. We had a good time."

The Plain Dealer ran several letters praising Joe's baseball work in 1972.

Joe Bajornas of Canton wrote: "Joe Tait resuscitated all my interest in Indians baseball with a World Series performance in announcing Gaylord Perry's 14th victory. He personified in one short 2-hour, 20-minute ballgame the enthusiasm that has been lacking since 1967."

That was a reference to Jimmy Dudley, who was fired as Tribe broadcaster after 1967.

Ron Bogner of Mansfield wrote: "Joe Tait was just superb. At first, I thought I was listening to Harry Caray. Then I realized it was the voice of the Cavaliers. . . . When will Nick Mileti and WERE and the rest of the brass wake up and get those two yokels—Score and Neal—off the airwaves?"

In a *Plain Dealer* story, Harry Jones praised Joe's work: "He's one of the most capable announcers that I've heard in a long time. He had no television experience but did a superb job."

The story also reported that due to his heart attack, Jones said it was the first time he'd missed a game in 25 years covering the Tribe—13 as *The Plain Dealer*'s baseball writer, three on radio and nine on TV. Jones was 51. *The PD* reported that he was the third Tribe broadcaster to suffer a heart attack on the job. It happened to Dudley in 1963 and Neal in 1969.

*   *   *

In 1973, Joe received a call from Mileti.

"Joe, remember when I said I'd make it up to you," said Mileti.

Those were Mileti's words when Joe agreed to do the Cavs' games for $100 each in 1970.

"Well," said Mileti. "Today, I'm doing just that. You're the new voice of the Cleveland Indians, along with Herb Score."

Mileti also brought back Harry Jones to do the TV games with Rocky Colavito.

In 1972, Joe's salary was bumped to $150 per game for the Cavs—Mileti kept raising him $25 per game each year.

For the 1973 season, he received $30,000 for the Indians and $15,750 for the Cavs. Add in some other radio gigs, and Joe had turned a $7,400 job in 1970 to $50,000 in income by 1973.

"Nick always kept his word to me," said Joe. "I owe him a lot."

Suddenly, Joe's schedule changed dramatically. He was almost never home. He did the Cavs (82 games) and Indians (162 games) on the radio. When there was a conflict, he did the Cavs games. He also did some hockey.

"I had to really figure out how to live on the road," he said.

To protect the guilty, Joe doesn't name the "veteran baseball writer" who decided to show the young broadcaster how to handle the beat.

"The writer said the plane left at 11:30 in the morning—we were still traveling commercial—and to meet him at the airport at 10," said Joe. "I did. We had a drink at the airport bar. When we got to the hotel in New York, we had another drink at the bar—we were waiting for the team to unload everyone's luggage. I was drinking vodka and tonic. There was a third drink in the afternoon before leaving for the park on the team bus. And another drink after batting practice in the pressroom. And another drink right after the game, waiting for the players to dress and get on the bus. And yet another drink back at the hotel bar."

The next morning, it was more than a hangover that hit Joe.

"I realized two things," he said. "At this rate, I was going broke because we took turns buying the drinks. And I also was turning into an alcoholic."

He paused.

"I quit, cold turkey," he said. "I haven't had anything stronger than a nonalcoholic beer ever since."

*   *   *

Joe had a few advantages in taking over the Tribe games on radio:

1. Fans knew him from doing three seasons of the Cavs.

2. He had done a few Tribe games on radio and TV.

3. He was replacing Bob Neal, who was not beloved. There were very few letters of protest to the Indians or the newspapers when Neal was fired.

4. Joe sounded a little like the popular Jimmy Dudley in terms of enthusiasm. Fans missed Dudley, and were willing to embrace Joe because of his style and obvious love for the home team.

5. Herb Score made it clear that he liked Joe and enjoyed working with him.

"Herb was great to me," said Joe. "I was the lead broadcaster. I did the first three and the last three innings. Herb did the middle three. If that did bother him, he never said a word about it. He made it easy for me."

Nancy Score said her husband "just liked Joe. We all did. Herb was very happy because Joe did all the statistics. Herb hated doing the numbers and was glad to leave them to Joe."

"I learned more baseball from Herb Score than anyone else," Joe said. "He could have been a general manager and done a great job running a team. If I owned a baseball team in the 1970s and 1980s, Herb would have been the first guy I'd have hired to be general manager. He knew players. He knew everything about the game. Whenever something was happening on the field and there was a meeting with the umpires, I'd ask Herb what was going on. Sometimes, I had absolutely no clue. Herb always knew. I'm telling you, he ALWAYS knew what was the problem."

Joe discovered a few things about Herb—the former Indians pitcher didn't like to talk much about himself or his career.

"Herb used to say that sometimes it was best just to keep quiet," said Nancy. "Let them think you are a fool—it's better than to open your mouth and prove it."

Score didn't want to be viewed as a guy who lived in the past. While he never was a polished broadcaster, he took pride "in never talking down to the fans." He wanted to sound like a guy enjoying the game, talking to his buddies about it—but not acting like an expert.

Off the air, Score had very strong opinions. They were solicited by former general managers Gabe Paul and Phil Seghi. Several Tribe managers also took Score into their confidence, and asked his thoughts on various issues having to do with the team.

But Score would never give an opinion unless asked. And he would never betray a confidence.

"I know he talked to [the Tribe brass] about things, but I have no clue what was said," said Nancy Score. "I knew better than to ask Herb. You could always trust him to keep things quiet."

Score came to the games and trips impeccably dressed.

"That's because Nancy picks out my clothes," he used to say.

That was true to an extent, but Herb was a very neat man. It never seemed that he needed a haircut or that a single strand was out of place. His jackets, ties and everything about his appearance shouted that this was a very classy man.

"I never saw Herb pitch, but I did see his stats," said Joe. "I remember talking to [former catcher and Tribe manager] Birdie Tebbetts, who said he believed Herb could have been the greatest left-hander ever had he stayed healthy."

Score came up to the Tribe in 1955 billed as the next Bob Feller. He threw that hard and looked that good.

At age 22, Score was 16-10 with a 2.85 ERA and 245 strikeouts—as a rookie.

The next season, he was 20-9 with a 2.53 ERA and 263 strikeouts.

He had led the American League in strikeouts in his first two seasons. He completed 27 of 68 starts, throwing seven shutouts. He was 2-1 with a 2.00 ERA on May 7, 1957, when he was struck in the eye with a line drive off the bat of the Yankees' Gil McDougald. He missed the rest of the season and never was the same after that. He was 38-20 before the injury, 17-26 after. Score always insisted that it was an elbow injury after being hit in the eye that destroyed his career—not the eye injury.

"Once during a long rain delay, I got Herb to talk about his injury," said Joe. "He said the real problem was when he pitched off a wet mound in Washington. He slipped, and he hurt his arm. It was diagnosed as a sprain, but it really was a tear in his elbow. It never healed properly. He talked about it with the same emotion of a guy saying he had cornflakes for breakfast this morning and he may have pancakes tomorrow morning."

And Score would only reveal that to those he trusted, and he kept the discussion very short.

But Joe did find one area of Score's career that could be discussed on the air: "Herb loved it when I made fun of him as a hitter, and he joined right in."

Score batted a miserable .128 in his major-league career.

"One day, someone told me that Herb hit two home runs off Gaylord Perry when both of were in Class AAA," said Joe. "And that someone was Gaylord Perry, who was with the Indians at the time. I mentioned that on the air, and Herb shrugged it off by saying, 'Gaylord just didn't get enough grease on the ball.' He was talking about how Gaylord threw the Vaseline ball. But that's all he said."

But Score went absolutely giddy once during a game in Texas.

"I opened my mouth to say something, and a moth flew right in," said Joe. "I said a word, then it flew back out. Herb was laughing so hard, I thought he was going to have a heart attack. In our seven years together, I never heard him laugh that hard."

*   *   *

Right after Joe was hired, Bob Neal gave a long interview to *The Plain Dealer*'s Dan Coughlin. Neal was angry about being fired and how he was fired. Mileti announced his new broadcasting team at a banquet, before he was able to talk to Neal. He did call Neal a few times but never made a connection.

"For 18 years, I broadcast for a losing team," Neal said. "It hasn't exactly been an exciting adventure. When a team loses 102 games, you've got to be a miracle worker to maintain interest for the whole season."

There are a couple of points in that statement worthy of discussion.

Herb Score watched more bad baseball than anyone. He never viewed it as a grind-it-out job. He truly liked being at the ballpark and being around baseball people. For 33 years, he seemed grateful to have the job. He'd tell Joe that each day there was a chance to see something on the field that he'd never seen before.

Along with having the obvious talent, the best broadcasters are those who know thousands of well-qualified people across the country would love to have their jobs—and could do it well. Look at how Joe stepped into a major market in 1970 . . . and three years later, he was doing both the NBA and Major League Baseball.

"There are a lot of guys like me out there," said Joe. "But they never got a chance."

The other point is that each game is entertainment for someone. Yes, the team may stink, but people with health problems, people with personal problems, people who just want a break from the pressure of daily life look to their favorite teams for a diversion. The broadcaster's job is to make it as interesting as possible but not be phony. Fans immediately responded to Joe doing baseball because he came across like they would in the booth.

Think about his opening line for each game: "It's a beautiful day for baseball."

How often was that true in Cleveland, given the weather on the lakefront?

But Joe knew that a baseball game that day made it beautiful for someone.

Most of the broadcasters in Cleveland sports history are good guys off the air. Most fans have good memories of meeting the likes of Nev Chandler, Jim Donovan, Doug Dieken, Tom Hamilton, Rick Manning, Mike Hegan, Joe Tait, Jimmy Dudley, Les Levine, Mike Snyder and so many others. Fans always were stunned at how kind and polite Pete Franklin was when encountering him away from the microphone.

In his story, Coughlin correctly portrayed Neal this way: "He can be vain and pompous and doesn't have to reach far to find a nasty streak of invective in his soul. On the other hand, he is oversensitive about himself and reacts like a wounded cheetah to the slightest offense or imagined insult . . . he has a penchant for alienating people."

Part of being a broadcaster is understanding that you are in the people business. Yes, your check may come from the station and/or the team, but it is the fans who pay the cost either through ticket sales, cable TV bills or at least buying some of the products that are advertised.

Joe and Herb understood this.

On July 12, 1973, they did a game from the bleachers. *The Plain Dealer*'s Russell Schneider wrote: "The bleachers were filled almost to capacity with the presence of Joe Tait and Herb Score. The play-by-play duo was seated at the right side of the scoreboard and did the broadcast in semi-nudity. The gabbers removed their shirts to take advantage of the bright sun on a pleasant afternoon."

Members of the media may view that as a publicity stunt, but fans loved it. Score often sat in the stands for a few innings with his shirt off at the old Hi Corbett Field in spring training to catch some sun while his partner did a few innings on the air. When those innings were up, Herb put his shirt back on and returned to the press box. In the meantime, fans shook his hand, asked for autographs and just got to know Herb.

*   *   *

Not everyone loved Joe doing baseball.

In August of his first full season, *The Plain Dealer*'s Howard Preston (an editorial writer) began a column like this: "I do not know Joe Tait from any other siren in the night, but he is looked upon as a comer by some people in the field of sports broadcasting and he has a zest for his job. My own preference is for a less strident voice on radio, but then maybe other people enjoy being shaken out of their easy chairs when something sensational happens, such as a Cleveland Indian catching a pop fly."

He criticized Joe for not giving enough details, for saying, "He struck him out."

"Tait shows promise," wrote Preston. "But he may be dangerous if you keep your good crystal near your radio set. In the event of a Cleveland rally his shrill tone can crack glass from a distance of Kansas City."

The Plain Dealer's William Hickey wrote: "It's my considered opinion that Joe Tait is the most maddening baseball announcer I've ever been forced to listen to . . . and my ears go back to the 1930s. A thoroughly likeable and pleasant man away from the microphone, Tait must lie awake nights dreaming up new ways to torture listeners of Indians."

Hickey didn't like the fact that Joe sometimes said, "There's a DRIVE, which the left fielder is camping under."

Something else was happening here.

Remember when *Plain Dealer* critic Raymond Hart warned Joe that criticism was coming? Well, it arrived. Hart and Hickey were the media critics for the same newspaper. For years, Hart backed Joe, Hickey ripped him.

In another story, Hickey criticized Joe for saying, "There's a fly ball down the left field line. It could be fair. It could be foul. IT IS!"

Actually, it is something an excited Herb Score said . . . more than once. But not Joe.

Hickey added, "Tait is considered one of the best play-by-play sports announcers currently working. Of course, many of the really good ones have either retired or recently taken up other activities."

In 1974, a woman named Emma Blue wrote to *The Plain Dealer*: "Could you let Joe Tait go some place and listen to a real announcer and learn how? Or better yet, let him shut up for nine innings and listen to Herb Score. To listen to Tait is disgusting, all that hollering and exaggerated calling."

This brought a pile of letters to *The Plain Dealer* backing Joe. Most were like Jake Lane, who wrote: "I wish to sound off on Emma Blue's comment . . . to infer Joe Tait is a poor announcer because he livens up the game is erroneous. . . . Joe Tait comes the closest to making me feel like I'm there. . . . Even when the Indians are at their worst, Tait and his sidekick, Herb Score, make the game interesting and worth listening to."

Score's response to the debate over the baseball broadcasts?

"Joe, first of all, don't read it," he said. "If you do, don't pay attention to it."

It was good advice.

*   *   *

Joe and Score were together in the radio booth for seven years.

"When we were on the road, we rented one car," said Joe. "I used it during the day to go chase trains. Herb used it at night to go to his favorite restaurants. They'd keep places open for him. He was a star at some places—people knew him by name and came out of the kitchen to say hello. That happened in restaurants in cities all over the American League."

Score was a former player who had other baseball people as his set of friends on the road. He had been traveling the American League since he was a rookie in 1955 with the Tribe. Joe was new to baseball in the 1970s, and most of his friends were other media people. Herb liked to stay up late after games and eat with friends. Joe tended to go to bed after night games and get up early for breakfast.

"We probably had breakfast three times together in seven years," said Joe. "I went out with him about three times. We saw each other 162 times a year for games, so we spent a lot of time together."

"Herb always felt very comfortable with Joe," said Nancy Score. "They hit it off right away."

Joe enjoyed the slower pace of baseball.

"It's more relaxed," he said. "You have five minutes of excitement, 25 minutes of no excitement. Baseball is much tougher to do than basketball because you have to keep the level up in the broadcast. You can't go into the tank because it's a bad game and become moribund."

While Joe believes the NBA can and should be done solo on the radio, baseball needs a partner to fill in the dead spaces. It's why Herb and Joe did so well together—they seemed to like the game and each other.

While Joe kept doing the Cavs on radio, why did he leave the Tribe radio team after the 1979 season to do the Indians on television?

"Money," he said. "I was offered more money to go on TV, and it was for fewer games."

Joe also had been traveling at a reckless pace—one year, he said he was off and at home for only nine full days. It took a toll on his marriage, as he would be divorced in 1980.

"A lot of things fell apart there," he said. "I sort of needed to regroup."

Thinking back, Joe loved those days on the air with Herb Score.

"It was like we had been friends for 30 years almost from the moment we began working together," said Joe. "Herb made it easy for me, and I'll always be grateful for that."

Joe and Baseball

In the 1970s, Joe was broadcasting Indians games. I was about 12. I'd always try to hear the first pitch because right before the start of the game, my beloved Herb Score would say:

"And here is Joe Tait to tell you THAT . . ."

Joe Tait (always in a very upbeat tone): "It's a BEAUTIFUL day for baseball."

Of course, Joe would say this every game, regardless of the weather. It could be 40 degrees with a 20 mile-per-hour wind, but Joe would still belt out that it was a beautiful day for baseball.

But what I really waited for was the response Herb would give to Joe when Joe would say how beautiful it was when the weather was actually horrible. Herb's comments like "You're nuts" or "You're crazy" never failed to put a smile on my face.

—Tom Tornabene, Port Washington, Ohio

I loved Joe's sarcasm. I remember when he and Herb Score broadcast the Indians games in "foul" weather, he would say as he opened the broadcast, "It's a beeeaaauutiful day for baseball, if you're a DUCK!"

—Jerry Craig, Kent, Ohio

I especially loved how he started the broadcast with "It's a beautiful day for baseball" no matter what the weather was. I truly believe that any day is a beautiful day for baseball!

—Tony Mollica, Athens, Ohio

I grew up listening to Joe Tait and Herb Score doing Indians baseball on the radio. I also enjoyed him doing the games on TV with Bruce Drennan. My favorite catchphrase was "Wherever you are ... UP ON YOUR FEET for the seventh-inning stretch, the score Indians 3, Yankees 1."

—*Pat Hoover, North Ridgeville, Ohio*

After the handoff from Herb Score, Joe goes right into: "And it's a BEAUTIFUL night for baseball! Thank you, Herb, and good evening, everybody ..." Rain, snow, sweltering heat, it didn't matter. Every day, every game, it was a beautiful day for baseball.

—*Gregg Bollinger, Columbia City, Indiana*

I listened to Joe doing the play-by-play with Herb Score from the time he started until I left Cleveland in 1977 to live in Spain. I absolutely loved the two of them as a team. There weren't many games on TV back then, so I tuned in on the radio almost every night from April to October. I even took my radio to games at the old Stadium so I wouldn't miss a single detail. Even though I was only able to listen to Joe for four years, I will never forget how vividly he brought the games to me, and how often he made me smile with his repartee with Herb.

—*Cindy Chadd, Colmenarejo, Madrid*

My brother and I were 6 and 7, respectively, when we got our first transistor radio for Christmas in 1972. I began suffering, celebrating and sweating with Joe Tait during the Cavs' season. But it wasn't until spring when we listened to the second game of the Indians' season that I learned to love him. We'd gone to Opening Day with my dad. It was really cold, and I could see my breath when the game started. Tait comes on the air and describes the scene: "The skies are gray over Municipal Stadium, the temperature is a chilly 40 degrees, and it's a beautiful day for baseball." To me, that last line is like one of the great truths of man's history. "It's a beautiful day for baseball." He said it every game, no matter the conditions. The Cubs had Harry Caray, the Phils had Harry Kalas, the Cards had Jack Buck, but to me, the greatest baseball broadcaster will always be Joe Tait.

—*Patrick Salem, Downers Grove, Illinois*

I grew up in southeastern Ohio with the Pittsburgh teams on local TV and radio. Occasionally, I would use the motorized antenna rotation device and try to pick up Cleveland games, usually without success. Once I was able to tune in an Indians game on UHF channel 43. I remember thinking it was so funny that the one announcer didn't like the other one. Turns out it was Joe Tait and Bruce Drennan! There was a batting helmet promotion, and Drennan was mugging for the camera with a helmet on, and it was annoying the heck out of Joe. That was an early instance of Joe not hiding his feelings. I love his curmudgeonly side and his biting honesty, whether he was critiquing a ref, a player, or complaining about the noisy pregame intros.

—*George Mauersberger, Cleveland, Ohio*

When I was a young teenager in the 1970s, Indians games were broadcast on TV only on the weekends. So on many, many summer evenings, I would settle down in my bedroom with my transistor radio and follow the team by listening to Joe Tait and Herb Score call the games. . . . I scored the games on score sheets I designed myself and my Dad ran off on the mimeograph machine at work. I always appreciated the fact that Joe made sure to keep me up to date with all the pertinent game facts— substitutions, scoring decisions, and the like—while bringing the game and the atmosphere at old Cleveland Stadium alive through his play-by-play. On school nights, I often fell asleep listening to Joe on the little speaker I plugged in to my radio and placed under my pillow.

—*Dan Curwin, Twinsburg, Ohio*

Besides Joe's great ninth-inning call on Dick Bosman's no-hitter in 1974, the other game I won't forget that year was the last win in Gaylord Perry's winning streak—also in 1974 versus the Brewers. Saying his catchphrase, "It's a beautiful night for baseball," then later describing how bad the weather was when John Lowenstein hit the big home run into a strong wind to keep Gaylord's streak alive.

—Tom Oden, Akron, Ohio

One of the greatest memories I have is when Joe and Bruce Drennan were calling the Tribe. Drennan was describing a player as "he's got a little hot dog in him" and Joe started busting up and said, "So do you." It was like a picture, and you just know that Drennan had been pounding dogs that night in between innings. That to me was Joe. He was priceless. AND HE WAS OURS!!!!!

—Jim Metzler, Brunswick, Ohio

While Joe Tait was a fantastic basketball announcer, it was his start on Tribe games that blew me away. We didn't have good Indians teams, but Joe could make a foul ball sound exciting. If we could hear some old tapes of Joe on Indians broadcasts, they would sound up to date and modern. I believe many modern-day announcers were influenced by Joe Tait.

—Kevin Krippel, Garfield Heights, Ohio

I worked for the Cleveland Indians during the 1970s. Joe used to do the postgame interview with a player after each game. We were all up in the front office where the radio broadcast came over a loud speaker. Well, one particular night, Joe interviewed Charlie Spikes. He asked Charlie a question, Charlie would answer, and Joe would ask him another question. Not one of us could understand a word Charlie said, nor if he was really answering Joe's question. Don't think Joe knew either because he just kept asking him questions for about five minutes, said thank you to him and signed off!!!

—Peggy Wagner, North Olmsted, Ohio

I met Joe in 1971 by gate "A" of old Municipal Stadium. I was in my early teens. As we were waiting outside for some autographs from the players, Joe came out of the media entrance alongside John Fitzgerald and another gentleman. I went right up to him and asked for his autograph. Joe said, "I'll bet you don't even know who I am." I answered, "Sure, I do! You're Joe Tait—you do the Cavs games." And he burst out into that now-familiar laugh.

—Kevin Lynch, Mayfield Heights, Ohio

I met Joe back in the middle 1970s when the Indians sponsored a "Rally Around Cleveland" day at one of their night games to boost the team's anemic attendance. Early in the season, my friend and I had bought two "choice" tickets to that game that were located in the Upper Box seats behind home plate. Joe and Herb Score were the Indians' radio announcers. For that game only, they announced the game from the grandstands. My friend and I sat directly behind Joe and Herb. It was one of the best times I ever had at an Indians game. All types of food and baked good treats were brought to Joe and Herb. Since they didn't want to eat while on the air, we were the beneficiaries of this food. Joe only reprimanded my friend one time for using foul language when Charlie Spikes struck out with men on base. The highlight of the evening came when Joe and Herb signed my scorecard.

—Dave Grendel, Independence, Ohio

Doing radio for both the Cavs and the Indians took a toll. One year, Joe said, he was off and at home for only nine full days.

The Coliseum

A few years before the Coliseum opened, Nick Mileti drove Joe to a spot in Richfield, the Interstate 271 exit at State Route 303.

"There was nothing more than a huge hole in the ground," said Joe.

Mileti told Joe: "This will be where the Cavs will soon be playing. And that's only the beginning."

Mileti talked about how a shopping mall would soon be built there. And a hotel. And restaurants. And other businesses. The Coliseum would be a magnet. Who knew what it would attract?

Joe just saw the hole. He saw some sheep grazing at a nearby farm. He saw trees and lots of empty land near Cuyahoga Valley National Park.

"Nick, if you're wrong, you will have the biggest corn crib in Summit County," said Joe.

Milcti just laughed.

He was sure that somehow, it would all work out.

"I loved the Coliseum," said Joe. "It was a big building but didn't feel big. You could walk all over the place, find friends and sit with them. It had great sight lines. Now that it's gone, people out there forget how they hated the idea of it in the first place."

Looking back, it's hard to believe Mileti ever managed to get it built.

Then again, it was amazing how Mileti was able to find enough people to invest so he could buy the old Cleveland Barons and the Cleveland Arena for $1.9 million in 1968. He did that with the backing of Leo McKenna, a friend from the army who later worked on Wall Street.

Or how he bought the Cavaliers for $3 million in 1970.

Or the Indians for $10 million in 1972.

Or radio stations WWWE (now WTAM) and WWWM for $3.5 million—also in 1972.

Or a World Hockey Association franchise—called the Cleveland Crusaders—for $250,000.

When talking about Mileti, former Cavs coach Bill Fitch kept saying, "He did it all with other people's money."

At one point, Mileti had 54 different investors in the Indians.

"I had no choice but to buy the Indians," Mileti insisted for years. "Otherwise, they were moving to New Orleans."

Not quite.

The Indians were owned by Vernon Stouffer, of Stouffer frozen foods. His stock had collapsed. He was in big financial trouble, and he had to sell the team. Yes, New Orleans wanted the Indians.

But so did another group headed by a couple of guys with strong Cleveland connections. One was Al Rosen, a former Tribe All-Star third baseman. The other was George Steinbrenner, a Cleveland native. They offered Stouffer about $8 million in cash. Mileti came in at $10 million, but it was to be paid out over several years.

Stouffer was sold more on Mileti's charisma and big vision for the team than his offer.

Mileti talked his way into owning the Indians. Yes, he thought he was the best owner for the team. Mileti thought he was the best owner for almost anything in Cleveland—it was how he was wired. But it's not fair to insist that had Mileti dropped out of the bidding . . . well, the Indians would have left town.

No, they would have been owned by Steinbrenner, Rosen and their investors—the same core group that bought the Yankees about a year later and turned them into an American League power once again.

*   *   *

Mileti's biggest and most expensive gamble was the Richfield Coliseum.

According to a 1975 *Plain Dealer* story by Amos A. Kermisch, the Coliseum cost Mileti $32 million. That included 107 acres on the intersection of State Route 303 and Interstate 271 in Richfield. It was farmland on the edge of Cuyahoga Valley National Park.

"Middle of nowhere," was what the critics charged.

Mileti had research revealing about 4.7 million people lived within a 60-minute drive of Richfield. He said 2.8 million were within a 30-minute drive.

"Nick was just ahead of his time," said Joe. "He saw how people were moving to the suburbs. He saw how Akron and Cleveland were moving toward each other—in terms of where people were buying houses."

While the location was a problem for some people, the real trouble for Mileti was financing.

In this case, the "other people's money" came from Chase Manhattan Bank. According to *The Plain Dealer*, Mileti was financing nearly all of the $32 million with loans at least 4 percent over prime: "Even at the lowest interest rate (11.5 percent), the Coliseum would have to generate $3.7 million annually to meet the interest payment alone," wrote Kermisch in his *Plain Dealer* story.

In a July 3, 1973, *Plain Dealer* story, Hal Lebovitz wrote: "The gangsters who occupy the bar stools at some of our town's better taverns have come up with a Mileti Cocktail. It works this way: The gent who orders one throws down a quarter for the ginger ale, and everyone else in the bar is supposed to buy a whiskey for him. . . . The Mileti Cocktail gag is an outgrowth of his own actions. Nick provides the token two bits and somehow cons everybody else into putting up the rest while he savors the drink. That's the way it seems to the public, and it's not far from the truth."

Mileti never owned more than 10 percent of the Indians or Cavs, according to a *Sports Illustrated* story by Jerry Kirshenbaum. He compared Mileti to "a bouncy little man who resembles Danny Thomas."

According to *The Plain Dealer*, Mileti had "pledged 50 percent of the radio stations' profits to the two banks that put up a portion of the funds needed."

Joe doesn't disagree with any of this, but he was one of Mileti's most successful projects. While it was Fitch's idea to hire Joe, Mileti loved his work. He promised Joe that if he remained loyal, he'd "make it up to me."

Mileti did just that.

When Mileti bought the Indians, Joe became the radio voice. He did games for Mileti's hockey teams. Joe became tied to the Coliseum because he did so many games from there. Along with Pete Franklin, Joe was the star of Mileti's 50,000-watt station, WWWE.

And the checks from Mileti never bounced as Joe's salary was gradually raised.

In the 1970s, Joe's career reflected the Cavaliers. It began in the old dungeon of an arena on Euclid Avenue and East 36th Street.

"The visiting players hated it," he said. "They wouldn't even shower there. They stayed at the Sheraton across the street, changed in their rooms and walked into the arena wearing their uniforms. One winter, there was a tremendous snowstorm. It was almost a whiteout as I drove down Euclid to the game—and there was this purple thing in front of me. As I got closer, I realized it was Wilt Chamberlain in his Lakers uniform and warm-ups. Thank God I was going slow or I'd have killed him."

Joe paused.

"We really needed a new building," he said.

*   *   *

In February 1974, Mileti had to secure a $2 million loan from First Pennsylvania Bank and Trust so the Cavs had enough money to pay their bills. Rumors persisted the team was in financial trouble, even as its new home in Richfield was being constructed.

The Cavs' average attendances in their first four seasons at Cleveland Arena were 3,518, 5,222, 4,548 and 4,013. So when they received the loan, they were in their third season of declining attendance.

Bill Fitch was quoted in the *Plain Dealer* story by Bill Nichols about the loan as saying: "This bank has been in business for many, many years. Anyone who has doubts about us can just look at the bank. It's confident of our future, and so are we . . . this loan is built on our strengths. We wouldn't have done this if we didn't have faith in our future."

Most Cavs fans were not aware of the franchise's fragile finances.

At the same press conference, Mileti bragged that the team was making its final $175,000 payment to the NBA to pay off the purchase price of the franchise. Sounds good, but this was the team's fourth year of operation. Mileti then blamed the team's low attendance on "10 lawsuits" filed by various groups that wanted to prevent the building of the Coliseum in Richfield.

"This should be our third year there [in Richfield]," Mileti insisted.

His version of reality didn't exactly match the math, but Mileti didn't worry about that. He was more concerned with buying time to get his basketball team in the new building—and generating more revenue.

"Guess who he assigned to sell the Coliseum to the public?" asked Joe.

You know the answer.

"Now that it's gone, everyone tells me how they loved the old Coliseum," said Joe. "But I spoke to all these groups around Richfield, and they were angry about Nick building it there. They were worried about the traffic. They thought it would destroy the pristine little towns in the area. They were afraid of it."

Joe said it would be great for the area, great for the Cavs—even if the projected shopping mall and hotels never materialized.

"Turned out, I was right," said Joe. "I wish the Cavs had stayed there."

*   *   *

Mileti was 44 when the Coliseum opened with a Frank Sinatra concert on October 26, 1974. It was reported that Sinatra was paid $250,000 . . . remember, this was 1974. That's more than $1 million in 2011 dollars. *The Plain Dealer* reported the building contained 3,300 tons of structural steel, 490,000 cubic feet of concrete. Some of the windows were 28 feet high. There were 11 restrooms—six for women, five for men. It had 18,000 seats for hockey, nearly 20,000 for basketball—basically twice the size of the old Cleveland Arena. The *Plain Dealer* story by Roy W. Adams about the opening of the building also stated: "It could swallow three football fields, 37 million basketballs or seven billion hockey pucks. Do 189 pucks really equal one basketball?"

Some questions, such as the ratio of hockey pucks to basketballs, just can never be fully answered, but the only parking lot could hold 6,000 cars, and the Coliseum hosted about 300 events some years—everything from sports to the circus to the Ice Capades to tractor pulls.

When it opened, there were traffic problems (when the crowds were large) on Interstate 271, and it often took at least 30 minutes to get out of the parking lot after big games. But the building was terrific. The worst move Mileti made (other than his usual risky financing) was putting the corporate suites up near the ceiling, instead of near the floor where they would have been more attractive to businesses.

In its first season (1974–75), the Cavs averaged 8,161 fans—more than double the 4,013 of the final season at the Cleveland Arena. But his other teams were losing money. According to a *Plain Dealer* story by Amos A. Kermisch on May 25, 1975, the Indians were $2.8 million in the red during the first three years of Mileti's ownership. The Crusaders lost $1.2 million in their first year. The Cavs lost $779,000 in their four years at Cleveland Arena. Their only profitable year was 1971—$38,353.

The Coliseum created another problem for Mileti: What to do with the now-obsolete Cleveland Arena? He tried to sell it. There were no buyers. In the end, Mileti had the building demolished and donated the land to his alma mater, Bowling Green. The university eventually sold it to the Red Cross, which put up a building.

While the Coliseum was a very successful venue, Mileti was being chewed up by all his other investments and teams—and the nearly 12 percent annual interest on the building.

Broadcasting from the floor at the Coliseum.

"I was talking to [former Cavs assistant coach] Jim Lessig," said Joe. "He said Nick was the best at putting deals together and the worst at keeping them together. That's really true."

By 1980, Mileti had sold the Indians, the Cavs, the radio stations and lost the Coliseum to Chase Manhattan Bank.

Enter Gordon Gund.

"In 1976, when my brother George owned the Cleveland Barons [of the National Hockey League], he asked me to join him," said Gordon Gund. "Nick Mileti owned the Cavs. Both of us played at the Richfield Coliseum. By 1977, Chase Manhattan Bank had foreclosed on the building and taken over the Coliseum. We didn't think hockey could make it in the market, and we were ready to move the Barons. The bank said they'd give us a significant ownership in the Coliseum if we'd try to keep the Barons there for one more year [1977–78]. We did, but we couldn't draw enough to make it worth our while. We moved the Barons to Minnesota, where they combined with the North Stars."

But he kept the building and eventually ended up with the Cavaliers in 1983.

The Cavs moved to Gund Arena (later named Quicken Loans Arena) in downtown Cleveland in 1994.

"When Gordon was negotiating with Gateway about them building an arena in downtown Cleveland, he also had plans to put about $40 million in upgrades into the Coliseum," said Joe. "He was going to move the suites down from the ceiling and really make it into a great place. But he'd only do that if the plans to move downtown fell apart."

But they didn't.

"Too bad," said Joe. "I would have loved to see what they'd have done to the Coliseum."

Today, that site is not the biggest corn crib in Summit County. But the building is gone, the hole is filled in and it belongs to the National Park Service.

"Now, when I speak in Summit County and people say they wished the Coliseum were still around, I remind them of when I was there years ago and they gave me all kinds of crap about it being built in Richfield," said Joe. "I tell them that I don't want to hear it. . . . But I'm like them, I do miss it."

The Miracle Year

When the Cavaliers were the Miracle of Richfield, radio ruled. "I believe there were only 10 games on TV that season, none at home," recalled Jim Chones. "Everybody was listening to Joe Tait and Pete Franklin—even the players. I think almost all of us had Joe and Pete on the radio as we drove home from the games."

This was the 1975–76 season. There was no Internet, no cable television, no ESPN. There were a few games on WUAB, TV-43. But there was radio. Joe did the pregame, the games and the long postgame shows. Then came Pete Franklin with *Sportsline*.

It was a time of sideburns, bell-bottoms, Afros and long, scraggly hair. It was Nehru suits and mustaches. Very groovy, right? Actually, when most men see pictures of themselves from that era, they wince. They want to confiscate every print and have them burned.

But when it came to basketball in Cleveland, it was a season for the ages.

And Joe on the radio, along with the two Cleveland newspapers and the *Akron Beacon Journal*, told the story of how the Cavs made the playoffs for the first time in team history.

This was the Cavs' sixth season.

Here's what happened in the first five:

Year	Record	Avg. Home Attendance
1970–71	15-67	3,518
1971–72	23-59	5,109
1972–73	32-50	4,474
1973–74	29-53	4,013
1974–75	40-42	8,161

For five years, there were no winning seasons, no trips to the playoffs and few large crowds. Attendance doubled from 1973–74 to 1974–75 when the Cavs moved to the Richfield Coliseum, but their largest crowd was 20,239 for the final home game. It also was fan appreciation day with lots of giveaways. That was one of only two crowds over 15,000.

The Cavs were not catching on with the public, despite playing in perhaps the best NBA arena. But even that was disdained by a large chunk of Cleveland sports fans, because the Richfield Coliseum was in . . . well . . . Richfield. It was surrounded by sheep and cornfields. To hear some people describe it, you'd have expected a buffalo to suddenly trot onto the floor in the middle of game, followed by a wagon train.

Chones was traded to the Cavs in May 1974. He had been playing in the American Basketball Association with the New York Nets. His NBA rights belonged to the Lakers, who considered Chones immature and not likely to mature in the near future. Chones was 6-foot-11 and 25 years old. When Fitch coached at Minnesota, he tried to recruit Chones to that Big Ten school. Instead, Chones (who lived in Racine, Wisconsin) was charmed by Marquette's Al McGuire.

"I knew Chones going back to high school, and I knew I could coach him," said Fitch.

Chones knew he had to get out of the ABA before there was no ABA.

"I also respected Fitch," said Chones. "I didn't know anything about the Cavaliers or Cleveland, but I knew he could coach."

After signing with the Cavs in late spring 1974, Chones flew to Cleveland—expecting someone to meet him at the airport. No one did. He took a taxi to downtown—the Cavs still had their offices at the old Cleveland Arena, as the Richfield Coliseum wasn't set to open until the fall. He said when he arrived at the Arena, a guy name "T" approached him with a .22-caliber pistol. He was a friend of Nick Mileti's, and the Cavs owner yelled, "Don't kill the big man!"

"That was my welcome to Cleveland," said Chones.

Mileti drove Chones to Richfield, showing him where the team would play. It seemed as if they were heading to Nebraska, the ride went on and on, the houses became fewer and fewer, the farms bigger and bigger.

"I had no idea what was about to happen in Richfield," said Chones. "None of us did."

Chones found himself being challenged by Fitch.

"He cussed me out, and I cussed him out," Chones said. "I'd never had a coach like that. Bill's approach was, 'If I can scare them, then I can teach and coach them.' He wanted things done a certain way. But he also knew that we were getting close to being a winning team. So he pushed us even harder."

Chones averaged 14.5 points and 9.4 rebounds. He looked around the dressing room and saw Austin Carr, Bingo Smith, Dick Snyder, Jim Cleamons, Dwight Davis, Jim Brewer and Campy Russell. All were players in the early to middle 20s. All had at least average NBA talent, with some better than that. This was not a team that should have a losing record.

The only older key player was Snyder, a native of North Canton, who was 30 when the Cavs acquired him from Seattle. They also received $250,000 and the No. 8 pick in the 1974 draft in exchange for trading the No. 3 choice.

Fitch knew Seattle wanted 7-foot-3 Tom Burleson. The Cavs coach liked Chones better as a center. He also knew the $250,000 would help the cash-challenged Mileti. And he believed the experienced Snyder would be an asset because of his shooting. He picked Campy Russell at No. 8.

So in the spring and summer of 1974, he added Chones, Snyder and Campy Russell. He also took a little guard named Foots Walker in the third round of that 1974 draft.

"We missed the playoffs on the final game of the season," said Joe. "We were playing Kansas City, but the game was in Omaha, Nebraska. They did stuff like that back then to try and draw some extra people. Kansas City had a [95-94] lead, and we had the ball for the last shot. Fitch drew up a play, and of all the guys on the court, the last one who was supposed to shoot it was Fred Foster."

Since these were the pre-Miracle Cavaliers, you know who ended up with the final shot.

His nickname was "Smooth." But he wasn't so smooth on that last shot at the buzzer.

"I can still see Ron Behagen slapping the ball back into Foster's face," said Joe.

Joe's description of that play on the radio: "This has been a season of struggle, a season of injuries, a season of comebacks . . . three seconds . . . who will take the last shot . . . Cleamons throws it to Foster at the foul line, he shoots . . . blocked . . . and the Cavs' season ends in Omaha, Nebraska."

Foster was averaging 6.3 points, shooting 42 percent that season. It would be the last shot he took with the Cavs.

"Making it worse than just missing the playoffs was that Buffalo made it," said Joe. "They came into the league as an expansion team with us."

"That was hard on me, because I really injured my knee that season," said Austin Carr, who played only 41 games. "Had I been healthy, I know we would have made the playoffs."

But he wasn't . . . and they didn't.

Yes, after five years, the Cavs had improved, but would they ever matter to anyone besides their few hard-core fans?

*   *   *

Six weeks into the 1975–76 season, no one saw any semblance of a miracle in Richfield.

The Cavs were 6-11.

"Guys were mad at Fitch and upset because they weren't getting enough shots and playing time," said Chones.

Fitch was uptight, because his young team had been picked to at least make the playoffs. This was his sixth season as coach; if he wanted to be around for a seventh, he had better start to win.

But there was a problem. For all the talent that his young team had, and it was considerable, not a single player had been a key part of a team that had won a playoff series. Most had never been to the playoffs.

Dick Snyder was 31 and a career 13-point scorer, but he was not suited to be the team leader.

"He just hated Fitch," said Joe. "I think it's because Fitch rode him hard. I'm not sure why. Dick was a good guy, a real pro and a hard worker. But they just didn't get along at all."

Former *Cleveland Press* sportswriter Burt Graeff said several players thought Fitch's offense was too structured. He also was very strict. Other than when Lenny Wilkens played for the Cavs (1972–74), Fitch didn't consult with players for their thoughts.

Wilkens tells the story of how the Cavs had a rough trip, losing a few games by wide margins. Fitch put the team through a grueling workout. Wilkens had an ankle problem and didn't take part. Fitch sat down next to Wilkens and seemed pleased with the practice.

Wilkens asked, "What did you teach us?"

That led to a discussion about using a demanding practice to actually teach the players or just to punish them for poor play. The young Bill Fitch leaned toward punishment at certain times. As he matured as a coach, that stopped. He learned that over a long season, you can't allow your players to drain themselves physically in practice—especially veterans.

Fitch not only needed a veteran that the players could respect but one that he could trust and turn to for advice.

"Then we got Nate," said Chones.

That was Nate Thurmond.

"And I was mad," said Chones. "Because Nate was a center. He was older but still a center. Fitch said that I'd still start and my minutes wouldn't be cut, but I didn't believe him."

So Chones was acting like most of his teammates—wondering what was in it for him.

"But Nate changed everything," said Chones.

Thurmond was 34 when he came to the Cavs. He had played 11 years with Golden State and was in his second season with Chicago. The Bulls had two centers in Tom Boerwinkle and Thurmond. They were 3-11. They played a high-post offense that stressed the ability of a center to be about 15 feet from the basket and pass to teammates cutting to the rim. Thurmond had many superb center skills, but passing was not one of them. The Bulls were glad to trade Thurmond and his hefty contract to the Cavs for two backups: Steve Patterson and Eric Fernsten.

While Thurmond loved the West Coast and still lives in the Bay Area, he had a strong connection to Northeast Ohio. Thurmond grew up in Akron. His father worked at Firestone for more than 30 years. Nate went to college at Bowling Green.

Thurmond also loved expensive places to eat. He drove a Rolls Royce and, as Joe said, "No one knew how to be more charming around the ladies . . . he was just a classy gentleman. Socially, he was a cut above any player we had."

He also had more experience, more respect and more success than anyone on the roster. Every Cavs player knew Thurmond was headed to the Hall of Fame, even if his cranky knees meant he could play no more than 20 minutes most games. On the court, he was the 6-foot-11 son of the rubber worker who played with his elbows out. He HATED it when anyone drove down the middle of the court and made an easy layup against his team. He didn't defend the opposing post player, he smothered him. He pushed him. He told everyone that his job was to block shots.

"With Nate on the court, guys like [Bob] Lanier didn't shove us around," said Chones. "Kareem [Abdul-Jabbar] hated playing against Nate, because Nate knew Kareem's favorite spots to catch the ball—and he took those spots on the court away from Kareem."

While Thurmond looked like a collection of arms, legs and knee pads, he was surprisingly strong. He was one of the few centers who could hold Wilt Chamberlain away from the basket. Chamberlain long insisted that Thurmond was the toughest matchup he ever faced.

Fitch knew all that, which is why he made the deal. Fitch also knew Thurmond had bad knees and hammertoes. So he couldn't practice much. He played in a lot pain, and when he arrived in Cleveland, he knew his career was near its end. He wanted to go out the right way in the area where he grew up.

"He wore checkered jackets and cologne that smelled like peppermint," said Chones. "When he spoke, we listened."

Joe said Fitch indeed knew there was something special about Thurmond off the court.

"Bill was death to anyone who was on the team bus who was not a member of the team or the Cavs organization," said Joe. "But once in a while, he allowed Nate to bring one of his lady friends to ride with us to the game. Bill would say, 'She can come, but she sits next to me.' It was a joke, but he did give Nate some special treatment. No one resented it, because everyone on the team knew what Nate meant to us."

Thurmond said many of the same things as Fitch, but because they came from a legendary center rather than a coach who had been in the NBA for five years and yet to have a winning season— those words carried more power.

"When I played power forward next to Nate, he got all the defensive rebounds," said Chones. "He knew that some people in the league were saying he was done, and Nate wanted to prove them wrong."

Fitch developed a platoon system after the trade.

He started Jim Brewer and Bingo Smith at forward, Chones at center with Dick Snyder and Jimmy Cleamons at guard. Coming off the bench were Austin Carr, Campy Russell, Foots Walker and Thurmond.

"When Nate would take off his warm-ups and step onto the court, the fans exploded," said Joe. "They went nuts when they saw Nate. He'd play close to 20 minutes most games—the last 10 minutes of each half. Fitch wanted Nate on the court when it meant the most."

Chones said Fitch matched the players who loved to shoot and were never going to make anyone's all-defensive team—Russell and Carr (battling his own knee and foot problems) with Thurmond.

"Nate never cared if he took a shot," said Chones. "He was the ultimate team player."

The Cavs were 6-11 before the deal, 43-22 after.

*   *   *

Once the Thurmond deal was made and the Cavs began to win, the crowds came. The traffic was stuck in the Coliseum parking lot, waiting to get onto Interstate 271.

"When I first met Joe, he was still tall and sort of skinny," said Chones.

The center also discovered that Joe had a hard time convincing some players to stay around after the game for that long postgame show and interviews.

"But I loved it," said Chones. "When we started to win, the traffic was real bad. So I'd stick around after the games and talk to Joe and Pete Franklin."

That's also when he discovered the players were Joe Tait and Pete Franklin fans.

"The guys were in the cars, just like the fans, listening to those shows," said Chones.

This was the middle 1970s, long before satellite radio or iPods. If anyone had any sort of tape player, it was an 8-track.

Fans came to games an hour early and often stayed an hour afterward. The team was such a surprise, a pure basketball delight. After they staggered to that 6-11 start, it appeared this would be yet another disappointing season, another reason to forget basketball and wonder if the Indians would actually do anything—and try to guess who'd be the Browns' draft choices in the spring.

Then the Cavs started to win.

And the fans started to cheer . . . and scream . . . and chant.

"LET'S . . . GO . . . CAVS!"

"LET'S . . . GO . . . CAVS!"

Local disc jockey Larry Morrow and his production director, Dick Fraser, were directed by Nick Mileti to write a fight song for the Cavs. Morrow was the morning man on Mileti's WWWE radio station, the same station that carried Cavs games. Morrow also had written some commercial jingles for companies such as Smucker's.

Mileti wanted it to be the upbeat, much like the Globetrotters'

"Sweet Georgia Brown." Morrow and Fraser came up with a vintage 1970s Motown-like hoops song, heavy on saxophones, trumpets and a driving beat.

The chorus was simply: "Come on, Cavs—gotta make it happen."

Other lines included "Cavs basketball is what it's all about. . . . Come on, Cavs—gotta make it happen. . . . Keep on keepin' on. . . . Come on, Cavs—gotta make it happen."

There also is a vow in the chorus: "Never surrender—ain't no way."

Like much of what happened to the Cavs and the fans that season, you really had to be there to understand it. The Cavs were like the Coliseum, that beautiful building in the middle of nowhere with a team so unselfish, watching them play was to see a basketball masterpiece.

The Cavs' 49-33 record was second best in the Eastern Conference, behind Boston (54-28).

The Cavs had no player picked for the All-Star team. They had no player voted to the first or second All-NBA teams. Chones was the team's leading scorer at 15.8 points per game, modest in a season where 15 NBA players averaged at least 20 points. But the Cavs had seven players scoring at least 10 points per game. The second-leading scorer was Campy Russell (15.0), and he didn't even start. The Cavs had the second-best defensive team in the NBA, and they must have had the best bench with Thurmond, Carr and Russell in reserve.

"This wasn't a team where you could say, 'If you stop this guy, you stop the Cavs,'" said Joe. "It really was a true team."

As Morrow's song proclaimed: "Cavs basketball is what it's all about. . . . Come on, Cavs—gotta make it happen."

They made it a happening.

"This was before the corporate types took over," said Joe. "Real fans were at games—just check the ticket prices."

The top ticket was $12.50. You could sit in the Coliseum's lower bowl for $7.50 and $6. Upper concourse seats were $5, and there were $4 general admission tickets up high behind the basket.

"COME ON, CAVS! . . .

"LET'S GO, CAVS! . . .

"They cheered over and over," said Joe. "It was just the fans going nuts. They didn't have an electronic scoreboard or cheerleaders, or some guy in the middle of the court screaming into a microphone. They did it on their own. They loved that team because they watched it grow up—and then saw a local guy in Nate come home to lead them. No marketing department could create this, it just happened. It was real."

*   *   *

The Cavs drew the Washington Bullets in the first round of the playoffs. This was when only four teams in each conference made the playoffs. You played a best-of-seven series. If you won two rounds, you were in the NBA Finals.

Washington finished 48-34, a game behind the Cavs. It was a powerful team with 20-point scorer Elvin Hayes at power forward, massive Wes Unseld at center. The backcourt was Phil Chenier and Dave Bing. The small forward was Truck Robinson, who was anything but small at 6-foot-8, 230 pounds.

While the Cavs won one more game, Washington was favored. The Bullets had more experience, and three future Hall of Famers in Unseld, Hayes and Bing. Chenier was a career 17-point scorer. If you lined up the Cavs' starters against Washington's in that series, you'd probably take the Bullets at each spot.

But the Cavs' bench was much stronger—Campy Russell, Austin Carr, Foots Walker and Thurmond being the key subs.

"We thought we'd win the title that year," said Chones. "Our confidence was so high."

Fans arrived at the opener in the Richfield Coliseum at least an hour before tip-off. About 30 minutes later, fans were chanting "WE WANT THE CAVS! . . . WE WANT THE CAVS! . . . WE WANT THE CAVS!"

The Cavs weren't even on the court. They were in the dressing room, receiving last-moment instructions from Fitch.

Both Austin Carr and Chones remember it exactly the same

way—the noise and stomping was so loud, the floor and walls were shaking. Fitch drew up plays on a blackboard, and two Cavs had to hold it steady.

When they trotted on to the court, it turned to "LET'S GO, CAVS! . . . LET'S GO, CAVS!"

But on that night, it looked like the Cavs' first ever-playoff game. The Bullets were in front, 37-19, in the first quarter and eventually won, 100-95.

Game 2 was in Washington, and the Cavs won, 80-79. . . . Bingo Smith drilled a 25-footer with two seconds left. Joe was just screaming, "BINGO . . . BINGO . . . CAVS WIN!!!"

It was like that for the rest of the series, back and forth.

The Cavs won Game 3 at home, they lost Game 4 on the road.

Game 5 was a 92-91 victory at the Coliseum. Bingo Smith tried to win it again with another long jumper, but it was an air ball . . . only Jim Cleamons tracked it down, and the Cavs guard made a reverse layup at the buzzer for the win.

"Cleamons got it!" Joe yelled. "Cleamons got the rebound! Game over! Cleveland wins, 92-91. UNBELIEVABLE . . . THE CAVS HAVE WON IT, AND THIS PLACE IS GOING CRAZY!"

It was the second time the Cavs had won in the final six seconds.

Game 6 was in Washington, and the Cavs lost, 102-98, in overtime.

"About every game came down to the last minute, and a few, to the last second," said Joe. "So you had the Cavs, who had never made the playoffs before, playing all these tight games—the fans just fell in love with the team. Remember, they started the year at 6-11 . . . and they were having a Game 7 at the Coliseum."

Here is how Joe described the final nine seconds of Game 7, after the Cavs had rallied to tie it:

"Score's tied at 85. Cleamons will inbound on the left side. Cleamons looks and waits. Flips to Snyder. Snyder sideline left. Snyder on the dribble-drive, to the hoop, put it up—GOOD! IT'S GOOD! Snyder scores with four seconds to go, and the Bullets take time. Cleveland 87, the Bullets 85. Four seconds to go!"

Washington had the ball, Joe continued: "Here comes the play. Unseld lobs it underneath. Snyder knocks it free. It's picked up by Chenier. Shoots it—NO GOOD . . . NO GOOD! CAVALIERS WIN! THE CAVALIERS WIN, 87–85! The Cavaliers have defeated the Washington Bullets, 87-85. . . . The crowd is going berserk at the Coliseum!"

For the four home games, they drew record crowds of 20,784 . . . 21,130 . . . 21,312 . . . and 21,564. The fire department determined that 21,564 were the most the Coliseum could hold.

"If only Chones hadn't broken his foot . . . " said Joe, his voice trailing off.

This is perhaps the biggest IF ONLY in Cavs history.

Chones was the Cavs' leading scorer in the Washington series, averaging 15.0 points and 7.2 rebounds.

It was on to Boston, the winner going to the NBA Finals.

"I can still see it," said Fitch. "Right at the end of our last practice before that series, Chones came down with a rebound . . . "

"I heard a snap," said Chones. "I thought I broke my foot."

It was a stress fracture. Chones was done. So were the Cavs, who were eliminated in six games by Boston. The Celtics advanced to the NBA Finals and defeated the Phoenix Suns.

"There is no doubt, we would have won the title that year," said Joe. "By the end of the season, we were the best team in the league."

Chones said: "Joe Tait made the Miracle of Richfield. Everybody was listening to him go crazy on the radio. Fans told us about the broadcasts. We heard the highlights the next day."

Joe disagreed.

"The Miracle season made me," he said. "There was no TV in the playoffs. People had no choice but to listen to me, and I had some great games to call."

More on the Miracle

[FANS WRITE IN]

At age 11, I heard one of the most endearing radio calls known to Clevelanders: Joe Tait's *Miracle in Richfield*. It hit me harder than I realized. I ended up with a copy of that album from the series and had it signed by every player on the team— including Joe. Foots Walker is the only signature still missing. I showed the album to Joe at a game one night. He got quite the laugh, while I was falling in love with basketball.

Since that initial meeting, I was at games with Joe that defined him. The four-overtime thriller versus the Lakers in 1980 was declared by Joe as his favorite game. I was unfortunate to watch "The Shot" live. I went to Joe's last game when Ted Stepien was in charge.

The 1985 series versus Boston, the Mark Price-Brad Daugherty years, the LeBron James domination—all spent with Joe. Being there, though, did not create the memories. Those came from listening to Joe in the basement of my parents' house where I grew up. One light on . . . Joe on the radio . . . hanging on his every word. I can proudly say that I literally went years without missing a game.

TV games were rare when I grew up, so Joe (thankfully) is what we had. I was so nervous during one of the Jordan-led Bulls games that I took the radio into my closet and listened to Joe in the dark. I figured I could handle it if it was just him and me.

I graduated from college in 1988 and received a degree in— you guessed it—radio and TV broadcasting. That didn't pan out, but Joe's influence did. I stayed with basketball, began coaching at the ninth-grade level and earned my teaching degree. I would eventually, and proudly, serve as the head boys' basketball coach at Copley High School. I was there, in total, for 15 seasons.

Basketball led me to many of the greatest relationships in my life, and I can't help but feel that Joe's voice was the trigger that began a fabulous journey. That journey also includes thousands of kids who have created immeasurable influence upon my life. I feel indebted to a man I've only met once, but whose voice I have felt for nearly 35 years.

—*Dana Addis, Wadsworth, Ohio*

I was 8 years old in the spring of 1976. I knew Joe Tait from the Tribe radio broadcasts on 3WE with Herb Score. My parents were raised on radio. My Dad and I listened to baseball games as early as I can remember. He often worked late but would crawl into my bed when he got home and turn on the game. I carried a transistor radio with me to listen to Joe and Herb start the game earlier in the evening. We started that routine for Cavs games just in time for the "Miracle at Richfield." I could hardly contain myself when the Cavs closed out the Bullets and Joe described the crowd as going "berserk." At the time, my second-grade class at Fairlawn Elementary was writing a newspaper gazette to celebrate the Bicentennial. It was supposed to be written as if it were 1776. The day after the game, I wrote a piece predicting that in 200 years, the Cavs would defeat the Bullets, and the crowd would go berserk. I still have the gazette, with some combination of letters looking remotely like "berserk," but thanks to Joe, I knew the word and understood exactly what he meant.

—*Alan Abes, Montgomery, Ohio*

My dad used to listen to the "Miracle of Richfield"-era Cavs games on our old stereo in our living room. I started listening, too, I think, just so I could stay up late—at first. But I got hooked, too. My parents would make me go to bed early most nights because I was little then. I am 44 now, and I remember having to go to bed during halftime of the game where we beat the Bullets to win the series on Dick Snyder's shot. I had been lying on carpeting on my bedroom floor and was trying to listen under the door to see if we would win. I could barely hear Joe's voice over the static, but I could tell we won when my mom yelled and my dad tried to quiet her down. I used her yelling as an excuse to come out to see if she was OK. They couldn't stay mad at me since we won.

—*Sam Santilli, Kirtland, Ohio*

I owned a little Lakewood bar in the late 1970s, long before ESPN and sports bars with a dozen TVs. I would shut off the jukebox during the "Miracle of Richfield" games (not without resistance), and a group of guys would huddle around a small radio. Joe would bring those games to life like no one else.

—*Kevin McDonough, Lakewood, Ohio*

Growing up in Fairview Park, I followed my father's lead and became a huge Indians, Browns and Cavs fan in the 1970s. I remember "borrowing" my sister's red AM transistor radio, a promotional giveaway from Sinclair gas stations. I listened to Joe Tait and the Cavs in my bed. During the "Miracle of Richfield" year of 1976, I tuned in each night under my bed covers with my Sinclair radio and earphone listening to Joe, sometimes falling asleep before the end of the game.

Jim Cleamons, Dick Snyder, Nate Thurmond, Austin Carr, Bingo Smith, Jim Chones . . . they became legends in my 8-year-old ears as I listened to Joe paint a picture "from right to left across your radio dial."

Later, as I attended Miami University, one of my friends obtained a WWWE tape recording of one of Pete Franklin's shows documenting the fall of the Cavs from the "Miracle" year to the Ted Stepien era. The tape featured many of Joe's legendary calls, including the deciding game against the Washington

Bullets. As college students from Cleveland, we bonded over the Cavs tape because it seemed we all had grown up with Joe. Sometimes, after lamenting over "The Shot" or another Cleveland heartbreaking loss, we would dust off the Cavs tape to hear Joe's re-broadcast of the "Miracle" year one more time.

—*Dave Dillman, Loveland, Colorado*

Joe interjected the fun factor into the game: From yelling "BINGO!" to talking about Whitey's Burgers to the interviews with Bill Fitch. My favorite was when the CAVS made a trade (forget the details). Joe complimented Bill on a great trade, and then Bill replied, "Now I am worried."

Joe gave the Cavs a personality when, without him, it would have been torturous to follow a losing team. Sitting in my kitchen, listening to the radio, I would envision the kitchen table as the basketball court, and with Joe's play-by-play, I would picture who has the ball where on my virtual basketball court—"Footsie Walker taking the ball left to right" and "Snyder from the corner."

—*Nick Horiatis, Woodinville, Washington*

I was 14, and my brother, Jerry, was 17. We had our own bedrooms separated by a wall. We'd each be lying in our beds, pretending to do homework, as we'd listen to Joe call the Cavs' games. We'd pound on the wall between us when something exciting happened. Those games were so exciting, and we were pounding away on our walls so much—at some point Jerry put his fist through the wall! Mom wasn't too happy, but we sure were crazy for those Cavs.

—*Daniel Colbert, Santa Barbara, California*

I was only 6, but I can remember listening to the Cavs' "Miracle of Richfield" playoff series with Washington on the radio with my dad. We were in Eastern Pennsylvania, so the reception wasn't always the greatest. Thanks to Joe Tait, we could follow every game to its gut-wrenching conclusion. My

dad worked third shift at the time. I remember telling him on
the phone about the finish of the game where Jim Cleamons
scored at the buzzer.

Years later, when I got married, my dad contacted Joe, and
Joe sent me best wishes and an autographed picture. After I
sent him a thank-you note in which I mentioned how I remembered the '75-76 playoff series, he sent me an audiotape he had
with the series highlights. I have listened to it many times.

—*Darren Donato, Fleetwood, Pennsylvania*

I was 7 years old at the time and vividly recall listening to
the Washington Bullets series each night on the radio. I can
still hear Joe saying the names of the Cavs players as well as
Phil Chenier, Elvin Hayes and Wes Unseld. This was an era in
which most basketball games were not shown on television. So
I had to imagine what these players looked like, and Joe painted
the perfect picture. He captured the action so expertly that I
felt like I was sitting courtside rather than anxiously jumping
around in my bed full of excitement and fear.

After the excitement of the "Miracle in Richfield" season, I
listened to Joe call games on the radio even when the Cavs were
on television. Joe's ability to describe games in far-off, "exotic"
locales such as New Orleans, San Antonio, Denver, Los Angeles,
San Diego and elsewhere sparked my lifelong interest in travel.
Fortunately for me, my business career has involved extensive
travel, which is something that I still enjoy. I am certain that
my curiosity about U.S. cities comes from listening to Joe Tait
describing the arenas, cities, food, and culture of different cities
in the U.S. Even now, when I have been to the cities listed more
than a dozen times each, I still get geeked just before landing in
these cities.

—*Marc Insul, Solon, Ohio*

I was a teenager when the "miracle" of Richfield was going
on. While many kids probably wanted to be a Cav during those
times, I want to be Joe. People thought I was nuts, but that is

how much he inspired me. Alas, a trip to NASA intervened, and I ended up with a degree in biomedical engineering. But to this day, a part of me wants to "grow up and be like Joe."
                                        —*Mark Matthews, Akron, Ohio*

I was 12 years old during the "Miracle of Richfield." The games were not all televised then. We had a console stereo that played 78 and 33 records and had an AM/FM receiver. The receiver would barely pick up enough signal so I could follow the game. After everyone went to bed, I would lie in front of the console and listen to Joe call the game. His descriptions were so good ("to the line, to the lane" . . . was my favorite). Joe's calls of Austin Carr, Bingo Smith, Nate Thurmond, Campy Russell, Jim Chones and all the rest are my best memory of Cavaliers basketball. I have lived in Columbus for the past 23 years and have picked up WTAM in Columbus when the stars align and the signal is strong enough.
                                        —*Mike Vaughan, Westerville, Ohio*

It was the time of the Miracle at Richfield. It also was the time of the Metropolitan Opera's annual spring visit to cavernous Public Auditorium with its seating for 10,000 opera lovers. At each intermission, swarms of opera lovers would flee to the locked exit doors along the sides of the vast rectangular building to press the numerous hand-held transistor radios against the crack in the doors to hear the excited voice of JOE TAIT. . . . By the third act, approximately 500 to 1,000 men had not returned to their seats. They were glued to the cracks in the doors and to JOE TAIT's voice. Opera lovers, yes; but Joe Tait and Cavs fans first.
                                        —*William (Bill) Goldstein, Gates Mills, Ohio*

What I most fondly recall and still have on cassette tape today tucked away somewhere are the "Miracle of Richfield" highlights, Joe Tait's radio broadcasts against the Washington Bullets. I can still hear Joe in those highly tense moments with a thunderous crowd describing Dick Snyder's "dribble drive" to the basket and shooting it in off the backboard . . . Jim Cleamons' reverse put-back in the last second off of a missed shot . . . Elvin Hayes at the line with the game almost over and Joe blasting out, "He missed them both!"

What could be more exciting and memorable than hearing Joe Tait with all he could muster with nothing more than a hoarse voice yell out "The Cavaliers WIN, the Cavaliers WIN" at the end of that series as the boisterous crowd took over the court? I can still vividly hear all of those calls in my head after all these years, something that I cannot repeat for any other Cleveland sports memory or broadcast. With all of the technology I have at my fingertips today, there is nothing that can compare to hearing Joe Tait on my 1970s-era AM clock radio!
                                        —*Randy Tolen, Lyndhurst, Ohio*

It was the spring of '76, and the Cavs were in the playoffs for the first time. As fate would have it, my friend and I, who were huge fans, were going with my parents to North Carolina on spring break. We had my dad's Zenith SuperRadio, so we were able to pick up the games on 3WE . . . a little. During Game 2 versus the Bullets, we were hanging on every play, every bit of static and every complete drop out of sound. As it came down to the wire, the signal was especially dodgy. On the last play, it sounded like Joe said "BINGO! Bobby hit it!" I said, "I think we just won." When the signal came back, we found out I was right. Thanks, Joe, for yelling loud enough so we could hear in the mountains of western North Carolina.
                                        —*Clint Scroggs, Canton, Ohio*

I was at the final game of the Bullets-Cavs series during the "Miracle." Joe was so big back then. Joe was a giant during that "Miracle" year, as he is always in Cleveland. But that year truly was special. Joe was very much the nerve center of that passion regarding the Cavs and what they did.

What do I love about Joe? He is humble. He is brilliant in

so many ways. He really did tell it like it is, which fans love. He was both objective yet partisan for the Cavs. He is not arrogant, even though he worked around arrogance every single day in his profession. He loves trains. He is retro. Joe holds good, decent, traditional American values. He loves his country and is not ashamed to admit it and act like it.

Talking with Joe Tait was like talking with your old man having a beer after a Sunday dinner. Joe made the players and coaches seem more human just by the way he treated them. The players and coaches, in turn, would relax and loosen up. The fans loved that. Would the fans really know Jim Chones and Austin Carr without Joe Tait? Joe made the players and coaches seem like good neighbors to the fans.

—*Paul Kline, Parma, Ohio*

Joe's Dad and Nate Thurmond

Joe often has said that Nate Thurmond was one of his all-time favorite Cavaliers. Most of us assumed it was because Thurmond was the veteran presence that sparked the Cavs to the Miracle of Richfield season. He was a class act, a Hall of Famer. But he only played with Cleveland fewer than two seasons.

But there's more to the story.

"He meant a lot to my father," said Joe.

Growing up in the Tait home was not easy for Joe. His parents were often distant with each other. His father was called "The Judge," because he was considered wise and decisive when it came to making decisions. But someone called "The Judge" is not a man who is quick with a compliment, a smile or an encouraging word. Joe's dad thought his son was wasting his time (and part of his life) chasing his dream of being in radio.

That began to change when Joe became the voice of the Cavaliers, even though Joe's dad still thought sports were rather frivolous.

Then his dad met Nate Thurmond.

"The Cavs were in Chicago, and my father came to the team hotel to meet me," said Joe. "I had cleared it with the Bulls so my father could sit with me at the press table at the old [Chicago] arena. Fitch set it up so my dad could ride with us on the team bus to from the hotel to the arena."

As each player came to the lobby, Joe introduced them to his father. The players were all pleasant, shook hands—but nothing more than being nice to someone who was the dad of a guy they knew and liked.

But the 6-foot-11, balding Thurmond immediately began talking to Joe's father. Joe's dad knew nothing about sports and had never heard of Nate Thurmond.

"My father also had some problems when it came to race relations," said Joe. "He never used any racial slurs or told racial jokes. But he was very fearful of black people and didn't have a high opinion of them in general. But there he was, talking to this huge black man. I have no idea what they talked about, but they talked in the lobby, and they talked on the bus. After the game, they talked again on the bus coming back."

At the arena, Joe's father asked his son, "What kind of player is Nate Thurmond?"

"He's in the twilight of his career, but he's still an outstanding talent, and he's one of the greatest players in the history of the league," said Joe.

Joe's dad said: "Well, he's an outstanding human being. Really an impressive guy."

Joe's was stunned, because his father rarely passed out those compliments.

The next time the Cavs were in Chicago, Joe's dad also was at the hotel. The players came down, and Thurmond walked over and said, "Mr. Tait, it's good to see you again!"

They shook hands like old friends.

"My father was always impressed that Nate remembered his name," said Joe. "I really believe those were the first times that my father ever had long, serious talks with a black person. Where he lived was a rural area in Amboy [Illinois], and it was all white. The people he worked with at the phone company were mostly white women. His talks with Nate made him think differently about a lot of things."

Joe said he didn't inherit the racial prejudices of some people around him because he interacted with minorities in school.

"In high school, there was a car pool for four of us," he said. "Two of us were white, one was black and one was a racial mix. One of the mothers drove us to school, and we all kicked in for gas. Our school was integrated. Being around black people was not a big deal for me, and it continued when I covered sports."

But Joe said the NBA can teach some life lessons because the vast majority of the players are black. Often, the coaches are black. Whites are the distinct minority.

"After I joined the Cavs, my first roommate was Joe Cooke—a black guard from Indiana," he said. "In those days, if you wanted a single room, you had to pay extra. I didn't have any extra money, so I had a roommate. I didn't think twice about the color of the roommate. You just wanted to be with a good guy, and most of the guys in my early years with the Cavs were really good guys—and I got to know them well."

*   *   *

Thinking about Thurmond and his father reminded Joe of a different story.

It begins after a game in Milwaukee. This was 1975, so the team still flew commercial. The airlines had a problem with the tickets. Not enough seats for the players for a flight from Milwaukee to Cleveland. Finally, the airline decided to bus the team from Milwaukee to Chicago, where they could catch a flight to Cleveland.

But when they arrived in Chicago, there still were no seats on a flight to Cleveland.

Fitch was outraged. The airlines were of no help. The team had a home game at the Coliseum that night.

Finally, trainer Ron Culp arranged for Wright Airlines—a private company based in Cleveland—to send a plane to Chicago to get the players and bring them back to Cleveland. That meant hours of waiting around the airport.

"Nate sensed the players getting upset and restless," said Joe. "I watched him walk over to every guy and tell them how lucky they were to be in the NBA, to have the jobs they had and the money they made."

Joe heard Nate say at one point: "You're a pro. Now, damn it, sit there and relax. We are going to play a game tonight when we get home, and we need to get ready for it."

The plane showed up about 5:30 p.m. By the time they arrived at the Coliseum, it was 10 p.m. for a 7:30 game.

"We were playing New Orleans, and they had warmed up about six times by the time we got there," said Joe. "The game started about 10:45. We just beat the crap out of them."

Joe's memory is correct, the final score: Cavaliers 112, New Orleans 90.

"We won that game because Nate made sure everyone's head was in the right place," said Joe.

*   *   *

Joe believes Thurmond also had an impact in how Joe's dad viewed his son. They began to accept each other, and Joe's dad had a new sense of appreciation for his son.

That's because he saw Joe at work in Chicago, sitting next to his son courtside. He saw how Joe was liked and respected by men such as Thurmond and Bill Fitch. He realized that all the work Joe had put in to reach major-league radio had been worth it. His father never exactly said those things, but Joe knew their relationship was changing for the better.

"In the last 10 years of his life, we got along well," said Joe. "I'd visit him on the farm, and we'd take long walks in the country, talking about society and life in general."

Joe can't recall any specific conversations, but there was a general sense of peace and comfort between the two men.

"My dad died in 1980," said Joe. "He was 79, I was 43. He and his second wife were visiting Vicksburg, the Civil War battlefield. He called that night to say hello and said they went to the museum. The old fellow selling the tickets said, 'You better come in here quick, because we're still winning the war.' My father thought that was really funny. . . . That night, he died in his sleep."

Joe paused for a moment, trying to remember if his father ever said anything about his career choice.

"He did, once, near the end of his life," said Joe. "He said, 'This sure turned out better than I thought it would for you.'"

Beer Night

It was a night when fans were admitted to the bleachers at old Cleveland Stadium for 50 cents. It also was a night when a 12-ounce cup of beer was sold for a dime.

What could you buy for 60 cents?

Try six cups of beer, the purchase limit for one person.

How's that for restraint? You are limited to a mere six cups . . . 72 ounces . . . of beer. Of course, you could get into another line at another concession stand and buy six more beers, assuming you had another 60 cents.

So for $1.70, you could buy a bleacher seat to a Tribe-Texas Rangers game . . . and drink a dozen beers.

"But it was only 3.2 [percent alcohol] beer," the Indians would later plead, as if it were unsweetened Kool-Aid.

It was June 4, 1974. Joe was calling the game on the radio with Herb Score. Most Tribe fans know what happened. Drunken fans stormed the field in the ninth inning, starting a riot. The game was suspended.

But for several innings before that, drunken fans staggered onto the field. This was in the era of streakers, and a few folks shed their clothes and dashed across the outfield. At one point, a gallon jug of Thunderbird—yes, someone smuggled a gallon jug of cheap wine into Beer Night—was heaved out of the stands and landed near Texas first baseman Mike Hargrove. Yes, that's the same Mike Hargrove who later played for and managed the Indians.

Joe watched it all, and when remembering it 36 years later, he shook his head and said: "I was sick to my stomach. It was the worst thing that I ever saw during a broadcast."

This is not to stumble down memory lane of a beer-soaked

event that lives in infamy in the memory of many Cleveland fans. It's to tell the story behind the story.

"I called Beer Night a riot," said Joe. "I said it was 'a disgrace to the game and to the Indians.' I said the Indians 'have only themselves to blame because it was a STUPID promotion. . . . Members of the front office left early.'"

Joe paused and shook his head again.

"When I first heard about the 10-cent promotion, I knew it was stupid," Joe said. "Whoever is going to show up for 10-cent Beer Night was going to be there to get drunk. If he's not drunk before he gets there, he will be when he leaves. . . . We first had two streakers . . . then five streakers. . . . I think I counted about 20 by the end of the game. . . . Never knew why, but running around naked was a big deal back then."

Umpire Nestor Chylak called the game in the ninth inning, awarding a victory to Texas. By then, fans were on the field, trying to steal caps, gloves and anything else they could from the players. Some threw up on the grass, a few passed out.

"Even Herbie [Score] said this was getting totally out of hand," said Joe. "Then we saw some of the Indians hierarchy bailing out in the sixth inning. It got serious when a fan took [Texas outfielder] Jeff Burroughs' cap. Burroughs ducked and sort of stumbled. . . . [Texas manager] Billy Martin was worried about Burroughs, and he came out of the dugout with a fungo bat. A bunch of players went with him. Fans stormed the field . . ."

Joe shook his head yet again.

"Fans were swinging chains—don't ask me where they got to chains from. They broke off pieces of chairs . . . [Indians manager] Ken Aspromonte led his players to the field, and you had the picture of the Indians and Texas players fighting together, retreating back into the first base dugout . . . [Tribe pitcher] Tom Hilgendorf had his head split open when someone threw a chair out of the upper deck and it hit him."

The national publicity was horrible, a game in Cleveland destroyed by a bunch of beer-soaked fans. The team had a ridiculous promotion and not much extra security.

"[Tribe President] Ted Bonda wanted me fired because I called it a riot," said Joe. "Well, it was a RIOT. The only reason that it wasn't a worse RIOT is because I called it a RIOT on the radio, and a bunch of police heard me, and they came down to the Stadium to see what was going on. Some of them told me that they called the station house and said they better send reinforcements down to the Stadium to check it out."

So when Bonda confronted Joe about calling it a riot, Joe said, "That's because it was a RIOT!"

Joe said it's important to remember what life was like for Cleveland in the 1970s.

"Every week, the *Laugh-In* show did Cleveland jokes," he said. "It was when the mayor's hair caught on fire, the Cuyahoga River caught on fire. Cleveland was a butt of national jokes."

And then there was Beer Night.

Plain Dealer columnist Hal Lebovitz wrote this: "Joe Tait, who is going to get a National Basketball Association referee killed some night with his highly charged criticisms, didn't help on the Indians play-by-play broadcasts by his repeated huckstering 'Come out to Beer Night and let's stick it in Billy Martin's ear.'"

Reading the story 36 years later, Joe said, "What I said on the air was, 'Let's make a lot of noise and stick it in Billy Martin's ear.' For that, he wanted to blame me for what happened."

The Indians had a few near brawls with Martin's Rangers before Beer Night when they played in Texas. Martin had said his team had nothing to worry about when they came to Cleveland "because nobody goes to the games." He didn't know about Beer Night.

Lebovitz wrote: "The impression may not have been one that Joe intended, but that's the inference the listeners got. Thus, Joe, with his high-voltage delivery conceivably helped create an atmosphere that led to the final scene."

Joe countered with a charge about a cartoon in Lebovitz's own sports section of an Indian holding boxing gloves, as if preparing to fight the Texas players. Lebovitz came back with a second column, admitting the problem was not the cartoon or Joe's remarks. It was "only because the fuel was there . . . the alcohol. Without the fuel, it's impossible to have a fire."

The Indians sold 65,000 beers that night. Lebovitz estimated the average adult had about five beers. Bonda wanted to fire Joe to take the heat off what had happened on his watch. He was team president. The team was being ripped by nearly every media outlet across the country. Comedians used it for an endless series of jokes.

"Nick Mileti owned the team back then," said Joe. "He was out of town during the riot. He came back, talked to me on the phone about what happened. He talked to the ushers, the police and the players—anyone he could who was at the game. He also listened to the tape of the broadcast. He told Bonda something along the lines of, 'I can't see anything wrong with what Joe said. It obviously was a riot.' That was it. I kept my job."

Joe said he listened to the game tape "several times. . . . I don't regret a thing I said."

Then Joe remembered this story, meeting Chylak. They talked about Beer Night, and the umpire mentioned how the Indians were down, 5-0, then came back to tie up the game.

"Joe, I figured as long as they're not shooting or anything like that, we'll get it done," said Chylak. "All of a sudden, I felt some pressure behind the left heel of my shoe. I turned around, looked down and there was a hunting knife sticking in the ground right behind my shoe. That's when I said, 'Game. Set. Match. *We're outta here!*"

When I Became Joe Tait's Editor

[BY MARK MOSGROVE]

I was a couple of years out of college in the middle 1990s and had embarked on the crazy and challenging task of publishing a local newspaper in lower Medina County. I had graduated from Kent State with a degree in journalism, in part because I wanted to cover pro sports like Joe Tait. Instead, I was trying to run a local newspaper with no experience and no money.

In hindsight, it wasn't a very bright idea.

For the first year I ran the paper, it nagged at me that Joe lived in my very own hometown, the small community of Lafayette Township. We didn't even have a traffic light. It took me quite a while to obtain Joe's phone number. I finally got up the courage to call him to ask for an interview. I thought it would be the coolest thing, to be the local boy interviewing one of his idols.

I got his voicemail, and I left a message. I was so nervous; I must have sounded like a goof.

To my surprise, he called back and left me a message! I remember his message like it was yesterday: "Well, I don't know why anybody would want to interview me, but you can if you want to."

I pulled into his driveway and walked up to the front door of his house. I was a nervous wreck. When Joe answered the door, he was in an old T-shirt and had been working out in the barn. He seemed kind of tired, maybe just a bit inconvenienced that this snot-nosed kid was coming to his house. I tried to conduct the interview like I was a pro, but I had the sinking feeling that I was crashing and burning. I could hardly put two words together. Joe was quiet and unassuming. I had pictured him being more extroverted since he portrays himself that way over the radio. I mistook his quiet personality as being disinterested in being interviewed by me.

So after probably sweating 10 pounds off in one of the longest hours of my life, I started to wrap up. I thought Joe was thinking, "Kid, you've got a long way to go to be a journalist."

But then the strangest thing happened.

Out of the blue, Joe asked, "So, would you like me to write a column for you?"

After I picked myself back off the floor, I stammered, "Shh . . . shh . . . sure . . . if . . . if . . . if you want to."

So I gave him my mailing address and left. I thought for sure that Joe was just trying to make me feel better for my inept interview session, and I'd never see or hear from him again. A week or two later, an envelope appeared in the mail. I opened the letter, to find an article typed out on one of those old electric typewriters. With whiteout ribbon and a typing mistake here and there for good measure.

I was stunned. He sent me a story? He sent me a story!

One of the most memorable moments in my life was sitting down with his typed-out article and entering it into the computer. Then I had to decide if I should publish it "as is," or if I should edit the work like I would any other story.

To my utter glee, I started editing the article. With a flush of realization, it dawned on me.

"I can't believe this . . . I am Joe Tait's editor!"

After that, I didn't feel like a snot-nosed kid anymore.

Like clockwork, Joe continued sending me his columns. One regret I have in my life is that I abruptly sold the newspaper due to a personal situation, and I was not able to thank Joe properly for his time and interest in my newspaper.

When Joe was sick the past year, it really came to my mind. I kind of wondered if he even remembered me, or remembered sending in those articles to that little community newspaper for those few months—to that young guy who didn't know what he was doing. But it's something that I will never forget. And although it's about 15 years too late, I want to say, "Thank you, Joe."

If Only Pete Franklin Hadn't Gone to the Dentist

HOW JOE TAIT ENDED UP IN THE
MIDDLE OF A CONTROVERSY
WITH FRANK ROBINSON

The year was 1977, and a man named Pete Franklin ruled Cleveland sports talk. Knowing what media was like in 1977 is critical to understanding this story. It was an age of most television sets having only five channels—three national networks, a public TV station and an independent station. It was before cable television, before the Internet. It was when sports talk was just emerging from the radio cradle, and it was Pete Franklin who ruled the airwaves. A few others had weekend sports shows on smaller stations, but Franklin's voice boomed in "38 states and half of Canada" at night on 50,000-watt WWWE radio.

Fans really did listen to the outrageous Franklin not only for hundreds of miles, but the signal carried more than 1,000 miles on some clear evenings. He not only was the Godfather of Cleveland sports talk, but perhaps the nation's most popular sports show host—partly because the medium was so new. Hardly anyone else was doing it.

Certainly, no one did it quite like Franklin, who once asked a caller: "Explain this to me. . . . How can you dial a phone and wear a straitjacket at the same time?"

He called people idiots and morons and bozos and mental patients and sounded as if he meant every word on the air. But sitting with Franklin as he did his show, he'd smile and wink as he fired those insults. It was all show to Pete Franklin. He also loved to duel with *The Plain Dealer*, especially sports editor Hal Lebovitz and baseball writer Russell Schneider. It was a battle for the hearts and minds of Tribe fans—whom do you trust more? Is it Franklin or the newspaper guys?

Franklin called Lebovitz "Lo-Bo" on the air.

Lebovitz called Franklin "Frank Petelin" in print.

There were two Cleveland Papers—*The Plain Dealer* and *The Press*. They had their own grudge war, as there was a sense that eventually one of them would die. *Cleveland Press* baseball writer Bob Sudyk and Schneider didn't speak, despite being in the same press box, the same hotels on the road and in the same interview sessions. They acted as if they wished the other would drink a bottle of battery acid and endure a long, painful death.

And that was how they felt about each other on a good day.

That also was Schneider's opinion of Franklin.

Enter Joe Tait.

"Pete was having some serious dental work done, and they asked me to fill in for him," said Joe. "He was going to be gone for a month. I'd do *Sportsline* on the nights when the Indians were off and I wasn't calling the games. Back then, I was always looking for ways to make some extra cash, so I figured—why not?"

Joe couldn't recall what he was paid, but it was probably about $100 a show. At this point, Joe had no problems with Schneider or anyone else . . . he steered clear of all the Cleveland media feuds. He considered Franklin a friend, but he also was friends with several writers.

Near the end of April, the Indians were 5-11. This was Frank Robinson's third year managing the team. One night, a caller asked Joe, "If you were general manager of the Indians, what would you do with Frank Robinson?"

Joe said: "If I were general manager, I would not have brought him back. I would have fired him at the end of last season. But now that he's back, I see no reason to let him go. So maybe he'll get better."

At least, that's how Joe remembers it . . . and that part is fairly accurate.

But Joe also said: "I don't think Robinson has the mental or emotional capacity to manage well . . . It's tough for a superstar to communicate with guys of less talent. I just don't think Frank knows how to stir them up the way he stirred himself up when he played."

Remember that Robinson was the first black manager in major-league history. He also was 39 when he got the job, the Indians wanting him not only to manage—but to play. It's doubtful general manager Phil Seghi wanted to hire Robinson. It has long been believed that making Robinson the manager was the idea of team president Ted Bonda, who was interested in making a social statement and stirring up some interest in the incredibly mediocre franchise. Robinson had managed several winters in Puerto Rico but had never managed or coached in the minors. This was on-the-job training for him.

The Indians were 77-85 under Ken Aspromonte, a good friend of Joe's. The manager and radio broadcaster often had breakfast together on the road. But late in that 1974 season, the Indians traded for Robinson—and it seemed clear he was being brought in to eventually manage. It created a very sticky situation for Aspromonte, who indeed was fired after that season. Nonetheless, Joe and Frank Robinson got along reasonably well in the first two seasons. They occasionally played tennis together, part of a doubles group with sportswriters Bob Sudyk and Hank Kozlowski.

While filling in for Franklin, Joe candidly answered that question about Robinson. That led to this headline in *The Plain Dealer*: "TAIT RAPS ROBBY: Tribe broadcaster says the manager must go."

In the story by Bob Dolgan, Joe also said, "There is no attitude [on the team], the club is dead."

"But the newspaper story ignored the fact that I said since the season had started, I saw no reason to change managers at this point," said Joe.

Robinson was having problems with players. When he joined the team in 1974, the star was Gaylord Perry. They didn't get along, and Perry was traded to Texas in June 1975. He also was the fan favorite on the team, and that didn't help Robinson. He had conflicts with Rico Carty, a popular designated hitter. At a Wahoo Club Luncheon, Carty challenged Robinson to lead the team—this was from the podium in front a more than 100 fans and several media members.

When I wrote *The Curse of Rocky Colavito*, Robinson told me Carty had been second-guessing him in front of the players in the dugout during games. Catcher John Ellis countered that Robinson was second-guessing his pitch selection when calling the game behind the plate. So we had a player second-guessing the manager, who was second-guessing the catcher. These were the type of things that bothered Joe, because they so easily could have been solved with better communication and more experienced leadership.

Robinson had a game where two Minnesota players batted out of order, but he and his coaches failed to notice it. That same game, Robinson gave a squeeze sign . . . the bunt play failed . . . and later admitted that he didn't mean to give the sign. In 1976, Robinson was unhappy with an infielder named Larvell Blanks. Nicknamed "Sugar Bear," Blanks was unhappy with not being in the lineup and threw his equipment and uniform into a trash can. Robinson found Blanks in the clubhouse, sitting in his underwear, not ready to play. In another game, Blanks protested being fined by Robinson by wearing a piece of tape over his mouth when sitting in the dugout. There was an exhibition game in Toledo, home of the Tribe's Class AAA team. Bob Reynolds was pitching for Toledo. He was mad because when Robinson cut him that spring, he learned of it first from a sportswriter. Robinson played in that game—and Reynolds fired a pitch behind his head. Robinson didn't get hit. He hit a fly ball to the outfield a few pitches later. As he headed back to the dugout, Reynolds yelled at him. Robinson screamed back—then the manager charged the mound and punched the Class AAA pitcher.

When Joe was talking about Robinson lacking "the mental and emotional capacity to manage," Joe was not speaking in racial terms. He was referring to incidents such as these, showing a clear lack of maturity. It was not a statement on the ability of African-Americans to manage and coach—remember, Joe's first love is the NBA, which is dominated by minorities. He was talking about Frank Robinson in the mid-1970s.

"Joe Tait's comments were probably the last straw," Robinson told me when I interviewed him for *The Curse of Rocky Colavito*. "It blindsided me and really pushed me over the edge. I didn't care if he was being paid by the radio station, he was working for the club. The team had to OK him to do the games. I didn't think it was right for him to take a shot at me on the air. I really believe the front office coerced him into doing it."

Schneider came back with a column ripping Joe: "Who the hell is Joe Tait and why should his opinion of Frank Robinson mean so gosh-awful much? It's absurd that Tait's opinion of Robinson should be considered any more highly than that of any good fan who sees most of the Indians games . . . because when you get right down to it, that's all Joe is . . . Tait is almost as great a phantom in the clubhouse as his mouth colleague, Pete Franklin."

Schneider also hammered Joe for not being in spring training—of course, Joe was also doing the Cavs' games and traveling with that team when the Tribe trained in March. It obviously bothered the baseball writer that Joe's opinion received so much attention from the fans and credibility from many media outlets. Schneider also liked Robinson—who was terrific for the writers to cover. He was thoughtful and loved to talk baseball with those he considered to be serious about the game. Like many old-line baseball men, he preferred the writers to most in the electronic media.

Joe's comments led to a meeting between Bonda, Seghi, Robinson and Joe.

"When I sat down, Frank pulled out *The Plain Dealer* with the headline saying Robby must go," said Joe. "Of course, that was not what I said. But Frank was screaming, 'How could you do this to

me, you S.O.B? . . .' As for the rest of the words, I'd never heard
them all put together in such combinations before . . . not fit for a
family audience, that's for sure."

Joe said as Robinson continued his tirade, Seghi was lighting
his ever-present pipe, and he winked at Joe.

"Right there, I knew Robby was done," said Joe. "I looked at
Bonda, and he had his eyes closed. I realized that they had been
very close to firing him, and I probably had extended his career.
In fact, after he finally was fired, Phil Seghi told me that they waited about 10 days longer before finally firing him."

After the meeting, sportswriter Hank Kozlowski still wanted
Joe to take part in the doubles tennis games on the road. He asked
Robinson if he'd play with Joe, and the manager said, "I'll play
against him, but I won't play with him."

Sportswriter Bob Sudyk was also part of those games and
warned Joe that Robinson "may hit a ball about 120 miles [per
hour] right at you." But the manager never did. He played his normal game but also never spoke to Joe.

Robinson was fired about five weeks after Joe took him to task
on *Sportsline.* There were stories in both papers about the impact
of what Joe said on Robinson's future. Some backed Joe's right to
speak out, others said he should have been more subtle because
he did play-by-play for the team.

"I vowed to NEVER, EVER host a talk show again," said Joe. "If
someone were to come to me now about hosting a show—more
than ever, I'd never do it. It's even worse now with all the garbage
on the Internet. I don't listen to talk shows. I don't like talk shows.
Some are like cesspools. I am even reticent about appearing on a
talk show."

For months after Robinson was fired, more stories came out
that Tait and Franklin (also a Robinson critic) were wrong because the team didn't improve under new manager Jeff Torborg.
It was partly the print media's way of getting back at the new influence of sports talk shows.

"The two venues can't coexist, play-by-play and sports talk,"
said Joe. "Doing games, you are talking about things as they hap-

pen—not about if someone should be hired or fired. But in sports talk, you give opinions on about everything. The Frank Robinson thing was the first time that I ever said anything like that on the air . . . about firing someone. I haven't done it since, because I haven't done any talk shows. I'd tell any broadcaster to stay away from hosting a talk show because you end up talking to some half-wit who can barely dial a phone and who knows absolutely nothing about what he wants to say. It's just babble."

A few years later, Robinson was hired to manage the San Francisco Giants. Joe said he sent Robinson this note: "I'm not going to apologize because I said what I honestly felt. I really am sorry that I put myself in that talk show position when my real job was play-by-play. I wish you all the best. [Former Indians second baseman] Duane Kuiper tells me that you are doing a great job in San Francisco and I'm happy to hear it. Good luck."

Joe said he never received a response from Robinson.

I knew Robinson reasonably well because I covered the Baltimore Orioles in 1979 when he was a coach. He was never thrilled with Joe, but his real animosity was aimed at Seghi. To this day, it's a safe bet Robinson believes Joe made those remarks at the urging of Seghi. Anyone who knows Joe can be sure that's not true. If anything, a general manager pushing Joe in that direction would probably cause Joe to push back—and not do it. Joe simply didn't think that the Frank Robinson in Cleveland was prepared to manage a big-league team. Robinson did learn quite a bit from his time with the Tribe and matured into a very solid manager.

"When Pete Franklin got back from his dental surgery, he told me, 'I knew you were going to fill in . . . but WOW!'" said Joe. "They asked me to fill in again for Pete, and I said NOT NOW, NOT EVER."

Ted Stepien

Just the mention of Ted Stepien's name causes Joe to make a face as if he just bit into his favorite brownie and discovered someone had baked it with Drano. He can barely talk about it because it's the saddest time in Cavs history, and it led to Joe leaving the franchise for two years because he simply could not work for Stepien.

Joe doesn't do a Pete Franklin on the former Cavs owner. Some younger fans may not recall Franklin, the Godfather of Cleveland sports talk radio. But in the 1960s, 1970s and until he left for New York in 1987, he ruled the airwaves. There were a few other sports talk shows, but none were even close to the impact or audience owned by Franklin.

Not long after Stepien bought the Cavs in 1980, Franklin realized that the franchise was in huge trouble. Yes, Stepien's incredibly tasteless comments that occasionally bordered on racism along with his amazingly destructive decisions made for tremendous talk radio.

One of Franklin's typical rants about Stepien went like this: "In my judgment, Ted Stepien is the dumbest individual I've ever encountered in 30 years doing sports. He is an egomaniac, a colossal moron, an idiot and a boob. I would be remiss if I didn't call him a dumbbell."

He also tossed in a few Hitler references some evenings. His nickname for Stepien was "T.S." It stood for "Too Stupid."

Stepien made millions with a company called Nationwide Advertising, which placed ads in various newspapers for people looking to buy or sell a house . . . or hire people for their companies. Remember, this was before the Internet, before the advent of cable television. At one point, his Cleveland-headquartered company had 31 offices—24 in the U.S., six in Canada and one in England.

In the 1970s, he owned a small piece of the Indians. But that didn't stop him from feuding with Tribe owner Nick Mileti, or demanding that team President Ted Bonda be replaced. He once told a Cleveland reporter that if he owned the Cavs, he'd want half the team to be white—he didn't think white fans would buy tickets to watch a mostly black team. Guess he snoozed through the 1974–75 Miracle of Richfield season when they set attendance records and had only three white players: Dick Snyder, Luke Witte and Steve Patterson.

In 1979, Stepien told *The Plain Dealer*: "White people have to have white heroes. I can't equate with black heroes. I respect them, but I need white people. The Cavs have too many blacks."

A year later, he bought the franchise for $2.3 million after the 1979–80 season. A few months later, he wanted to have a promotion to bring attention to his Cleveland Competitors softball team. He also wanted to raise money for local charities.

*   *   *

In 1938, Indians catcher Frank Pytlak caught baseballs dropped off the top of the Terminal Tower in downtown Cleveland. Fans were mesmerized. Even better, no one got hurt.

That was 1938.

This was June 1980.

There were supposed to be walkie-talkies that would let the softball players below know when the balls were to be dropped by Stepien. But they malfunctioned. Stepien's first drop landed on the hood of a car parked at a red light. The next banged off a man's shoulder. Another broke a woman's wrist. Finally, the fifth throw was caught by one of his softball players.

As you can imagine, the new owner of the Cavaliers came across exactly like the "nut job" he was called by Franklin. He owned a bar called the "Competitors Club," which was supposed to be Cleveland's version of a Playboy Club. Provocatively dressed waitresses—"Teddi Bears"—waited on customers and served over-priced drinks.

At the club, Stepien would interview some of the waitresses to entertain his friends, asking them questions such as, "Would you ever want to go to a nude beach?" He hosted lingerie shows at his club. He once invited *Akron Beacon Journal* reporter Sheldon Ocker to his home—for an interview . . . right after church . . . when they also could watch porno films. Ocker insists that's a true story, although they skipped the porno films when he arrived at Stepien's home.

It's funny now, but it wasn't to Joe and others who loved the Cavs and knew how fragile the franchise was back in 1980 when Stepien took over.

"I didn't even know there was a Ted Stepien until he became the owner of the Cavs," said Joe. "I went to the Competitors Club at East 12th and Euclid Avenue. It was in the basement of the old Statler Hilton Hotel."

According to Joe, Stepien opened the conversation by saying: "I'm of the firm belief that the play-by-play announcer should be part of the PR department. He should always put the most positive spin on the team and the games."

Joe stared at him for a moment, not quite sure how to respond. In all his days of broadcasting, even dating back to being in college and working at the Monmouth station, no one had ever told him to so blatantly shill for the team. This was 1980. Joe had done the Cavs for 10 seasons, the Indians for eight years. He was the top radio broadcaster in Cleveland.

"Ted," said Joe. "I'm not going to change I how I do the games. If you don't like how I broadcast the games, I suggest you buy me out right now."

"I can't do that," said Stepien.

"Then you're stuck with me, and I'm not about to change," said Joe.

*   *   *

Joe had been given a new three-year contract by WWWE, right before he sold the team. The same was true for coach Stan Albeck. Others in the front office also had been given three-year deals. Mileti was taking care of his loyal employees, figuring the new owner would either keep them—or write a healthy check before firing them.

Not long after Joe met Stepien, there was a call from Albeck.

"Joe," said the coach. "I just met Stepien. Have you talked to him?"

"Yes I have," said Joe.

"I can't work for the guy," said Albeck. "I mean, what am I going to do? I can't work for the guy."

"I don't know," said Joe. "I'm just going to do my thing. He'll probably fire my butt, and I'll get my money—and that will be it."

Joe said Albeck then called Nick Mileti, and the former owner had an idea.

"Nick told me to check page 12 of my contract," Albeck told Joe. "But I couldn't find a page 12. Nick said that he must have inadvertently forgotten to give it to me. He said he'd send over a copy of page 12."

Joe smiled as he recalled this story: "When page 12 arrived, Albeck discovered that it allowed the coach to opt out of the deal within six months if the team were sold. So Stan naturally said he wanted out and left the Cavs."

Albeck was quickly hired to coach the San Antonio Spurs, where he had a successful three-year run.

Before Albeck resigned, Stepien had hired Bill Musselman as sort of a general manager. It was clear Stepien wanted Musselman to coach the team. The new owner had once talked to New York Yankees manager Billy Martin, who was a friend of Musselman. He told Stepien that Musselman would make a great pro coach.

Stepien thought he was hiring the "Billy Martin of basketball" when bringing Musselman to Cleveland. Instead, he had imported one of the most despised coaches to Cleveland-area sports fans. Musselman coached the University of Minnesota in 1972 when there was a brawl during a game with Ohio State. About that incident, *Sports Illustrated's* William F. Reed wrote:

With 36 seconds left and Ohio State holding a 50-44 lead, they rioted. For a scary, improbable interval of one minute and 35 seconds, they came swinging and kicking at the Buckeyes from all sides of the floor. Luke Witte, Ohio State's talented seven-foot blond center, took his most serious blows when he was on the floor, writhing in pain and completely defenseless. It was an ugly, cowardly display of violence, and, when it was over, when the police and officials had finally restored order, the fans had the audacity to boo Witte as he was helped, bleeding and semiconscious, from the floor. The final 36 seconds were not played, for fear that the Gophers and their fans would rage out of control.

In the Minnesota dressing room, Musselman posted this sign:

DEFEAT IS WORSE THAN DEATH BECAUSE YOU HAVE TO LIVE WITH DEFEAT.

Reed also wrote this:

With the Buckeyes ahead 50-44, Witte was driving in for what promised to be an easy layup. Instead, Minnesota's [Clyde] Turner cut in front of Witte and clobbered him. Almost instantaneously Taylor got Witte with a sweeping overhand right hook on the ear. The crowd cheered, and then booed when it was Turner who was called for a flagrant foul and ejected from the game. As Witte rolled over and slowly got up on all fours, [Corky] Taylor walked up and extended his right hand in what seemed to be a gentlemanly gesture. But when Witte was almost to his feet, Taylor abruptly pulled him forward and drove his right knee into Witte's groin. The big center crashed back to the floor. Then the arena erupted in a swirl of flying fists. Later Taylor claimed, through Musselman, that Witte triggered the incident by spitting at him. But an inspection of slow-motion films does not reveal the spitting.

There was even more violence, but you get the idea. Three OSU players were hospitalized.

*   *   *

Eight years later, this game was still fresh in the minds of Ohio sports fans. Minnesota later was nailed with major NCAA violations during Musselman's tenure. His last job before being hired by Stepien was as head coach of the Nevada Big Horns of the old Western Basketball Association, a pro basketball minor league. Musselman had no NBA experience. He coached twice in the American Basketball Association—a 3-8 record for the San Diego Sails before the franchise folded in 1975, and then he was 4-22 with the Virginia Squires before being fired. With Virginia, he once played all five of his starters the entire 48 minutes.

This was the man hired by Stepien to coach the Cavs.

Not long after hiring Musselman, Stepien had the idea of inviting Witte to the Coliseum. The former Ohio State star would meet with Musselman on the court right before the opener—with fans watching. They were supposed to embrace and make everyone feel good. Witte declined the ceremony. He'd received a long letter of apology from Taylor for the fight, but nothing like that ever came from Musselman.

Before they played their first game, veteran sportscaster Gib Shanley wore a black armband during his televised report because he believed the Cavs were already "dead," and had no chance of success with the new owner and coach.

As the season was about to begin, Stepien asked Joe how many games the Cavs would win. They were 37-45 the previous season under Albeck.

"You won't win 30 games," said Joe.

"You've gotta be kidding," said Stepien. "That's no problem. We'll make the playoffs."

"You won't win 30 games," repeated Joe.

"I'll make you a bet," said Stepien. "I'll bet you the finest suit of clothes in Cleveland that we'll win more than 30."

"You've got a bet," said Joe.

The Cavs actually came close to that 30-win prediction. They were 28-47 with seven games left.

With four games left, the team was still at 28 wins. In the middle of a game, Stepien walked over to the press table in front of Joe and dropped a note on his scorebook.

"Folks, I may as well not do the play-by-play," Joe said on the air. "I can't see the game because Ted Stepien is standing right in front of me. He's dropped this note on my scorebook, and here's what it says: 'With 28 wins and four games to go, it's time for Joe to eat crow.'

"Ted," continued Joe on the air. "You could play with this team until the Fourth of July and not win 30 games."

The Cavs lost them all, finishing at 28-54.

*   *   *

Stepien had a buddy nicknamed "Boot," whose claim to fame was biting into a beer can, tearing it into two pieces with his teeth. Boot sometimes did this on the floor during timeouts of Cavs games. Stepien also had well-built cheerleaders—Teddi Bears— wiggling courtside. The first time Boot did his beer-can act at a game, fans just stared as he triumphantly held up the two pieces of the beer can. The Teddi Bears cheered. A few fans booed as he walked off the court.

Boot had another trick where he ate raw eggs, shells and all.

Now that's something you don't see in the modern NBA.

And you don't see a coach playing one of his stars all 48 minutes . . . of an exhibition game. Musselman did that to Randy Smith. But Musselman wanted to impress the fans . . . and Stepien, by winning that first preseason game. But he also may have lost the team in the process. They'd already heard that Mussel-man was a bit unhinged in the gym.

The Cavs hired an assistant coach named Don Delaney, who coached Stepien's softball team. He also had been a successful Cleveland area high school and junior college basketball coach. Joe believed Delaney at least had a clue about the game. Delaney knew it was a bad idea to play anyone 48 minutes in any game unless a championship was on the line.

But Musselman didn't listen to Delaney. Another assistant was Gerald Oliver, who was an assistant in the college ranks and spent some time in minor-league basketball with Musselman. There were no experienced NBA people in the organization, other than Joe. After nine seasons with Fitch and another with Albeck, Joe knew how the NBA worked. He could have been a wonderful resource for Musselman.

Instead, Musselman viewed Joe as the enemy.

"One night in the regular season, Musselman had played Randy Smith all 48 minutes again," said Joe, referring to a 109-102 Cavs victory at Dallas. "After the game, I mentioned Mussel-man playing Randy every minute of the game, and how it was a heckuva warm-up for the game we had the next night in Houston. Stepien told Musselman that I had been ripping him on the air."

After the game, Joe was sitting with a few friends in a coffee shop at the Dallas hotel. Musselman appeared in coffee shop.

"His face was scarlet," said Joe. "He was walking towards me, both fists clenched."

Musselman yelled; "I've had it with you. I've taken all the crap that I'm gonna take, and we're going to settle this right now."

Remember, this was in the middle of a coffee shop in a major hotel—with lots of people watching and listening.

"I knew if I stood up, he was going to take a swing at me," said Joe. "So I stayed in my seat."

Oliver showed up and asked what was wrong.

"Ted just told me that this SOB said on the air that I played

Randy Smith 48 minutes just to wear him down for the game tomorrow night," fumed Musselman.

"Coach, he didn't say that," said Oliver. "I was standing right by
Joe as he did his post-game show. I was right behind him, reading his stats. All he said was Randy played 48 minutes and it's a
pretty good warm-up for tomorrow night's game. That's all he
said, Coach!"

Musselman looked at Oliver, looked at Joe, looked around the
coffee shop, unclenched his fists and walked away without saying
another word.

The next night in Houston, Joe walked to a Denny's after the
game.

"It was pouring rain," said Joe. "There was Musselman in the
bushes near the Denny's, watching who was going in and out—
and who the players were eating with. He was checking out the
media. It was just nuts!"

*   *   *

The fact is, Stepien craved attention and was resentful of Joe's
popularity. He wanted people working for him who would be
completely loyal, so he hired Musselman and others because he
knew no other NBA team would do so. They were his men, his
creations.

And when it came to Musselman, the coach became Stepien's
Frankenstein.

The man had a total disdain of draft choices.

He traded a No. 1 draft pick to Dallas for journeyman guard
Mike Bratz.

He traded Campy Russell for Bill Robinzine. Then he traded
Robinzine and two No. 1 draft choices to Dallas for Richard Washington and Jerome Whitehead.

About three weeks after joining the Cavs, Whitehead was cut
because Musselman insisted he was "a stiff."

He traded another No. 1 pick to Dallas for Geoff Huston.

Dallas coach Dick Motta joked that he never wanted to leave

the office because the Cavs might call with another deal. He had added FOUR first-round picks—1983-86—without giving up even one significant player.

Pete Franklin kept screaming that the Cavs were being run by a "DODOHEAD, A REAL BOOB!"

The NBA became so alarmed that the league instituted what became known as the "Stepien Rule." The Cavs were considered such horrible dealmakers that any of their trades had to be approved by the league before they could go through. That was lifted after Stepien sold the team. What has remained is the "Stepien Rule" that prohibits any team from trading away first-round draft choices in consecutive seasons.

Randy Smith—the 32-year-old guard who played all 48 minutes of an exhibition game—had landed in Musselman's doghouse. He was removed from the starting lineup. Then, he was playing fewer than 10 minutes per game. He was the NBA's Ironman, having played in a record 743 games when Musselman decided to show his authority by ending Smith's streak.

"There were about two minutes left in a game, and Randy had not been on the court," said Joe. "There was a timeout. Musselman still hadn't put in Randy. The players refused to take the court unless Smith went into the game. For a moment, the players and Musselman stared at each other. They repeated that they wouldn't play unless Randy did. Musselman put him in."

By January 1981, Joe couldn't take much more. Joe took questions after a speech to the New Philadelphia Jaycees. He characterized Musselman and his deals as "stupid." He called Stepien a "sadist and masochist," especially for hiring Musselman. He said he was glad that he was employed by radio station WWWE, not the Cavs: "I'm not under Stepien's thumb, thank God. It would be terrible to have your fate in the hands of an idiot."

Stepien responded by saying Tait wouldn't do the games next season—he'd hire Bingo Smith and John Havlicek. That must have been news to both players, especially Havlicek, who was a former Celtic.

Stepien then sent a letter to WWWE General Manager Peter Ir-miter that stated: "So Joe Tait feels he can say to the world that I'm an 'idiot' and my coach is 'stupid.' I resent this inconsideration. Let Joe Tait fend for himself for a while."

The letter said Joe was not allowed to ride on the team bus to games. The Cavs "preferred" that Joe not stay in the same hotel as the team or travel on the same planes. "We prefer him not to visit our locker room. We will not permit him to interview any players, coaches or front office personnel on his show."

The letter was made public, and Stepien was ripped widely for attacking Joe. The fans embraced Joe, believing he was standing up for them. The players thought it was a joke. Forward Don Ford hosted a party for Joe at a San Diego restaurant where all 12 play-ers attended—and they all sat by a window near the hotel where they knew they'd be spotted by Stepien. That indeed happened, and the players defiantly waved to the owner.

Joe did write a letter of apology to Stepien. He stood by the substance of his remarks about the trades, coaching moves and deplorable condition of the franchise. But he regretted the name-calling.

*   *   *

When the Cavs played in New York, Joe was asked to see NBA Commissioner Larry O'Brien. Joe wondered if the league was up-set about him ripping officials . . . which he had toned down over the years.

"I just hope I don't get fined," Joe thought as he arrived at O'Brien's office.

The commissioner invited Joe in, told his secretary to "hold all calls" and shut the door. He didn't sit behind his desk but in a chair next Joe—as if they were buddies. Joe had never before spent any time with O'Brien.

His first words were, "Joe, what in the hell is happening in Cleveland?"

O'Brien was especially concerned because the NBA All-Star Game was at the Coliseum that year.

"I've talked to people around the league, and they told me that you'd give me some honest answers," said O'Brien. "I want honest answers. With the All-Star Game there, I'm scared to death."

O'Brien then told the story of his last visit to Cleveland at a luncheon to publicize the All-Star Game.

"There were two lines of scantily dressed girls waving pom-poms and chanting; 'Larry, Larry, we love you, Larry,'" said O'Brien. "Then there's this guy who tears the top off a beer can with his teeth . . . and then swallows an egg . . . cracks an egg and swallows it. The thing that is left in my mind is that he took this powdered sugar donut, opened his mouth and put it in—round wise. Then he chomped down on it. There was this little cloud of sugar hanging over his mouth."

Joe began to tell stories. The crazy trades, all of it.

O'Brien asked, "What should we do about the All-Star Game?"

"You should take it over," said Joe. "Don't let Stepien have a shot at it. If he does, he'll turn it into a carnival, and you'll be embarrassed on national TV."

"That's a good idea," said O'Brien. "But we'll pitch it as something we had been planning to do all along."

That's exactly what the league did, and the All-Star Game actually went off well.

*   *   *

Stepien needed a scapegoat for his team losing and the crowds in the 4,000 range. As *Cleveland Press* columnist Don Robertson wrote: "I meant to tell you, the Cavs are slow. Maybe they invented slow. I was appalled by the team's general clumsiness. . . . In the end, they lost. Somehow or other, they almost always lose."

Stepien decided the best way to battle the criticism was to take the games away from WWWE—from Joe and Franklin. He sued the station for $10 million in damages and the right to void the remaining two seasons left on the contract to broadcast the Cavs. *Cleveland Press* columnist Doug Clarke wrote: "Little Teddy blames Franklin's negative comments as the reason no one goes to the games. He also is jealous of Tait's popularity."

The owner wanted to take his team from a 50,000-watt monster, a station heard "in 38 games and half of Canada," as Franklin insisted on his *Sportsline* show. Stepien thought he was hurting WWWE and that he could put together a network of smaller stations with a new broadcaster replacing Joe.

The suit was settled with WWWE canceling the remaining two years on the contract. The $10 million in damages was dropped. What Stepien didn't want to understand is that his team had become a burden to the station. Ratings were low. Many advertisers were appalled by the way the franchise was run and had stopped buying time on the games. The station was obligated to pay $188,000 per year annually for the rights of the games, and that erased as part of the settlement.

The Plain Dealer's Dan Coughlin wrote: "When Stepien sang the old song, 'Please Release Me,' the bosses at WWWE had to bite their tongues to stop laughing out loud. Two years ago, the station made $250,000 in profits from the Cavs' broadcasts. This year, they will lose money and next year will be a disaster."

Coughlin wrote: "When they took turns kicking Joe Tait, Cleveland basketball's version of Walter Cronkite, people in town thought they had gone mad. The perception of Cleveland basketball—both locally and nationally—is that the ship is being steered by a madman."

*   *   *

As the 1980–81 season finally came to a close, the lawsuit between Stepien and WWWE was settled. The Cavs would be on a new station with a new broadcaster the next season. The last home game was March 27, and suddenly it became "Goodbye Joe Tait Night."

Not from the Cavs, but the media and fans.

Cleveland Press columnist Don Robertson and Peter Franklin seemed to be the first to start it. Soon, many in the media and fans grabbed onto it.

"I had no idea what was coming," said Joe. "We were on a road

By January, 1981, Joe couldn't stand watching Cavs owner Ted Stepien and coach Bill Musselman ruin the franchise. He vented his opinions at a speech to the New Philadelphia Jaycees. A reporter took notes, Stepien took notice, and Joe was soon on his way out.

trip—six days, four different cities—and when we came home, Cleveland mayor Ralph Perk issued a proclamation that this was 'Goodbye Joe Tait Night.' I was stunned when the fans began to fill the Coliseum."

The final home game was against Philadelphia. There were signs everywhere:

THANKS JOE

BON VOYAGE

THANKS FOR THE MEMORIES, JOE

NO MORE SEASON TICKETS

WE WANT JOE, NOT TED

HEY TED, WE PAID TO SEE JOE

TAIT IS GREAT

With 3:38 remaining in left the game and the Cavs losing by 20 points to the Sixers, the sellout crowd began chanting: "WE WANT JOE! WE WANT JOE!"

The media and fans organized a "Goodbye Joe Tait Night." At the final home game of the 1980–81 season, there were signs everywhere.

"I wondered if I should stand up and wave or what," recalled Joe. "Finally, I just stood and waved."

Stepien left the court, and was showered with popcorn and hot dog wrappers.

After the 138-117 loss, Stepien met with the media and insisted the fans came to "see the Sixers, not Joe Tait. . . . If you want to honor a man, do it the right way and have a banquet for him."

The problem with that explanation is that the Sixers had drawn 6,153 and 5,829 in their previous two games at the Coliseum that season. And that until this crowd of 20,175 was more than double of what they had for any game—8,252.

But Stepien just babbled on, telling reporters: "If you media guys want to honor him, you should have had a dinner and charged $100 a plate. The Cavs would have bought a table . . . This thing was to discredit the Cavs. We came to play a game, not to see Joe. If you want to have a Joe Tait Night at a Cavs game next

Ted Stepien told reporters, "This thing was to discredit the Cavs. We came to play a game, not to see Joe." Fans disagreed.

year, then ask us to schedule one, and you guys sell 5,000—we'll match what you sell."

Then Stepien added: "If he's so good, we'll see what kind of job Joe gets now."

Joe left the air with his usual sign-off: "And have a good night, everybody!"

* * *

Thirty years later, Joe is still amazed and humbled by the fan turnout that night. He had been in town for only 11 years, but he also was the only basketball radio voice for the new team. He was associated with the Cavs. He was their soundtrack, their theme song. Yes, they had different songs over the years—Stepien replaced a Motown version with a . . . POLKA!

You really can't make this stuff up.

"Had I stayed another year, I'd have killed Ted, and I'd be in

Lucasville doing play-by-play for the prison softball team," said Joe. "I was upset to see the franchise being destroyed. People ask me if I hate Ted. I don't. I feel sorry for him and for what he did to the Cavs and the fans, but I don't hate him. He set the franchise back for years . . . light years."

Joe became known for wearing a variety of colorful sweaters. "This is the first one I wore for a Cavs broadcast," Joe said. "A listener knitted it for me."

Meeting Joe Tait

[FANS WRITE IN]

I was a local high school play-by-play announcer for many years in the Zanesville area. One year, my partner, Mark Todd, and I traveled to Cleveland to do one of the high school games the Cavs would have before one of their own. After our game was over, we ventured to the media room to grab a meal before finding our seats for the Cavs game. Mark was hoping to meet Joe. As we sat eating, Mark kept glancing around, waiting for Joe to enter. When he did, Mark just sat there in awe as the Cavs legend made his way around the room to talk with the regulars. He didn't or couldn't have a clue who we were ... and it was just an honor to listen to him.

The room began to empty as tipoff was nearing, but Joe still hovered around. As we began to get up to make the trek to our seats up in the nosebleed section, Joe turned to us and asked us how we were doing. We explained we were there for a high school game, and it sure was a pleasure to meet him.

It was then that his eyes widened. "Did you guys get to try the brownies? They're to DIE for!"

With that, he turned and began his own walk to his broadcast perch.

Mark and I don't do the broadcasts anymore, and we don't get to see each other very often. But when we do, at least at some point, we reference "They're to DIE for!" in our conversation.

—*Jim Rudloff, Zanesville, Ohio*

My father, Dave (Westie) Westphal worked for the Cleveland Cavs in Richfield and then in Cleveland. He was in sales in Premium Seating. When I was little, my Dad would take me to all of the home Cavs games on Friday night. We'd walk around greeting his clients. We'd often wave to Joe, and he would wave back. In grade school, I did a report on sports broadcasting. My Dad got me an official interview with Joe. It was great sitting in his Richfield office. Shortly thereafter, as my sister and I were going to bed, my Dad turned up the radio in the house and played a "play-by-play" tape Joe made for me. It was me, out on the court vs. Michael Jordan. My favorite line was: "Dan 'The Man' Westphal, playing like a man here tonight at the Richfield Coliseum." My father passed away in 2001. Seeing and hearing Joe brings nothing but warm feelings about my Dad.

—Dan Westphal, Hudson, Ohio

In 1973, I wrote a letter to Joe asking if I could interview him for my school newspaper. I was thrilled to receive a handwritten reply telling me absolutely . . . let him know the date. He'd meet me at the Cleveland Arena entrance and make me his guest for the evening. My dad took me to the game. I tagged along as Joe completed his rounds, including a pregame, taped interview with Bill Fitch. I spent the game next to Joe at the scorer's table, so close to the Cavs bench that I could hear Fitch imploring his troops and cracking wise from time to time in the huddle.

Joe could not have been more gracious. When I got home, I wrote my rather starry-eyed profile, which appeared in the next issue of our school paper.

A few years later, I was attending college in Southern California and caught a Cavs game at the Forum against the Lakers. A half hour before the game, I spotted Joe at the visiting broadcasters table, just a few rows from where I was sitting. I went over and introduced myself. He not only remembered me but greeted me like I was an old friend.

He asked how I was and what I was doing. I later heard from

friends back in Ohio that he sent a personal hello from me to
Cavs fans listening on the radio.

—Tom Delamater, North Canton, Ohio

I met Joe Tait in the middle of a snowstorm at the end of
February 1990 when I was in college at Bowling Green State
University. The campus radio station, WFAL, carried the Cavs
games and brought Tait to BG to meet fans at a downtown
sporting goods store.

The problem: It was snowing that night. Really hard.

There was no way to know in advance if the event was can-
celled. Two of my friends and I set out to make the long walk
from our residence hall to downtown Bowling Green. It was a
20-minute walk on a good day. The snow kept piling up. By the
time we got there, I was pretty well convinced Tait would not be
able to make it to the event.

When we got to the store, the organizers told us he was still
coming, so we waited. The snow kept the size of the crowd
small, but there were a few fans there to see him. His car pulled
up a little late, but the snow didn't stop him. He entered the
store as jovial and pleasant as he always is on the air.

I shook his hand and told him that listening to his broadcasts started me off as a lifelong Indians fan.

"Don't blame that on me," he joked.

I had one of the fliers for the event for him to autograph.
After he signed it, I folded it up and put it in my coat pocket
so it didn't get wet in the snow on the walk back to the dorm.
The little folded-up flyer stayed in my coat pocket until about
a year ago, when I cleaned out my closet and donated the coat
to Goodwill. The flyer is in surprisingly good shape. It is a little
dog-eared and faded, but everything is clearly legible.

—Jefferson Wolfe, Dumfries, Virginia

I put the gutters on Joe's house in Lakewood many years ago.
When we got the work order, his name was spelled Tate. We
got to his house and set up our ladders. No one appeared to be

home. While we were on the ladders, we heard his voice saying hello. Being a HUGE FAN of his and the Cavs, we almost fell off the ladders on our way down to meet him.

He was very gracious to us and signed autographs for us. When we were done, he brought out lemonade and we talked for a while. He also set us up with free tickets.

—*William J. Wall, Macedonia, Ohio*

I was in Seneca Allegany Casino for a night in May after working in New York for a couple of days, and I ran into Joe at the casino. I introduced myself as being from Cleveland. He said he was there to celebrate his anniversary with his wife . . . and the Cavs would come back after a loss to the Celtics in the playoffs. Later, while I was having a dinner at the steak restaurant by myself, Joe had approached me. He invited me to join him and his wife for dinner. I was speechless and told him "Thanks for the offer," but it was his anniversary dinner. What a nice gesture, and I'll never forget it.

—*Kevin Madell, Parma Heights, Ohio*

I went to Bowling Green State University from 1992 to '96. Joe would visit the campus, set up stage at a bar and tell stories all night long. It was like grandkids asking their grandpa to tell them the same story over and over again.

"Mr. Tait, could you tell the Gary Suiter story again?"

I had a friend who was a big Danny Ferry fan and would ask Joe about Danny every time. Joe would say, "I remember you!"

As for the Gary Suiter story, it was when he got his first chance to start, and at tipoff time, he was out getting a hot dog.

—*Mike Wallace, Mentor, Ohio*

When I was 8 years old in 1988, we had just moved to Philadelphia from Cleveland. My family had lived in Ohio for generations, so the concept of being "away from home" was very new to us. My father surprised us one day by getting tickets to see the 76ers play the Cavaliers at the Spectrum. My dad typed up a little message, doubting his plan to give it to Joe in the press box would actually work. Joe not only took the time to speak to my father, he read my dad's message on the air to our friends and family back in Cleveland who were listening.

—*Brian Klein, Orange Park, Florida*

I have been listening to Joe for as long as he has been here in Cleveland, with the Cavs and the Indians. But I really felt a special bond with him last year when he and I both had heart problems. It was his last radio broadcast, so I headed over to meet him before the Cavs game at The Q. I told him how much I appreciated his many years as a broadcaster and shook his hand. As he started to release his grip, I held onto his hand and said, "Joe, I had a heart attack last year, just like you. I will pray for you, and you keep plugging away!" I will treasure his autograph and the memory of that night.

—*Vince Granieri, Cincinnati, Ohio*

During Shawn Kemp's first year in Cleveland, my father bought a four-game ticket package. During our final game, a member of the Cavaliers staff met with us and mentioned as a token of their appreciation of the ticket package, we would have the chance of meeting a Cavaliers player and getting his autograph. My favorite player at the time was Zydrunas Ilgauskas. My father asked if we could have the chance to meet Joe Tait instead. I knew who Joe Tait was at the time, but being only 12, I didn't realize how much of a legend he was. I was in awe at how down to earth Joe was. He was super friendly with us. He thanked us for being fans and enjoying his broadcasts. Looking back, I feel lucky having met Joe and knowing my first Cavaliers autograph was his.

—*Joshua Czech, Hartville, Ohio*

During a noon sports call-in show on WOSU-AM, an NPR affiliate in Columbus, I called Joe. I thought I'd play "stump the guest" and catch Joe Tait off guard by asking him for a story on one of the most obscure Cavs ever—Edgar Jones. Jones played two totally and utterly uneventful years for the Cavs from 1984 to '86. He specialized in coming off the bench to dunk the ball in a spectacular way to get a rise out of a crowd that had long since given up caring about the outcome of the game, which was a foregone conclusion.

Joe Tait didn't miss a beat, sharing a story with such obvious relish that the listener quickly got to the core of Edgar's strange and unique character. Jones was on scholarship to the University of Nevada . . . Reno. He showed up at the University of Nevada, Las Vegas on the first day of practice and boldly and loudly guaranteed coach Jerry Tarkanian a national championship. The setup was perfect for Joe Tait to be the voice of coach Jerry Tarkanian, who had no idea who Jones was. He calmly explained the difference between Las Vegas and Reno to the bewildered 6-10 basketball player . . . a difference that goes beyond the 450 miles separating the two campuses of the University of Nevada. The story was delivered in classic deadpan, and you could hear the host, Bill Menner, in the background trying to keep it together as he had more calls to take.

—*Richard Sheir, Montpelier, Vermont*

Hearing from you that Joe doesn't email, I sent him a letter. It stated how I live in Atlanta, and to this day, when I play basketball with my kids, I always break into a radio call of Joe's from the Miracle in Richfield. I can't help it—when I make a long shot, it is the Bingo call, or if I rebound a ball and put it back in, it is the Cleamons call.

Or, "Sets, sights, shoots, good!"

I got a letter handwritten to me from the Sacramento Hilton. What is this? I don't know a soul from there. Joe wrote me back and used the stationery from his hotel. I still have the letter. He was so nice, he told me the next time the Cavs were in town to come down to his broadcast table and say hello.

I did, and he was so nice. I had a bunch of Cavs questions for him, but he kept asking about what I am doing in Atlanta and my job. He was more interested in my life, that I could not ask him questions about the Cavs. I felt like I was talking to a long lost uncle who had this vast knowledge about the Cavs instead of a radio announcer for the team.

I can honestly say, Joe's handwritten letter was the last one that I have received in the mail to this day!

—*Mark McLaughlin, Sandy Springs, Georgia*

In the 1970s, when the Cavs were battling Washington, my friends and I went five hours early to a game at the old Coliseum. We set up the grill and downed a few cold ones. A car came near us. We thought it was the police telling us to leave. To our surprise, it was Joe. He jumped out of the car, chowed down a hot dog and shot the breeze for a few minutes. To us, that truly was the Miracle at Richfield!

—*Gary Leininger, Salem, Ohio*

I met Joe at a Cavaliers-Nuggets game in Denver around 2000 or 2001. It was hard to miss his colorful sweater. I tried to head down to floor level as the game ended but was intercepted by a female stadium attendant and sent to the exit.

When I turned to see her heading in a different direction, I made my move and bolted down to courtside. I told someone down there that I was a huge fan and wanted to say hello. I did shake Joe's hand. I had a flurry of memories and jumbles of what I wanted to say to him floating in my head as I did so. I managed to mutter that I remembered him announcing Indians games with Bruce Drennan. He acknowledged.

What I really wanted to say to Joe was how much he meant to me as a child. How, fatherless and usually alone, I would sit and listen to his broadcasts of Indians and Cavaliers during the '70s and '80s. My life revolved around games on the radio. I listened to every play, on the couch or in bed, and always with a losing team. I wanted to tell Joe that he was, without him or me realizing it, about the closest thing to a father figure that I ever had.

I knew I could count on him to be there, to make his familiar calls, "Footsie dribbles the ball down past the time line and into the frontcourt."

Or, "It's a beautiful day for baseball!"

Or, "And have a good night, everybody."

Thanks, Joe, for being there.

—Mike Pies, Longmont, Colorado

I attended Bowling Green State University. Joe would come to M.T. Muggs for a trivia night. In 1992, my friends and I got to the bar four hours early for the show. We had to have the front table. Joe always brought plenty of "terrific items" to give away for the correct trivia answers. This year, there were two big items: an autographed pair of Larry Nance sneakers and two tickets to the Lakers game.

The Nance shoes were being given away to the best trivia question given to Joe from the audience. When it came around to me to ask Joe a trivia question, I asked, "What do you think of Whitey's Restaurant?"

I knew Joe loved the place since his picture was plastered all over it.

Joe said, "Son, you may have just won the shoes. That is where I met my wife."

But, alas, I didn't win the shoes.

It came time to give away the Lakers tickets, and Joe made sure not to have an easy question. The question was, when the Lakers come to town, a member of their organization will be honored at the game. Who will it be? Everyone was yelling out former players (Magic Johnson, Kareem Abdul-Jabbar, Pat Riley).

I had to think . . . OK . . . he said "organization," so it doesn't have to be a player. Who has been with the Lakers a long time? I raised my hand and said "Chick Hearn." He said, "You are correct."

Chick Hearn was being honored for his 2,500th broadcast. Joe said I couldn't win both the tickets and the shoes.

I went to the Lakers game with my girlfriend (now wife). Before the game, we went to Joe's perch at the old Richfield Coliseum. Joe was busy getting ready for his broadcast. I am sure at least a thousand people try to talk to him before the game.

I yelled, "Mr. Tait."

Without stopping his work, Joe says "What?"

I said, "Thank you for the tickets."

Joe stopped what he was doing, turned around, saw me and my girlfriend. He came over, laughing, and shook my hand. That act, to me, is why Joe is so loved by everyone.

—Mark Struhar, Lakewood, Ohio

In 2003, I was a freshman place-kicker at Mount Union. We were playing Muskingum on homecoming weekend. Joe was and still is heavily involved in Purple Raiders activities, one of which is calling the games on the radio.

In the second half, I was called on to kick an extra point. On the word of a relative who was listening to the game, Joe said something to this effect: "Ed Dick is coming out to kick the extra point. Looks more like a linebacker than a kicker."

I presume this was due to my bigger build and larger shoulder pads, as Mount recruited me as a safety. The kick was good to boot. I feel privileged to have had Joe Tait put his signature spin on something relating to me like he has done for the superstars of the Cleveland Cavaliers and Cleveland Indians. My family recalls that story from time to time, and it will be with me forever.

—Ed Dick, Brunswick, Ohio

In 1969, I had just graduated from Benedictine High School, where I played hockey. In the fall, I enrolled at Cleveland State, and I went about starting a hockey team at CSU. We scraped together a group of student hockey enthusiasts to form a club sport at the school. We played our games at the old Arena on Euclid Avenue. I did not have the talent to make the final roster, but I became the team's manager.

Joe was the radio voice of the Cleveland Barons of the American Hockey League, and we played a game before the regularly scheduled Barons games. Somehow, we were given time between periods for Joe to interview someone from the CSU team, and I was selected. To say I was scared to death would have been an understatement. Joe, the consummate professional, treated my interview as if he were talking to the commissioner of the NHL.

—*Ken Bubnick, Broadview Heights, Ohio*

Joe spoke at an APICS meeting many years ago. As a token of appreciation, the group presented him with a beautiful mantel clock. After he opened the gift and admired it, he said, "I have a perfect spot for this in my bedroom," to which someone in the back of the room said, "Joe, it's not a 24-second clock!" You just had to be there!!

—*Robert Buzzard, Olmsted Falls, Ohio*

I didn't actually meet Joe (this time), but I was at a luncheon honoring Herb Score where Joe was one of the speakers. He was sitting on the end. When it was his turn to speak about Herb, Joe said something like, "If someone had told me that someday I would be asking (a famous player) to tell (another famous player) to pass the butter, I would have said he was crazy."

—*Bob Rodman, Homerville, Ohio*

I met Joe Tait twice in my life, both times at a music store. Joe was looking the classical music section over and seemed to be studying the music very hard. I approached him, and he was very polite, saying hello both times.

—*Jim Buchanan, Bay Village, Ohio*

I first met Joe Tait on my 6th birthday, during the pregame warm-up before a Cavs game against the Buffalo Braves in 1976. Being the day after Christmas, I had brought a tin of my mother's homemade Christmas cookies to give to him, along with a card addressed to "Joe Tate." I used to take my transistor into the Coliseum to listen to Joe call the games, so I got to hear him thank me on air at halftime.

It was such a thrill to hear Joe say my name on the radio that it never even crossed my mind that I might have misspelled his name.

Years later, while in college, I wrote to Joe to belatedly thank him for acknowledging me on the air and to apologize for my gaffe. He sent back to me a glorious little autographed picture, which now hangs framed on a wall in my living room.

Back in those days, some of my friends and I in the dorms would tape record many of Joe's broadcasts off the radio and then trade them around in the same way that Dead Heads trade live recordings of Grateful Dead concerts.

A few years ago, I wrote to Joe to express my appreciation for all his work over the years and for the courtesy that he had shown me in the past. Once again, Joe responded graciously, with a two-page handwritten letter that he mailed to me to my home in Asia.

—*Shawn Kelley, Olmsted Township, Ohio*

I waited to get an autograph from Joe in 1973 at the old Arena after a Cavs game. I waited behind his seat on the hockey boards and got him to sign my autograph. I remember Joe's scorebooks going from steno notebooks to those big "record" books that accountants had to the big notebooks to the final portfolio, but one thing was constant with Joe: THAT BIC FOUR-COLOR PEN!!!

He used that model until his final broadcast. Almost 40 years, he used that same style of pen.

—*Evan Meyer, Brecksville, Ohio*

Joe normally worked games solo. But for Raquel Welch . . . "The Atlanta Hawks set it up," said Joe. "She was promoting a beauty book. She said, 'Don't ask me any basketball questions; just ask about the book.' But as soon as the mic went live, she started analyzing the basketball game."

Bruce Drennan

In 1980, Joe Tait was in the middle of a divorce, dealing with new Cavs owner Ted Stepien and starting a three-year television relationship with Bruce Drennan.

Nothing in life ever prepares you for a trifecta like that.

Joe's marriage fell apart after nearly a decade of traveling, doing Indians and Cavaliers games on the radio. He also did some hockey telecasts.

After the 1979 baseball season, WUAB (TV-43) made what was a lucrative bid for the Tribe games—nearly doubling the television schedule to 70 games. Station manager Jack Moffitt wanted to make a major splash.

"I loved doing the Indians on the radio with Herb Score," said Joe. "But when they offer to pay you more for 70 games on TV than 162 on the radio . . ."

Joe can't recall his salary, but he thinks it was about $1,000 per game from WUAB. He was making about $50,000 doing the Tribe on radio. Moffitt wanted a different approach to broadcasting. Rather than pair Joe with a former player who would supply the expertise, Moffitt wanted Joe to work with a colorful broadcasting personality. He considered Charlie Steiner, who later went to work in New York and then with ESPN. In 2005, he became one of the radio voices of the Los Angeles Dodgers.

In 1980, Steiner turned down a chance to work with the Tribe because he wanted to do at least three innings of play-by-play. Moffitt then turned to Drennan, the froggy-voiced host of a sports talk show on WBBG radio.

"They never had Joe and me work together before I was hired," said Drennan. "They offered me the job, and I took it. Then I got together with Joe at the old TV-43 studios on Day Drive in Parma. We rehearsed a bit while watching a tape of a game. But that was about it. There was not a lot of preparation."

In 1980, Drennan was 29, and this is how *The Plain Dealer's* Bill Hickey characterizes him: "As far as I know, he is the only man working in broadcasting who has no idea what his voice will sound like from syllable to syllable. More to the point, he's the only broadcaster in America who is as surprised as his listeners when he suddenly accentuates a word in the middle of a sentence for no apparent reason . . . I mean, how many sportscasters do you know or have ever heard of who command an eight-octave range?"

Mostly, Drennan growled . . . or roared . . . or seemed so excited, either his voice or maybe his entire skull was about to crack. He ended every broadcast by bellowing: "I LOVE YA, CLEVE-LAND!!!"

"I had met Bruce a few times before we worked together, but we really didn't know each other," said Joe. "It's impossible not to like Bruce because he's funny, and sometimes he doesn't know how funny he is. Either way, he is funny."

But not at first.

Remember that Joe did a little baseball on television with Rocky Colavito. Then it was seven years on radio with Herb Score. He was with two classy former players, both legends to veteran Tribe fans. Score was especially understated in everything he did. Not a polished broadcaster, Score had "incredible knowledge of the game," according to Joe.

Drennan said he'd done a lot baseball on radio, but it was mostly fast-pitch softball in Aurora, Illinois.

"It was 100 games a year," Drennan said. "Men's fast-pitch softball at that level is a great game. I also worked at a radio station where we covered seven different high schools and their sports. I also hosted a show for [former Ohio State football coach] Earle Bruce a few times."

And he did several years of sports talk.

Joe didn't say much about the selection. His disintegrating marriage meant he needed the money, and TV-43 offered a healthy raise. He'd sit next to anyone from Al Pacino to Jimmy Hoffa to Bozo the Clown to get it.

"Joe and I had a lot in common," said Drennan. "We both grew up in the Chicago area. We both paid our dues in small-town radio. But I couldn't tell if Joe liked me—at first. He's not easy to get to know right away. He can be a bit moody, especially back then because of what was going on [with the divorce]."

*   *   *

It didn't take long for Joe to realize he wasn't sitting next to Herb Score anymore.

"We were in Chicago, and Bruce ate three hot dogs in 90 seconds," said Joe. "On the air, I said that it was like watching one of those World War II submarine movies where they're sticking torpedoes into the tubes. That was Bruce . . . gulp . . . gulp . . . GULP! He should have gone into competitive eating."

"We talked a lot about eating," said Drennan. "Sometimes, it was more interesting than the game, given the kind of teams we had in the early 1980s."

The Plain Dealer's Chuck Heaton wrote: "The pair are obsessed with food. They should swear off talking about it. Who cares that the chicken in the Texas Rangers' press room 'looked like lamb' and even Drennan couldn't down it."

Heaton also wrote: "Tait is a polished professional who will do a good job in any sport and under any conditions. His style is best suited for radio where he can paint a word picture of the game. Tait loses something on television, where the picture tells almost the entire story."

Joe agreed that Heaton had a point: "In TV, the camera tells a lot of the story. I do prefer radio. But at that point in my life, making money was very important, and TV paid the most."

*   *   *

Here is how a 1980 *Plain Dealer* story described Drennan calling a game:

"We've got a real barn burner here, Joe. . . . Yessiree, a real donnybrook."

At this point, Drennan's face is scarlet. He has a cigarette in one hand, a hot dog in the other. He is into the game. . . . In fact, you have a feeling that he is so into the game that he may not make it through the game without having a coronary. . . . When the bases are loaded, it comes out in a voice that is all his own: "Joe, the bags are juiced!"

"Bags are juiced" meant the bases are loaded.

"Ducks on the pond" were runners on base.

A "barn burner" or a "donnybrook" meant a close game.

All of those phrases came from the 1930s and 1940s, but they seemed both new and strange to Tribe fans. Joe often stared at Bruce, shook his head and then said, "Ball two."

Joe said he had heard one baseball broadcaster with a Drennan-like voice—Halsey Hall, who did the Twins. Hall also ate raw onions, drank gin and smoked cigars during a game, according to Joe.

"But in all my years of broadcasting, I never encountered someone quite like Bruce," said Joe.

Drennan said: "We knew the Indians were going to be bad, so we decided that we were not going to dwell on the baseball all the time. So we wanted to add flair and personality."

That was Drennan.

"One night, we were in Kansas City and losing something like 7-0," said Joe. "I knew that Bruce had spent the previous evening at a pro wrestling match. He loved wrestling. So I asked Bruce about the matches, and he went on and on about The Mauler and all these other wrestlers. He kept saying how he loved it, and I kept feeding him wrestling questions."

Joe paused.

"I used to tell Bruce that he should have gone into pro wrestling as a broadcaster," said Joe. "His personality would have been perfect for that. He'd have made a ton of money—more than he did in regular sports."

*   *   *

Early in their first season, Joe and Drennan "acted like strangers on the air," according to *The Plain Dealer's* Heaton. Part of the reason was that they were strangers—they hardly knew each other. Joe had never worked with anyone like Drennan, and Drennan had never worked major-league baseball at all. Both were radio guys, not TV men. Joe also had no clue what Drennan would say—and wondered why Drennan said some of the things that he did.

"Many fans have been irritated by the booming emphasis on certain words or phrases by Drennan," wrote Heaton.

Other critics compared him to a carnival barker trying to draw attention to himself.

No one confused him with Score or Tony Kubek, the former Yankees shortstop who often did the World Series and games of the week on national networks.

"We were better when we did it more like show business," said Joe.

On an Easter broadcast, Joe introduced Drennan this way: "It's only fitting on Easter Sunday that we give you Bruce Drennan, who like the proverbial Easter egg, is half-cracked and always colorful."

Stuff like that drove hard-core baseball fans to distraction— and it had the opposite impact on the casual fan. They kept watching the game to see what dumb things Joe and Bruce would talk about next. Tribe President Gabe Paul absolutely hated the broadcasts and kept complaining to the executives at TV-43. In the first week, TV-43 received more than 100 calls and letters, most hating the broadcast. It also was a subject in newspaper stories and talk radio.

While most writers liked Joe's work, he had one constant critic in *The Plain Dealer's* William Hickey . . . the same William Hickey who marveled at Drennan's vocal range . . . and the same William Hickey who often took an opinion opposite of fellow *Plain Dealer* media critic Raymond Hart.

After praising Drennan, Hickey wrote: "Tait is the typical sportscasting nobody, a man who turns in a highly professional performance, no matter what sport he is assigned to cover. In other words, he's a real bore, reciting all his statistics and who's on what base and all that sort of nonsense in an accommodating monotone."

Of course, reading Hickey, you realize he sometimes didn't exit the same sentence that he entered.

WUAB General Manager Jack Moffitt got what he wanted by pairing the classic sportscaster (Joe Tait) and the outrageous Drennan—people were paying attention. The ratings were solid, even if the broadcasts could be "uneven," to put it kindly.

*   *   *

Drennan talked endless about one day wanting to catch a foul ball. It finally happened in Milwaukee.

"I caught it with one hand," said Drennan, 30 years later. "WHAT A GRAB! Now I had the ball, and I decided it would be a nice gesture to give it to the fans. I figure I'd throw it out of the booth. But the ball hit the screen behind home plate, and it rolled down."

It rolled down, all right.

Off the screen, onto the field, and the ball kept rolling until it settled right under the home plate umpire's legs. He had to call time out, wondering how a ball ended up there.

Tait laughed; Drennan was embarrassed. The game stopped, the ball was tossed into the dugout.

So no ball for Drennan or the fans.

"People still talk to me about that," said Drennan. "They remember the crazy things we did."

When Drennan told the story, he left out a few details, according to Joe.

"Bruce nearly hit the window when he threw it," Joe recalled. "And it nearly rolled onto home plate. [Umpire] Larry Barnett never did figure out where that ball came from."

Joe said that after the game, Drennan walked into the press

room. Herb Score was reading the paper.

"Herb, did you see my catch?" asked Drennan.

"That was quite a catch," said Score, looking up from the paper.

"Did you see me try to throw it back to the fans?" asked Drennan.

"Sure did," said Score. "Did you ever stop to think that if you had thrown it into the stands and hit someone who wasn't looking— they could sue the crap out of you?"

Thirty years later, Tait laughed telling the story.

"You should have seen Bruce's jaw drop," said Joe. "He'd never thought of that."

When he switched to television for the Indians games, Joe got a new broadcast partner: Bruce Drennan. "We talked a lot about eating," said Drennan. "Sometimes, it was more interesting than the game, given the kind of teams we had in the early 1980s." Here, Joe and Drennan ride in a convertible for the opening day parade for the 1979 baseball season.

*   *   *

After a game in Chicago, a couple of Tribe players were arrested and charged with having marijuana cigarettes on the streets of the Windy City. The front office was very concerned about how to present this to the public.

Joe told Bruce: "Don't say anything about this. I'll handle it."

Joe read a terse statement about the arrests and then turned to Bruce, who said, "And let's hope the Tribe comes out smokin' tonight!"

Joe fought hard for about 10 seconds and then completely lost it.

*   *   *

"Bruce used to tell everyone that he got his broadcasting start in Manitowoc, Wisconsin," Joe said.

During an off day in Milwaukee, Joe and TV-43 director Pat Murray rented a car and drove up to Green Bay. They wanted to see the home of the Packers.

"We stopped in Manitowoc and asked at a convenience store if they knew where to find the radio station—WCUB," said Joe. "Bruce had told us the call letters. Turns out, it wasn't in Manitowoc. It was in a place called Two Rivers."

Manitowoc is about 80 miles north of Milwaukee. From there, Joe and Pat Murray drove another 15 miles north and found Two Rivers.

"It was in the middle of nowhere," said Joe. "It was just a little building with WCUB as the emblem and a Chicago cubby bear in the C—I guess they carried the Cubs' games. We took a picture of the station and had it made into a slide."

After the fourth inning of the next game, Joe said to Bruce, "You've been telling us about how you got your start in broadcasting in Manitowoc."

Bruce said: "Oh, right, Manitowoc. I wasn't there long, but that's where I started."

The picture of WCUB came up.

"Bruce," said Joe. "Does that look familiar?"

"That's the station in Manitowoc," said Drennan.

"Bruce, no, that's not Manitowoc," said Joe. "That's a station in Two Rivers. People in Two Rivers only go to Manitowoc to do their Christmas shopping, who are you trying to kid?"

Drennan babbled, and it didn't make a lot of sense.

"Boy did they nail me," Drennan said 30 years later, laughing about it.

"Here's the amazing thing," said Joe. "Bruce used that bit in some of his audition tapes. He said it showed he had a sense of humor and could take a joke—which was true."

*   *   *

Remember that Drennan was hired to do the Tribe games at the age of 29. He had to be dealing with some insecurity.

"I won't kid you, I was in awe of working with Joe," he said. "He was the greatest basketball broadcaster that I had ever heard. By 1980, he was already a legend with a lot of Cleveland sports fans."

Drennan had come to town in 1978 to try and be a second sports talk-show voice, battling Pete Franklin. It was a battle where he had no chance, as Franklin was the godfather of sports talk. He did the first regular radio sports talk show in Cleveland and had enormous credibility with the fans along with skyrocketing ratings.

"Because of my show, people used to tell me that I owned Cleveland," Franklin once said. "I wondered, 'What the hell does that mean? I get to pay the mortgage?'"

It meant no talk show had a chance against him.

In fact, Drennan had lost his talk show right before he was hired by WAUB and teamed with Joe.

The stakes were high for Drennan. He needed the work, and he needed to make baseball work. If not, it could be back to Aurora, Illinois; Manitowoc, Wisconsin; or even dear-old WCUB in Two Rivers.

Because he was the same age as the players, he hung around with them. He was in their card games. He went out to eat with them. He seemed to try to act as if he were a part of the team.

"Bruce used to say he won a lot of money playing cards," said Joe. "All I know is that [outfielder] Miguel Dilone used to call Bruce, 'My fish.' He was convinced he could take Bruce's money any time."

Drennan still insists that he won more money than he lost in those games.

But there was a problem that Drennan didn't quite comprehend. The front office thought he was "too close" to the players.

"They knew I had all the inside information," said Drennan. "I was very careful how I'd use it. When Lennie Barker threw his perfect game, I was the first one to get the interview on the field. Joe knew I'd get Lennie. I knew Lennie would talk to me before anyone else because we were tight. My friendships helped my coverage. I was in the back of the bus with the guys, and the back of the plane. It's where media members were never welcomed, but the players welcomed me there."

But it's never wise for a member of the media to be in a card game involving money with the people whom he is covering. That can lead to hard feelings between the players and the media member. It also can cause a media person to be strongly influenced in his coverage by either winning or losing a lot of money to certain players.

That didn't appear to be the case with Drennan, but the front office was concerned about that.

After three years, Tribe President Gabe Paul convinced WAUB to dump Drennan.

"I was devastated," Drennan said. "I was angry, crushed, confused. I thought I had done a good job. They complained I was too close to the players. I didn't understand it."

He said he had a long talk with Joe after his firing.

"Joe was the best," Drennan said. "He told me how I won't feel it right now, but no one can take those three years away from me. For three years, I did major-league baseball in a major market. I had experience. I had tapes. I had built my reputation. He said it would help me get jobs for the rest of my life—and it did."

While Drennan never did any more baseball broadcasting, he hosted various talk shows. When Pete Franklin left Cleveland and went to New York, Drennan replaced him on *Sportsline*.

In 2006, Drennan went to prison for five months after being charged with filing false tax returns. The reason behind the charges was his association with sports gamblers.

"When I got out of the joint and got my TV show on STO, some media people turned their backs on me," said Drennan. "But you know who was one of my first guests? It was Joe. He has always been a great friend, and he stuck by me."

Hearing that, Tait smiled and said, "Hey, I always liked Bruce. If not, I'd have tossed him out the window sometime in that first baseball season after some of the stunts he pulled!"

Joe Does New Jersey... and Chicago... as the Cavs are Sold

From the moment the 1980–81 Cavs season ended, Joe never thought he'd call the games of his favorite NBA team again.

"I didn't think there would be a Cavs team in a few years," he said. "I thought they'd just fall apart or that the league would take over the franchise and move it. Ted Stepien even tried to move the team to Toronto, but [radio broadcaster] Pete Franklin found out about it and called into a radio show in Toronto where Ted was being interviewed—and he just ripped into Ted. He also helped keep the Cavs in town."

After Stepien fired Joe, the Cavs' owner told several people, "Let's see what kind of job he gets now . . . and how long it takes him to get one."

Not only did the Cavs lose Joe, the radio station (WWWE, now WTAM) was thrilled to give the broadcasting rights back to Stepien. The owner thought this was wonderful: He could build his own radio network and not have to deal with Pete Franklin or Joe. Most media experts believed this was a disaster for the Cavs, who were losing one of the nation's most powerful stations—those 50,000 watts really did bounce over half the country most nights.

Despite Joe's obvious popularity in the Cleveland market and the fact that he also had been broadcasting Tribe games since 1972, Stepien convinced himself that Joe was just another voice on the radio—and one is just as good as another. He also ignored the fact that Joe already had gained respect and recognition in the NBA, far beyond the Cleveland market.

A week after Stepien fired Joe, the phone rang. It was Mike

DiTomasso, who entered the NBA in 1970—just like Joe. He was an official for only two seasons but also earned a law degree and went to work for the New Jersey Nets.

"Joe," said DiTomasso. "I hear you are looking for work."

DiTomasso had to quit being an official because of an inner-ear problem. Joe mentioned that he indeed was a broadcasting free agent.

"How about doing the Nets?" he said. "We are moving to the Meadowlands and need a play-by-play man. Are you interested?"

"Absolutely," said Joe.

He needed the work and the money. He had been divorced, had kids heading to college. He was still under contract with the Indians, but it was only for 70 television games.

Larry Brown was hired to coach the Nets, and he brought along several assistant coaches. But the Nets had one who was under contract but not wanted on the bench by Brown.

"His name was Al Menendez," said Joe. "They said to make Al my color man, letting him finish out the final season on his contract. Al had never done radio before, and he had no idea that was what they had in mind for him."

When Joe and Menendez met, the former assistant coach said, "What do I do?"

"Nothing," said Joe.

Menendez stared him.

"Nothing," repeated Joe. "Just sit there and don't say anything until I talk directly to you—and then you can respond."

Joe said Menendez, " . . . did a beautiful job. He could sit there for 10 minutes and not say a word—and when I'd point to him, Al would come up with something good."

Joe said before one game, the Nets had a ceremonial jump ball with Yogi Berra, Miss New Jersey and official Bob Rakel.

"As the ball went up, Menendez said, 'There they are, the good, the bad and the ugly,'" said Joe.

Joe enjoyed doing the games and lived that winter in a terrific house that belonged to Rich Gossage, the Yankees relief pitcher during that period. Gossage lived elsewhere in the off-season.

While Joe had the talent to work in the New York market, he never had the desire to live on the East Coast.

"I've always hated New York," said Joe. "It's too big. It's too dirty. It's too rude. New York is like dropping some diamonds into a two-holer—yes, there are some diamonds in there, but you have to go through a sea of manure to get them. That's New York to me."

And it's why he was hoping to get a basketball job somewhere else. He knew it wouldn't be Cleveland. Stepien still owned the team. The Cavs' record was 15-67, matching the worst in franchise history. The other 15-67 record was in 1970–71, the first season. The Cavs had four coaches that season—Don Delaney, Bob Kloppenburg, Chuck Daly and Bill Musselman. They used 22 players. They finished the season on a 19-game losing streak. The average announced attendance was 5,769—although it was much lower than that in terms of actual people in the seats.

"To top it off, they didn't have another first-round draft choice until the next ice age," said Joe. "The situation looked hopeless."

*   *   *

Then Joe received another offer—from Jerry Reinsdorf and Eddie Einhorn. They were starting something called Sportsvision, a prelude to what became SportsChannel. It was the beginning of all-sports cable television stations, this one based in Chicago. Joe would do the Bulls' games on cable TV with Johnny Kerr, a former star NBA center and Bulls coach.

"Not long after I got the job, I was driving to Chicago across the Skyway Bridge with the sun setting," said Joe. "Lake Michigan and the city sparkled. I was thinking that I had finally made it. I grew up dreaming of working in Chicago—and here was my chance."

But it didn't turn out quite as Joe expected.

This was 1981, and sports cable channels were so young, they were making up their approach to programming—almost from week to week. The Chicago station had both the Bulls and the Blackhawks of the National Hockey League.

"The Bulls weren't good, and the Blackhawks got hot," said Joe. "They began to bump the Bulls for hockey. I was teamed up with Johnny Kerr, and they sent us to do college games all over the state. We did games from Notre Dame to Northern Illinois to De-Paul to Northwestern and Loyola of Chicago. The Bulls had collapsed under Paul Westhead, who was a terrible coach."

Joe recalled coming back to Cleveland with the Bulls, and "My engineer and I counted there were 137 people in the seats. I'm not kidding, 137. It was sickening to see what happened to the franchise. In our worst moments in that first year at the old Cleveland Arena, we never had only 137 people there."

The Bulls were 28-54. Joe did 18 of their games on radio, filling in for Jim Durham. But Durham was solid as the radio voice of the team.

Joe also did some college games on radio for CBS, "just enough to know that I never wanted to work for a big network."

Chicago may have been his dream once upon a time, but not now.

"I really missed Cleveland," said Joe. "I had married Jean, and she lived in Richfield. I did the Indians' games on TV in the summer. But I still didn't think I'd ever do the Cavs' games again—because I didn't think there would be a Cavs franchise in Cleveland for long."

Once, Joe listened to Paul Porter, who was hired by Stepien to be the Cavs' radio voice.

"I just caught a few moments because they no longer were on WWWE [with its 50,000 watts]," said Joe. "I heard Paul Porter scream, 'And Dr. Late, James Silas, hits one from the corner . . . and the Cavs are now down by 54 in Portland!!!'"

Joe laughed, recalling the story.

"From his voice, you'd have thought it was a tie game," he said. "I like Paul Porter. He later became the public address man for the Orlando Magic. He was the kind of broadcaster that Ted wanted. Paul is a good man. He called me when I retired . . . and I was impressed he lasted those two years with Ted."

Joe paused.

"I really believed the franchise would die at the end of that [1982–83] season," Joe recalled.

*   *   *

In 1982–83, Stepien still owned the team, but quietly, things were changing. Harry Weltman was hired as the team's vice president, supposedly to help Stepien put together a Cleveland sports television cable channel. But soon, Weltman was running the basketball operation. A week into his new job, Weltman fired Musselman as coach—replacing him with Tom Nissalke. Weltman was a former general manager of the St. Louis Spirits of the old American Basketball Association. Nissalke had been a head coach in the ABA and three different NBA teams. Weltman knew Nissalke would as least bring some sanity and stability to Stepien's chaos. Nissalke was hired two weeks before the regular season, and the Cavs started 2-13. From the outside, it looked like more of the same.

The Cavs opened the season with five consecutive losses, making their losing streak 24 games—dating back to the final 19 losses of the 1982–83 season. But Weltman and Nissalke at least had a clue of how to run a pro team. In December, Weltman traded for World B. Free. They began to win a few games. More importantly, Stepien had lost so much money that he finally knew that he had to sell the team. NBA Commissioner David Stern had the perfect buyer in mind—Gordon Gund. He already owned the Coliseum, purchasing it for a mere $300,000 in 1981 after Nick Mileti had money problems—and the building was taken over by Chase Manhattan Bank.

Stern called Gund and said, "I can get the Cavs for you cheap."

Gund said, "Why would I want it?"

Stern said, "It's an NBA franchise. You own the building. It would be good for you. You can turn it around."

Gund said: "How can I turn it around? All the draft picks are gone. The reputation of the team in town is awful. It's a mockery. There are more flies than fans in the stands. I own the building. I know there aren't 800 fans there some nights."

Stern said that it made no sense for the Cavs to lose and Gund to have no major tenant in the building. Gund said since he only paid $300,000 for the building, "It's cheaper to wrap it up [close it down] than buy the Cavs and have them eat my [financial] lunch for years."

Stepien was threatening to move the team to Toronto. The NBA wanted a franchise in Cleveland and Stepien as far as away from it as possible. Siberia would have been too close. Gund knew this. Stern also knew Gund owned an investment company that often purchased depressed businesses, built them back up and then sold them for a profit.

Gund told Stern: "Paying anything for this is too much. It's buying the right to lose money for a long time."

The main problem was Stepien and Musselman traded away draft choices for the next four years. The Cavs had no No. 1 pick until 1987. Weltman, then the general manager, was working with Gund to cut a deal with the league to buy draft choices.

Gund was able to purchase the Cavs and Nationwide Advertising from Stepien for an announced price of $20 million. But it was only $2.5 million in cash, with the remaining $17.5 million paid out over the next 10 years.

This happened because the NBA agreed to sell the Cavs draft picks—four first-rounders from 1983 to 1986 for a grand total of $1 million, or $250,000 each. This was unprecedented, and it showed the NBA's desperation to get rid of Stepien.

In Stepien's three seasons, the Cavs' average attendance was 5,475, 5,769 and 3,916.

The announced attendances for the final four home games were 2,441, 2,039, 1,952 and 2,495. They had four crowds of fewer than 2,000 that season.

Gund and Weltman hoped the addition of first-round picks over the next four years would help rebuild the team. But they also had another idea of how to stir some interest in the Cavs, one that involved Joe Tait doing what Joe Tait always did best—build interest in the Cavaliers.

38 States

Living in Wisconsin and Iowa these past four years has left me depleted of watching my beloved Indians, Browns and Cavs. Then in 2009, I remembered something I learned from my communications classes—when the sun goes down, you are able to get AM stations that you normally don't get. I excitedly dialed up 1100 on my way back from a church council meeting, and I heard, "WHAM! And a right hand!"

One of Joe Tait's many unmistakable catchphrases!

It was like I was back home driving on I-271 coming home from work—except I was in the middle of rural Wisconsin (and it snows just as much!). I sat in my parking lot of my apartment for the rest of the fourth quarter and listened to the Cavs beat the Nets that night. It all ended with, "Have a GOOD night, everybody!"

It didn't get any better than that—even when my wife complained that I was gone longer than normal. How could she even begin to understand?? For me, it was all worth it!

—*Rev. James Lotz, Naperville, Iowa*

Back in 1973, I was driving home from California. I had just been discharged from the Navy. I had just crossed the Mississippi River, and I was channel-surfing with my radio, and I heard Joe Tait's voice. I believe he was doing an Indians game then. I began to cry. I hadn't been home in over two years, and I'd been driving for at least three days, so I felt that I was finally home—even though I was many miles away from Cleveland.

You can't ever think of Cleveland or home without also thinking about Joe Tait.

—*Roy Borgerding, Euclid, Ohio*

I used to sneak my transistor radio into bed with me as a kid just to listen when the Cavs were on the West Coast. Joe and my Dad were the two people most responsible for my love for the Cavs. It's because of Joe that I got into broadcasting, and I have been doing it since 1985. My favorite broadcast, which I still have on cassette, was in 1985—the game in which the Cavs clinched the playoff berth against the Nets. That was when the Cavs team carried coach George Karl off the floor.

—*Jeff Tolcher, La Verne, California*

I was on a business trip to Germany with my ex-husband that was supposed to last a few weeks. I was 24 years old and very excited to go to Europe. While he went to his job every day, I was sitting in an upstairs apartment in the home the company had rented for us. I had no car. Our trip turned into months. Although we did some wonderful weekend traveling, I was very lonely and homesick. In the middle 1970s, even television didn't come on until late afternoon, when the men came home from work. I had a radio, but because we lived in the mountains, I could rarely pick up Armed Forces Radio. That was my only tie to home. Mail would have a three- to four-week turnaround. One night, I was feeling particularly lonely, so I tried one last time to find something on the radio. "BINGO" was the first word I heard . . . Joe Tait calling the Cavs game! I felt like I was at home!

—*Gail Stilwell, Brunswick Hills, Ohio*

I grew up listening to Joe announce the games. I drew a photo of a Cavaliers player shooting the ball, and it had Joe on the sideline sitting behind a 3WE banner. I think the player was Mike Bratz. I'm now 45 years old, and I still have the picture. I was a college student in Chicago, and I'd tune in Cavs games on AM 1100. It would fade in and out with the amplitude modulation, like waves on the water. But it was carrying a piece of home to me in Chicago.

Joe was there telling me about the games between the Cavaliers and the Bulls in the playoffs as my first daughter was born in the early 1990s. I remember driving to the hospital to visit my wife and new daughter, listening to the games. I was still in Chicago, but I chose to listen to the weaker signal of WTAM so that I could hear the picture being painted of Mark Price, Hot Rod Williams, Brad Daugherty, Larry Nance, Mike Sanders and Craig Ehlo. That daughter just entered college this fall.

—*Bob Butts, Solon, Ohio*

True story. I was on my honeymoon in 1976. My wife and I were married on February 28th. We drove to Miami in my Volkswagen Beetle. We didn't have much money, so we were staying in a cheap motel somewhere on the beach. I left the room and drove to pick up some snacks. The Cavs were playing that night. On a lark, I turned on the car radio to 1100. Lo and behold, I could hear Joe calling the game. I pulled back into the motel parking lot and continued to listen. I was in the car for maybe 45 more minutes. Finally, my new bride peeks out the window and sees the car. She comes running out of the room and asks where I have been. I said: "Honey, you won't believe this, but you can pick up Joe Tait down here. The Cavs are winning!" It was the first time, but unfortunately not the last time, I made my wife cry. Thanks a lot, Joe!

P.S. My bride and I have been mostly happily married for 35 years. I love my wife and Joe Tait, too!

—*Terry Maloney, Youngstown, Ohio*

I was born in Cleveland, Ohio, and moved when I was 7 in July 1988. My family decided that for the next several years we would live on a sailboat going from port to port every day. We

sailed through Canada, the Chesapeake, Florida and the Baha-
mas. Living on this sailboat was an amazing experience, but a
big part of me missed Cleveland.

I found what I was looking for in the form of 1100
WWWE . . . the 50,000-watt monster on the lake. Every night, I
would wait until the sun went down because that meant I was
able to pick up the station on the radio—with the help of my
dad, who rigged a copper wire to the top of the 50-foot mast that
ran down to the radio antenna.

We would sit there as a family every night and listen to Joe
call each Cavs game. My dad would tell stories about how he
was at the Miracle at Richfield, and I would yell "from the line
to the lane" every time Joe said it. When we finally ended our
journey, we moved to Annapolis, Maryland. My dad got courtside seats to see the Cavs and Bullets play. I got to meet John
"Hot Rod" Williams, Tree Rollins and several other players . . .
BUT the person I was most excited to meet was Joe Tait.

—*John Davison, Yonkers, New York*

We moved to Atlanta just a few years prior to popular use of
the Internet. One night, I pulled into the driveway feeling tired
from a long day and a little homesick. I wondered how my Cavs
were doing. No way to know unless . . . I figured, why not try
finding the Cavs' Cleveland broadcast on the car radio? I felt a
little foolish, since—after all—I was 700 miles away. Darned if it
didn't work. Hearing Joe's voice was like getting a surprise call
from an old friend, and knowing I could dial in was like finding
$100 in a coat pocket.

—*Jim Hibbard, Snellville, Georgia*

Joe Tait is the Cavaliers. Or maybe more appropriately, Joe
Tait is the voice of Cleveland—occasionally cynical, constantly
hopeful and always sincere.

My fondest memory of Joe is from a time when I couldn't
even pick him out of a lineup. During the Cavs' memorable
57-win season in 1991–92, I was 15. I discovered I could pick

up a weak signal from 3WE from where I lived 250 miles away, outside of Dayton. Every game night, I'd carefully turn the radio dial like a safecracker hoping to pick up the broadcast. When I'd hear Joe's voice, my ear would latch onto it. I knew I was going to be treated to an evening of basketball in the theater of my imagination—all because Joe was so good at painting a picture with his voice.

I'm quite certain I never would have even attempted to try to listen to a crackly, static-clogged broadcast while lying on the cold floor in the darkness of my family room if I didn't know Joe would make it worth my while. At 15 years old, though I'd never laid eyes on him, I considered Joe Tait one of my best friends.

—Jonathan Knight, Columbus, Ohio

With groundbreaking sports-talk host Pete Franklin. "He would join me at halftime, then I went up to his booth for the postgame," Joe said. "Here, we were complaining on air about being cold and someone got us a blanket."

Gordon Gund

Harry Weltman had several moves in mind once Gordon Gund bought the Cavs.

"But one of the first had to be getting Joe back," Weltman said. "It was the easiest and best decision that I ever made as general manager."

Joe was finishing the 1982–83 season in Chicago, where he worked some college games along with the Chicago Bulls. He still lived in Northeast Ohio. While Chicago was once his dream, Cleveland had become home.

"I was doing 70 Indians games on TV," he said. "So I really liked the idea of coming back to the Cavs—once Stepien sold them. I had known Harry Weltman over the years. We weren't close, but he'd call me, and we'd talk. I liked Harry very much and believed he'd bring some sanity to the Cavs. They also had Tom Nissalke as coach, and I knew Tom was a legitimate NBA coach. So I could see how things would improve. They would be a normal basketball team again."

When Weltman asked if Joe had an interest in doing the games for the 1983–84 season, Joe had a one-word answer: *"Absolutely."*

Gund was all for it, even though he had never met Joe.

"I live in New Jersey, but I'd heard Joe on the radio," Gund said. "That was back when it was WWWE, and you could hear it clearly at night. I loved Joe's voice and how he did the games. You can see a game when Joe does it."

Gund has been blind since the age of 30, so radio is an important vehicle of communication for him.

"After buying the Cavs, the biggest challenge was bringing back some legitimacy to the franchise," said Gund. "In the minds of the fans, Joe was associated with the good times of the franchise."

And the fans also knew that when Joe simply couldn't tolerate the Stepien regime, he left. So Joe returning was a signal that things had changed for the better with the Cavs.

"We knew that we weren't going to be a good team right away," said Weltman. "Not after all the crazy trades. Joe was very important to us letting the fans know that we were serious about changing things."

The 1983-84 Cavs also introduced a new logo. The media guide described it like this: "Burnt orange, white and royal blue. The logo featured the word CAVS in block lettering in orange with a blue backdrop. The V is shaped like a basket with a white netlike outline in the middle of the letter and a basketball positioned above it."

Gund thought hiring Joe was a wiser idea than changing the logo and team colors. They wanted to distance themselves as far as possible from the look of the Stepien teams. But they didn't want to go back to the old wine and gold of the early 1970s. Hard-core Cavs fans didn't embrace the new uniform, colors and logo—but that was a minor issue. More important, Joe was doing the games and telling them that in a few years, this new ownership could put a winning team on the court. Joe had clashed with important people with teams before because of his candor—not only with Stepien, but he battled with Tribe manager Frank Robinson. So the fact that Joe was positive about the Cavs was a major endorsement to fans who loved his broadcasts and knew his history.

"We also thought it was important to be on 3WE and have Pete Franklin as part of our broadcasts," said Gund. "So we had Pete's show from the Coliseum, and the fans loved that. Joe and Pete were key to helping us win back the fans."

To Joe, it was a chance to return to his first sports love—the Cavaliers. He also didn't enjoy spending part of the season in Chicago, the other part in Cleveland doing the Indians. He didn't have to be told to sell the new Cavs—he was happy to be back.

"When they traded for World B. Free, it really made basketball fun again," said Joe. "Only those of us who followed the team closely back then realize what World did for the franchise."

Weltman traded guard Ron Brewer to Golden State for Free on December 15, 1982. So World was on the team when Joe arrived, and Joe had a 22-point scorer with a charismatic personality to talk about. Free was listed at 6-foot-3, but he was closer to 6-foot-1. That was short for a shooting guard. But the veteran could really shoot. He was 29 and balding, and he'd hold the ball above his head. His jumper seemed to arch up near the scoreboard, then drop way down through the rim. He ate cheeseburgers before games at Whitey's. He loved to sign autographs and pose for pictures with fans.

Joe has never wavered in his belief that Free's No. 21 should be retired. Like Nate Thurmond, Free wasn't here long—four seasons—but they were four years when the Cavs were digging out of the rubble of the Stepien Era. He also is the team's second all-time leading scorer—averaging 23.0 points—behind LeBron James. He shot a respectable 45 percent from the field, 38 percent on 3-pointers. He isn't the best player in Cavs history, but he is the most under-appreciated.

*   *   *

If you listened closely to Joe's broadcasts, you heard him mention the colors of the uniforms and other things that he hopes "paints a verbal picture of the game." He paid even more attention to these details after meeting Gund. The Cavs owner mentioned how Joe's style was especially appreciated because of his blindness.

One of Joe's biggest fans is Cathalynn Thompson, who has never seen a Cavaliers game. She was born three months premature. All she can see is light, dark and a faint outline of people. Joe was her eyes on the Cavs, the radio broadcaster's voice the soundtrack of every Cavs season for her since the days of Nissalke coaching the Cavs in the early 1980s.

So yes, Cathalynn became a Cavs fan just as Gund bought the team and Joe returned.

"To the line, to the lane, to the hoop . . . wham with the right hand," said Cathalynn, repeating her favorite Joe call. She works for Mobile Meals in Akron, taking calls from clients. On game days, she wears her Cavs sweatshirt as she settles in front of the radio. If the game is also on network television, she turns the sound up on the TV.

"And I listen to Joe, too," she said. "I like the TNT guys, so I want to hear them . . . but I also like to hear Joe."

Cathalynn was exactly the kind of fan that Gund and Weltman had in mind when they hired Joe. Obviously, they needed the big spenders who sit in suites and at courtside. But they also wanted to connect with Cathalynn, the average fan who wanted to have a reason to fall in love with the team. They needed Joe to preach the gospel of Cavs basketball, and they loved it when fans repeated some of Joe's favorite catchphrases.

"'Three ball . . . got it!!!'" said Cathalynn. "That was another of my favorites."

"I've met Cathalynn and her parents several times," Joe said. "When I do the games, I think about people like her and Gordon Gund. I know that several blind people do listen to me. That's why I describe the color of the uniforms, the color of the lines on the court, anything I notice that they would like to see."

By the time Joe retired, Gund had been listening to him for 28 years—the same as Cathalynn.

"What a voice Joe has," said Gund. "It's so full, like a pipe organ."

Then Gund did his Joe imitation . . . "'Wesley Person for THREE . . . GOT IT!'" Gund wasn't exactly sure why Person was one of his favorite players to "watch" through Joe's eyes, but the shooting guard who was here from 1997 to 2002 appealed to Gund. Probably because he shot 42 percent on 3-pointers as a 12-point scorer—and Joe made those 3-pointers sound as if they were shot from somewhere south of Columbus.

Gund said he also appreciated Joe's sense of humor.

"When we had people selling tickets, Joe would read the advertisement and phone number to call, they he'd say, 'Operators are standing by. Why doesn't someone get them a chair?'" said Gund, laughing.

When Gordon Gund bought the Cavs, he quickly hired Joe back as the team's radio voice. "I loved Joe's voice and how he did the games. You can see a game when Joe does it" Joe's blunt style did sometimes cause him to wince. "He was so damn candid," Gund said. *(NBA Photos courtesy Cleveland Cavaliers)*

Gund then mentioned Joe saying, "'Left to right on the radio dial.'"

With digital radios, most people don't have dials. But when Gund last had his vision, radios did have dials—and that phrase has special meaning to him.

There were times when Joe's sarcasm "did make me wince," said Gund. "If we were playing poorly, you could tell right away from listening to Joe. He was so damn candid, utterly unvarnished."

Did he ever tell Joe not to say something?

"Once or twice, I thought about it," said Gund. "But knowing

Joe, it wouldn't matter. He'd say what he wanted to say. That's another reason we wanted him—for his honesty and credibility."

Joe said the only time he backed off was when the team would announce a larger crowd than appeared to be in the seats. At Gund Arena, the seats were blue. Joe used to call those attendance figures, "Blue Seat sellouts."

When Gund had the team colors changed to the "new" wine and gold before the 2003 season, the owner asked Joe to see them first.

"I want to hear what you say before you say it on the radio," Gund told Joe.

"I told Gordon that it looked more like tomato juice and mustard than wine and gold to me," said Joe. "But because he really tried, I wasn't going to be critical. At least they were much better than the other uniforms."

Gund has never seen Joe, "But I do have a picture of Joe in my mind. He's a big man with a round face, at least that's how his voice sounds. I know that he is kind of wide and stout, probably bigger than he wants to be. But I sense a steady presence."

Pretty close, as Joe would attest. About all that's missing would be Joe's beard.

Gund paid special attention to Joe's final games with the Cavs.

"He had been having some physical problems, so I knew the day was coming when he'd quit," said Gund. "But it really was a sad day for me. I will miss hearing him, because no one does a game quite like Joe Tait."

A Hall of Fame Voice

[BY FRANK KURTZ]

I first met Joe at the age of 13. It was March 30, 1978, right after the Cavaliers suffered a heartbreaking 99-95 loss to the San Antonio Spurs. I have a mild case of cerebral palsy, and I'd just been released from the hospital following hip surgery. I didn't know it, but the father of one of my classmates had written Joe several months earlier. He addressed the letter to Joe and Pete Franklin. Joe found it in Pete's mailbox while substituting on *Sportsline* one evening. In the letter, my friend's dad told Joe about my desire for a career as a sportscaster. He asked Joe if it would be possible for me to meet him.

Joe wrote back and told my friend's dad that he'd get us tickets whenever we wanted to come to a Cavaliers game. After the game, we went down on the floor and visited with Joe. He gave me a Cavs media guide along with official statistics from that night's game. He said he would get tickets for me whenever I wanted.

I didn't know then that Joe would be a lifelong mentor and friend.

I took Joe up on his offer by writing and asking for tickets to games occasionally. Sometimes I wrote just to let Joe know how I was doing. Joe penned a personal handwritten reply to every one of my letters as if we were old friends. When I got to Indians games early, I'd go to the press box and wait for Joe to arrive. He always took time out of his busy day to spend a couple of minutes visiting with me.

In the fall of 1983, I enrolled in Kent State University's telecommunications program with the hope of one day following in Joe's footsteps. I did play-by-play of a Kent State football game that autumn. I sent the tape to Joe and asked him if he would listen to my work and evaluate it.

He replied and agreed to assist me, saying that he honestly felt I had a future in the business if I worked hard enough. Everybody who knows Joe well understands that he's as honest as the day is long. He always encouraged me to keep working hard, but he also made it very clear when he felt like my work wasn't up to par.

I thanked him for his honesty on more than one occasion, and he always replied, "It doesn't do you any good not to hear the truth."

There were some funny moments in those days, too. I walk with crutches because of my cerebral palsy, and one night I tripped on one of the many cords on the Coliseum's press row. I got back up and walked past Joe, who shouted, "I saw it all, Frank! You were clipped, and that should be a 15-yard penalty!"

One of my fondest memories is also one of the funniest. My dad took my brother and me to see the Indians play at old Tiger Stadium in the summer of 1987. I found Joe at the press box, and we visited a bit. I handed him a note and asked him to say hello to my grandparents on the air.

During the broadcast he says, "Frank Kurtz and his brother and father are here tonight, and he wanted me to say hello to his grandparents, Ruth and Carl Sullivan, back in Brewster, Ohio. It is my understanding that Grandma is a big Tribe fan. . . . Unfortunately, Grandpa's not so interested, and Grandma doesn't always get to see them. . . . Better straighten up, Grandpa!"

My grandparents couldn't get over that, and they talked about it with family and friends for the rest of their lives.

I was approaching my final year in the broadcasting program at Kent State in the fall of 1988, but something was wrong. I'd been hoarse all summer. When it didn't go away, I consulted a specialist. It was later determined that I had a malignant tumor on one of my vocal chords that would have to be removed. My mom called many friends and family to explain what was happening. Four or five days after surgery, the phone in my hospital room rings. I had a tracheotomy and couldn't talk, so my mom put the phone up to my ear.

"Frank, this is Joe Tait calling. I want you to take it easy and do what the doctors tell you, and I'll look forward to seeing you when you're feeling better and back on your feet."

Joe's words of encouragement were very uplifting, and they meant more to me than anyone will ever know.

Joe and I have continued to keep in touch since then with many letters and phone calls. He helped teach me that people are the most important thing in life. I'd always want to talk basketball, and he'd always turn the conversation around to how things were going. Joe's just a regular guy with a Hall of Fame voice who never forgot where he came from, and I'm very grateful that he's part of my life.

Shawn Kemp and the New NBA

For years, the NBA had been slowly eating away at Joe's basketball heart.

The league he loved, the league of the 1970s when basketball in Cleveland was like a toddler trying to find a way to stand on its own feet while being watched only by family and a small circle of friends.

Then the marvel of the miracle season in 1975–76 . . .

Then the Cavs came back from the rubble of Ted Stepien in the early 1980s to a team in the late 1980s and 1990s that was a contender and a delight for basketball purists . . .

The teams of Bill Fitch and Lenny Wilkens . . . just thinking about them makes Joe smile.

By the middle 1990s, they were gone . . .

"It's not just the basketball," said Joe. "I respect what Mike Fratello did as coach. I liked him, and he got most of his teams to play extremely hard."

But the game was changing.

"I'm not sure when I first noticed it, but there was never a moment of silence," he said. "There was blaring music. When they couldn't get the fans to clap their hands, they played the sounds of hands clapping to wake up the crowd. They had junk thrown into the stands, some clown screaming into a microphone during timeouts. The sound effects never ended."

Joe paused.

"Then came the cheerleaders," he said. "We had the Cavalettes in our first year. Unfortunately, a few of them ran afoul of the law, and the entire group then went away. And that was a good thing. But then they came back with dance teams . . . the Cavalettes were demure young ladies compared to them. Some of the dance team routines look like they came straight from a strip club."

For several years, Joe was the Cavs' vice president of broadcasting in addition to doing the games on radio.

"I sat in on those marketing meetings," he said. "They didn't talk about the game. They talked about the 'complete entertainment experience.' It's like the game was secondary to all the crap they wanted to do."

Joe's first love was the Miracle team built by Bill Fitch. But he never felt closer to any group than the Cavs of the early 1970s, guys who were just like Joe—young and fighting to survive in the league. When he runs into the players from those years, they embrace like old army buddies—and quickly start telling their basketball war stories.

Joe also appreciated how Harry Weltman brought some stability back to the team after the Ted Stepien Era.

"I will say it until my dying day—they should retire World B. Free's No. 21," said Joe. "He was all we had right after the Stepien Era. World came here with this bad reputation, and he was great to the fans and media. I loved World, and he meant a lot to this franchise. Getting World was a great move by Harry Weltman."

Joe was thrilled with owner Gordon Gund hiring Wayne Embry as general manager. Next came Lenny Wilkens as the coach.

"They are two of the classiest men in basketball," said Joe. "Look at the team they put together and how they played so unselfishly."

He mentioned the names: Mark Price, Brad Daugherty, Larry Nance, Craig Ehlo, Hot Rod Williams, Mike Sanders, Winston Bennett . . .

"We had All-Stars on those teams, and they didn't need anyone to carry their bags," he said. "They didn't have personal assistants, or whatever they call those guys who hang around the players and travel with them now. Somewhere along the line, some of these guys went from being basketball players to celebrities."

Wilkens left the Cavs in the summer of 1993; his last record was 54-28. The Cavs were knocked out of the playoffs by Michael

Jordan and the Chicago Bulls. It was the fourth time in six years the Bulls had wiped the Cavs out of the playoff picture, and the frustration was mounting. The problem wasn't simply the Cavs couldn't beat the Bulls—no one could in that era. History tells us that now. But in the middle of it, the Cavs thought a different type of coach could help. So they went from the quieter Wilkens to the more confrontational Fratello. Just as Wilkens' last team was swept by the Bulls, so was Fratello's first.

From 1994 to '97, Fratello's teams were 1-9 in the playoffs. They were good enough to win a few more games than they lost, but not talented enough to even make it a serious series in the first round.

"That's when they made a decision that they wanted a star," said Joe.

What's wrong with that?

"I said they wanted a star, not necessarily to win," said Joe. "They wanted to sell more tickets."

In the summer of 1997, the Cavs no longer had Nance, Daugherty, Price, Ehlo and Hot Rod Williams. All had retired or been traded to other teams. They had missed the playoffs. They were heading into their fourth year at the new Gund (now called Quicken Loans) Arena in downtown Cleveland. Fans were not renewing their season tickets. In the first three years downtown, the average attendance dropped from 20,238 to 17,807 to 16,895. The last season, there were only three sellouts. Embry was assigned by ownership to find a "star." It was about selling tickets and luxury suites. It was not about building a winner. Embry no longer had his power base. Joe believed the marketing types had convinced ownership that the team needed sizzle. The biggest name available was Seattle's Shawn Kemp.

Gund has always said great basketball teams have at least one star—and that Cavs team had none. You don't always contend for a title with a star, but virtually every contender has a star.

"But it has to be the right star, the right kind of guy," said Joe. "When I heard we were after Kemp, I knew this was trouble."

In the summer of 1997, Kemp was only 27. He had averaged 18.7 points, 10.0 rebounds and made his fifth All-Star team. He had entered the NBA at 18, and his body was an "old 27" because of all the years that he'd played. He also was packing on the pounds. He was best with about 250 pounds on his 6-foot-10 frame, but was listed at 270 when the Cavs traded for him.

Embry did his research. He had page after page about Kemp's battles with Seattle coach George Karl. And about Kemp being late for practices and flights. About Kemp getting out of shape. About Kemp and some episodes in bars. About Kemp and some rumors of drug use.

Most of all, a question lingered: "Why was Seattle so anxious to deal Kemp only one year after he took them to the NBA Finals—and when he was only 27?"

The Cavs could get him as a part of a three-way deal with Milwaukee and Seattle—the Cavs sending Terrell Brandon and Tyrone Hill to the Bucks. When the trade was being discussed, Gund went around the room, asking his advisers if they favored the deal. All of them did. Embry was the last to speak. He reluctantly went along with it, a decision that he regrets to this day.

"I knew Wayne didn't want to make a trade like that," said Joe. "Kemp wasn't his kind of guy. But things were changing at that point with the team—and in the NBA. Everyone just wanted a player who was a star, or at least they thought was a star. Create some buzz, that's what it was all about."

The Cavs then made another major mistake. They reworked Kemp's contract.

Here was a guy who had his contract reworked twice in Seattle, a deal which still had three years left. And here was a guy who was fined several times for his poor attitude and work ethic. And here was a guy who was getting heavier, a guy whose off-the-court reputation was questionable.

The Cavs took this guy and gave him $100 million over seven years before he played a single game in Cleveland. They wanted to make Kemp happy, hoping he'd respond by playing harder and taking conditioning seriously. Instead, Kemp saw it as a reward for what amounted to bad behavior. He acted like a jerk, forced a trade and then signed one of the most lucrative contracts in the NBA.

Embry did put a weight clause in the contract. He wanted it to be 265, but the Cavs decided to make it 275. Kemp showed up at 290 pounds but wasn't fined. Why make him unhappy?

"Crap like that bothered me," said Joe. "Shawn Kemp is a very nice man, always friendly to me. But I knew it wouldn't work."

In his first season with the Cavs, Kemp was heavy but still averaged 18 points and 9.1 rebounds. They won 47 games, making the playoffs. They added only 47 season ticket holders. But the main thing was the season ticket total didn't decrease.

"Everyone said that the trade worked," said Joe. "Then came the lockout, and Kemp came back fatter than ever. We didn't play well, Mike Fratello was fired. Randy Wittman was a rookie head coach when he replaced Fratello. Kemp had no respect for him. Kemp was constantly late for airplanes. I'm not talking about 10 minutes, but 45 minutes or an hour. We'd sit there in the private plane, waiting. I sat up by the coaches. Trainer Gary Briggs would tell them that we needed to go, but Wittman let Kemp run the show."

Joe then said during one of the waiting-for-Kemp flights, Briggs was saying if the Cavs didn't leave soon, they'd miss their "window" to fly into Newark . . . and that would cause problems with the control tower.

"But Randy didn't want to leave Kemp," said Joe. "Finally, Briggs was so frustrated about the indecision, he told the coach, 'If you don't have any balls, you can borrow mine.' Wittman just sat there, stone-faced."

Joe said after they arrived in Newark, guard Bobby Sura said, "Joe, have you ever seen anything like this in all your years in the league? The man [coach] has no control.' Everyone knew what was going on, but the Cavs did nothing to stop it."

The Cavs fell apart after Kemp's first season, missing the playoffs. He got fatter and fatter. In 1999–2000, he paid $300,000 in fines to the Cavs for violating his weight clause. Kemp didn't care because he had $70 million left on the contract. In the summer of 2000, General Manager Jim Paxson was able to convince Portland to take Kemp and his huge contract.

One of Joe's favorite phrases for the modern NBA is "the inmates running the asylum."

During Wittman's tenure (1999 to 2001), Joe remembers sitting in a marketing meeting with the coach and Cavs radio producer Scott Zurilla. The marketing people were talking about "the total entertainment experience." Their idea was "to have a full house at the game, even if the team doesn't show up," said Joe. He had been telling the marketing people that the game and the team are the main things, that a second of silence won't kill anyone.

"Finally, I had just heard enough," Joe said. "I told them, 'This is all bull crap,' and then I got up and walked out after to listening to 90 minutes of that garbage. Wittman was stunned and asked Zurilla if I planned to come back. Scott said that he doubted it, and I didn't go back."

Joe said he noticed himself "bitching too much on the air about all the noise and crap going on." He tried to keep the criticism to a minimum.

"Usually, I just ripped them for all the hugging and kissing and crap they did before the opening tap," he said.

Something else was happening. Joe was getting older.

He was 33 when hired by the Cavs in 1970. By 2000, he was 63. He went from being the age of the older players . . . to the age of the coaches . . . to being the oldest guy on the bus and plane in most seasons. He felt like their grandfather. He was more distant from the players and was alarmed at their growing sense of entitlement.

"I got so sick of the players all needing their 'guys' to take care of them," he said. "I went from loving the NBA to liking it. By the end, I just tolerated it. I divorced myself from much of the game, and I concentrated on the broadcast—doing a good job there. I did it for the fans, the people who have listened to me, year after year."

Joe admired the skill and athleticism LeBron James brought to the Cavs, but he remembered hearing how some in the marketing department were taking credit for all the sellouts.

"If there is no LeBron, no 50-game-winning seasons and going deep into the playoffs—do you really think they will pack the house?" Joe asked. "They drew 20,000 a night because of LeBron and the team winning. It had nothing to do with cheerleaders who were nearly topless or some guy on the court with a microphone screaming his head off. To me, the NBA was getting to be too much like a circus—and I'd had enough."

LeBron

When LeBron James was playing for Akron St. Vincent-St. Mary High School, Joe hated the hype. He hated the team playing a national schedule, traveling all over the country for tournaments. He hated how some of those high school games were televised on ESPN, the first high school team to be featured on the national sports network. He hated how James was on the cover of *Sports Illustrated* and other national magazines. He hated how James' team was covered nearly as well as the Cavaliers when James was a senior. He hated how James was called "The Chosen One" and "King James."

But he never hated LeBron James.

"I don't blame him for all that," said Joe. "It's just the professional sports mentality permeating all the way down into the high schools. Some of the summer teams are just cesspools."

Joe loves small-time high school sports, which is why he'd broadcast a few high school games each winter—usually from small towns with teams where most kids won't play after high school. It reminds him of the high school games he called as a young broadcaster at small stations in the Midwest.

For Joe, it's like taking a professional shower after all the noise and glitz he endured nightly in the NBA for decades. Because Joe started his career in the Cavs' first season, his best memories are when the team was fighting for its survival. In 1970, there were two basketball leagues—the NBA and the American Basketball Association (ABA). Part of the reason Cleveland, Portland and Buffalo were granted NBA expansion teams in 1970 was so the upstart ABA would not put teams in those cities. Joe and everyone associated with the NBA in the early 1970s knew two pro leagues would never survive. They knew some franchises would fold or move.

They knew the last thing pro basketball needed was an overblown sense of entitlement.

So it's hard for Joe and most others from that basketball generation to comprehend the star system that transformed James and some other high school players into instant celebrities and ordained superstars at the age of 16. While some players could go straight from high school to pro ball in the 1970s, very few did. The three most notable were Moses Malone, Bill Willoughby and Darryl Dawkins. Most players waited at least three years before leaving college for the pro draft.

But starting in 2001–02—James' junior season—pro scouts were drooling over a 16-year-old from Akron.

Like any sane adult, Joe knew this was not a healthy situation for any young player.

As Joe said, "So much of it was embarrassing."

And as he stressed when talking about James—he doesn't blame LeBron.

"Somewhere, there was a report that LeBron never talked to me," Joe said. "That's just not true. I never had a problem with him. He'd say hello to me, I'd say hi to him. We never carried on any long conversations, but we were always cordial and professional."

Joe was 66 years old when an 18-year-old LeBron James was the Cavs' No. 1 pick in the 2003 draft. They didn't have much in common. In Joe's final decade with the team, he didn't have much connection with the players. They were generations apart in age and interests. You could say that an NBA lifer such as Joe could have been helpful to a young LeBron James . . . or any other young player . . . but most young millionaires don't think they need much advice.

Joe realized James was unlike any Cavs player—ever. Not one was as physically gifted. Not one was marketed so aggressively. Certainly, no Cavalier ever had more media attention, commercial endorsements and demands on his time.

"I asked simply that LeBron do one postgame interview a year with me," said Joe. "So many of our games were on national TV, and they always wanted him. He usually did his one interview a year. One time, I remember him coming over to the press table, sitting down in front of me. I said, 'Well, look who is here!' LeBron said, 'I told you that I'd come.'"

And they did a nice interview.

*   *   *

LeBron was not Joe's favorite member of the James family.

"He was fine, but his mom [Gloria James] was always super-friendly to me," said Joe. "Whenever she saw me, she'd run up and give me a big hug. I enjoyed her."

Then Joe smiled, laughed and told this story . . .

"At halftime of my 3,000th Cavs broadcast, my family was up in a loge that the Cavs had provided," he said. "My son Joe looked down at the broadcast area and saw a woman sitting in my lap. He asked my wife [Jeannie], 'Who is that woman sitting in Dad's lap?' Jeannie looked down and said, 'Oh, that just Gloria.' She knew that Gloria liked to run over and give me a hug. Gloria loved listening to the games on the radio."

*   *   *

In his final decade doing the Cavs, Joe noticed how players suddenly had "guys." They were personal assistants. Or posse members. Or hangers-on. Or whatever you want to call certain people who were always around the players.

LeBron James had a guy—Randy Mims.

He was allowed on the team plane and stayed at the team hotel. As Joe said, "LeBron would tell Randy to get something—and Randy would get it. Or he'd tell Randy to call someone—and Randy would make the call. You could say he was LeBron's 'Bobo' or whatever, but he was a nice guy and never really got in the way—at least as far as I know."

For decades, the team had one bus from the hotel to the arena for players, coaches and media members who regularly traveled to the games. But not long after James arrived, they added a special bus for the media.

"I guess they didn't want us with the players and coaches," said Joe. "For a while, they had a full-sized bus, and the only ones on the second bus were Randy Mims and me. Then they went to a 24-seater, and it was still the two of us. We got a laugh out of that. Then LeBron wanted Randy on the first bus, so I rode alone. Then the TV guys starting using the media bus, and sometimes they had some corporate types and contest-winning fans on that bus."

While Mims was with James from the start of his pro career in 2003—even sitting right behind the bench during games—he never had an official position with the team until 2006. Then he was named "team liaison" by Cavs owner Dan Gilbert's front office.

"Dan overdid it trying to placate LeBron," said Joe. "There were times when we had one travel schedule, but LeBron would want to stay an extra day in a certain city because he had a commitment or whatever, and we'd change it to suit LeBron. I'm sure Dan felt that he had to do about anything he could to keep LeBron happy . . . he sure was packing the arena with fans. LeBron could have run naked down Euclid Avenue, and everyone would say how great it was that he was working out to stay in shape. People just loved him, and everything he did was great."

It's fair to say James added about $100 million to the value of the franchise.

"But it's like raising a child," said Joe. "If you give him everything he wants, anytime he wants it . . . that kid is going to come back one day and steal your car."

*   *   *

In James' final season with the Cavs, Joe had a sense something was wrong.

"I had no idea about him going to Miami, but I just sensed he was not coming back to Cleveland," he said. "I look back now, and I'm convinced that LeBron, Dwyane Wade and Chris Bosh all knew what they were going to do even before LeBron's last Cavs season. I have no cold, hard facts; I just sensed it."

Joe said that while James and former Cavs coach Mike Brown

usually got along, "Mike was never LeBron's kind of coach. He was a defensive coach . . . and LeBron would probably rather play for someone like [his former high school coach] Dru Joyce II. I heard there were some problems with LeBron in the dressing room that last season, but I never went in there after the game. So I really don't know, and I didn't make it my business to find out. I just had a feeling that LeBron was like a guy who knew he was going to be somewhere else next season."

Joe said watching the Cavs lose to Boston in the 2010 NBA semifinals, James' lack of leadership was on display for everyone to see.

"He never was a real leader," Joe said. "When we got into the playoffs with Boston and it was clear they were playing their best basketball—and the Cavs just weren't good enough—it had a real detrimental effect on his game. I don't know how much his elbow was hurting. I do know that he just didn't play as hard or shoot as much as he should have. He looked defeated, almost as if he just wanted the playoffs to be over and done with. He never has been, never will be a leader. And down deep, he knows it. That's why he left to go with Wade. He'd rather let Wade be the leader."

*   *   *

Joe did watch the entire *Decision* show on ESPN, a marketing ploy by James and his associates. They sold the 60-minute special to the all-sports network on which James would talk to sportscaster Jim Gray (who was hired by James, not ESPN) to announce his decision about what team he had picked.

"He knew what he was doing, and he didn't feel right about it," said Joe. "He barely looked at the camera. He seemed very uncomfortable. He never dreamed how this would come off—the negative effect. He still can't believe how it turned the fans against him in every city where he plays on the road. He just didn't get it."

James clearly had ventured out of the safety zone of his hometown team and adoring fans. He went from one of the most likeable athletes in the world to one of the most despised—according to several marketing surveys.

"In Cleveland, if he had a bad game or made a mistake—people would just say that was OK, he'll play better next time," said Joe. "He could do no wrong. No wrong at all. Everyone loved LeBron. That's why he was so surprised by the negative reaction to the ESPN show. . . . He thought everyone would like it because everyone always seemed to like about everything he did."

When Gilbert wrote an email ripping James and calling him a quitter, Joe said the first thing that crossed his mind was, "Dan, you created the monster, now you have to live with it."

But Joe also said he appreciated how Gilbert stood up for the fans and reflected what most of them were feeling about *The Decision*.

"Dan Gilbert did everything, I mean everything, he could to make LeBron happy," said Joe. "And then LeBron turned right around and took a hike to Miami."

*   *   *

While Joe didn't watch the 2011 NBA Finals, he was very pleased that Dallas upset James and the Miami Heat.

"The fact that LeBron and Wade and the rest could decide to get together and make their own team, it was great that they lost," said Joe. "I don't care what these guys get paid. But I don't want the inmates running the asylum. I don't want the players acting like this is some summer league all-star team that they put together themselves—it makes the fans feel something is really wrong with the league. You could end up with all the good players in a few cities, and the league will die a miserable death. The fans will know something rotten is going on."

Joe knows the TV ratings for the Finals were high, "because about everyone outside of Miami wanted to see the Heat lose." Joe said he often was turned off by Dallas owner Mark Cuban, who "can be an insufferable ass." But he found himself laughing at and with Cuban when the Mavericks' owner stood next to the championship trophy and puffed on a victory cigar.

"It was a very good thing that Miami took gas in that series," said Joe.

LeBron James was distant toward the media. But his mother, Gloria, was a Joe Tait fan. "Whenever she saw me, she'd run up and give me a big hug," Joe said. *(NBA Photos courtesy Cleveland Cavaliers)*

Joe did watch some of the postgame press conferences and saw how "LeBron suddenly looks like and feels very old."

He said James "still has a hard time with the idea that fans can't stand him. He is having a terrible time dealing with defeat. Then when he said that the people who were against him were still going to have the same problems in their lives when they wake up the next day . . . of all the stupid things to say. I wonder if he'll ever win a championship. I don't know if he has the guts to do it. All the stuff is piling up on him now, and for this, he has only himself to blame."

*   *   *

Zydrunas Ilgauskas is the last Cavs player who had a close relationship with Joe.

"He went to Miami to try and get a championship ring before he retired," said Joe. "He wasn't even in uniform for some of those games in The Finals. He wanted to be a contributor, playing 15, 20 minutes a game and helping a team win a title. He loved, absolutely loved Cleveland. But when LeBron left, he knew they couldn't win here—and the team wanted to rebuild and get younger. So he went to Miami. I'm telling you, the culture shock was hard on him."

Joe said one of Ilgauskas' friends visited the veteran center and his wife in Miami.

"I was told they were never happy, and the longer they were there, it got progressively worse," he said. "Mrs. Z is from Cleveland. That was a zoo down there. I feel bad for him, because I'm sure it's not anything close to what he expected."

Working With Joe

[BY SCOTT ZURILLA]

I worked with Joe for 17 years in the Cavs radio network. Here are some thoughts:

Growing up, I wanted to play for the Cavaliers or work alongside/replace Joe Tait. I never missed a Cavs game. I can't count the number of times I would wake up in the middle of the night to the sound of the radio because I fell asleep listening to Joe call a West Coast Cavs game. I also pretended to be Joe and called the play-by-play of myself practicing in my backyard.

When I was hired by Dave Dombrowski to produce the Cavs' radio broadcasts, I couldn't believe that I was not only going to work for my Cavaliers . . . I was going to work with Joe Tait! I was TERRIFIED to meet him. It was Joe TAIT!!! I remember asking Dave a couple times, "How am I supposed to correct Joe when he messes up while recording a spot?" or "How am I supposed to tell Joe to do that again, the first time wasn't good enough? I can't tell Joe he screwed up!"

Joe would test you at first . . . bust your chops about it to see how you would react, and then redo it, no problem. And boy, did we have to redo some things. After a while, he would spout off in the recording booth in frustration. Not at me, just sometimes he would have trouble with a particular line or word and get all tongue-tied, and he would say the funniest things . . . most of which I cannot print!

When the Cavaliers were playing in Atlanta during the 2009 playoffs, I finally got back to my room after Mike Snyder and I finished our postgame show. It was around 1:30 a.m. I was getting ready for bed when my hotel room phone rang. It was Joe. And as only Joe can say, I hear a "What are you doing?" I said getting ready for bed. He said, "Are you watching TV?" And I said no. He said, "Put channel 44 on." To which I see a bunch of Asian men fighting. Because of my background in the martial arts, Joe said, "What are they doing?" and proceeded to ask me if any of them were Bruce Lee or Jackie Chan, etc.

Joe, Dave and I would travel around the state to visit our radio affiliates every summer to smaller towns such as Bucyrus, McConnelsville, Dover and New Philadelphia. We would stop at small, local places for lunch. And that is where I learned of Joe's eating habits. Not that he ate a lot, but how fast he ate. He literally would be finished with his meal and contemplating dessert before I was half way finished with mine.

Joe loved the hot dogs at the arena. . . . Two hands, three bites. It was gone! He also loved peanut butter-and-jelly "Uncrustables."

When people find out that I work for the Cavaliers, the very first question I get is, "Do you know Joe Tait?" I not only work with Joe, but he is my friend. Joe and I got in the habit of sitting and talking in the air booth as he prepared for that night's game. Talked about everything and anything, but usually not basketball. Movies, TV, books, history, his interests, my interests. Next time you watch the movie *Death Race*, think of Joe; he is a big fan of Ian McShane. He and I have gotten in the habit of calling each other Ian McShane (him) and Jason Statham (me). He and I also talk a lot about the movie *No Country For Old Men*. He is a big Tommy Lee Jones fan.

Here is the message on Joe's home phone: "Hello, Joe and Jean Tait. We're not home. Don't know why. Neither do you, but leave a message, and we'll both find out together."

For his 3,000th Cavaliers broadcast, Joe was temporarily back on the floor. *(NBA Photos courtesy Cleveland Cavaliers)*

Joe was selected as one of the Cavs Legends. Here he's accompanied by Campy Russell, Austin Carr, Elmore Smith, Bingo Smith. "There's probably a plaque somewhere in the building," said Joe. *(NBA Photos courtesy Cleveland Cavaliers)*

Joe receives the Curt Gowdy Electronic Media Award at the Basketball Hall of Fame induction ceremony on August 12, 2010 in Springfield, Massachusetts. *(NBA Photos courtesy Cleveland Cavaliers)*

Joe and Jim Chones react as a banner is raised to the rafters of Quicken Loans arena in honor of Joe's career as the Voice of the Cavaliers. *(NBA Photos courtesy Cleveland Cavaliers)*

Have a Good Night, Everybody

When Joe came to Cleveland in 1970, he had no idea he would make it his home. He was thrilled to be doing the Cavaliers and working in a major-league city. But he had never held any job for more than three years. After all, that was—and often still is—life in radio.

"I had no idea that I'd become this attached to the area," said Joe. "In fact, I tried not to have my heart set on staying here during those early years because in the back of my mind, I feared that the franchise would fold or move. No one was going to the games, and [Cavs owner] Nick Mileti had no money."

Joe was 33 when he arrived in Cleveland. The city where he'd worked the longest was Rockford, Illinois. He was a Midwestern guy, so Cleveland immediately felt comfortable.

"I know this sounds silly, but another reason that I liked Cleveland was that it had a lot of trains," said Joe. "It was a big railroad town when I first moved in. I liked [Cavs coach] Bill Fitch. Three years into the job, Nick Mileti put me on the radio to do the Indians games. I got to know a lot of good people. The fans were great and accepted me. After a few years, I never wanted to leave. The only reason I did work in New Jersey one year and Chicago the next [1981–83] was because Ted Stepien owned the Cavs. I couldn't work for him. But in those years, I still lived in Richfield because I was doing the Indians—this was home."

Joe said when he married Jean and moved into her home in Richfield, "it felt a lot a like Amboy, Illinois, where I grew up. Richfield was smaller in the early 1980s."

Joe now lives in a rural area outside of Lodi, about an hour from downtown Cleveland.

"When Ed Keating was my agent, in the 1980s, I could have told him to find me a job in a bigger market," said Joe. "He had the connections to do it. He told me that he could get me a job somewhere else. But I liked it here, so why move? At one point in the 1980s, I had a chance to do the Cubs games with Harry Caray. I had a contract with WWWE and WAUB [TV-43]. WUAB was willing to let me out of the deal, but WWWE would not. I was told to get some lawyers and they'd work out a deal, but I believe that once you sign a contract, it's a contract. I also realized that once upon a time, doing the Cubs was a dream job for me. But I had married Jean and settled in Cleveland, so it had lost a lot of its appeal."

Joe said a mistake some media people make is to chase the next job, the next big market. He did that when he was in small-market radio, where no one had job security and no one made even a decent wage unless you owned the station.

"Al McCoy [voice of the Phoenix Suns] and I have talked about how just because you are doing well in one market doesn't mean you will be accepted in another market," said Joe. "Al has done the Suns for 40 years. I know of very good broadcasters who left this market, like Gib Shanley. He left the Browns and went to Los Angeles. He thought he had a deal to do the Rams games, but that fell through. He was doing sports news on TV in L.A., and it didn't work for him. By the time he came back to Cleveland, he was able to get a sportscaster job on TV, but he no longer was the voice of the Browns because Nev Chandler had been given the job."

Joe said, in the 1980s, when Art Modell owned the Browns, he was invited to lunch.

"I may have said hello to Art once or twice, but that was it," said Joe. "I didn't know him."

Modell told Joe, "You're probably wondering why you're here. It's because I believe you can do very well on the televised football broadcasts."

Modell meant on the national networks. He had connections with the NFL's television committee and with the networks.

"If you're interested," said Modell. "I will personally take you to NBC and CBS and see that you talk to the right people. I don't think there'd be any problem with you getting a job."

A few years earlier, when Joe worked in Chicago, he did the CBS radio college basketball game of the week.

"I'd had a taste of the networks where they had nine guys to do the work of one," said Joe. "I didn't like it. I told Art that I was flattered. . . . In fact, I was flabbergasted that he'd make that offer. But I loved Cleveland and wanted to stay. I also told him that no matter money, I'd hate living in New York. So I appreciated his offer, but it wasn't for me."

Joe talked about a legendary Detroit radio morning man named J.P. McCarthy.

"He had monster ratings on WJR," said Joe. "No one could touch him. Not the rock stations, nothing. He went to San Francisco and absolutely bombed. He was there for a few months, and then came back to Detroit—where he had huge ratings again. The lesson is not everybody loves you. If you can find a niche in a good market, you are wise to stay there."

*   *   *

In 2010, Joe was voted into the media wing of the Naismith Basketball Hall of Fame.

"It was not something that I thought about much," he said. "I was honored. It's nice. I went in with Karl Malone and Scottie Pippen, and I was surprised that they even knew who I was. They came over and shook hands. Charles Barkley was there, and he yelled at me from across the room. He was super to me."

Former Miami Heat broadcaster David Halberstam began to lobby for Joe to make the Hall of Fame in 2003. His email stated: "I made requests of folks like Lenny Wilkens, Marv Albert and others [to support Joe]. I've spent my life dedicated to sports on the radio and called hoops myself for more than 25 years, mainly St. John's University and the Miami Heat. Joe was the best NBA play-by-play announcer I've ever heard. There were many of us who benefited from the extensive signal of WWWE, which at night wafted into some 38 states. In the pre-cable TV days, it helped budding announcers like us hone our craft. Joe was the best because of his unique style, description, command, voice inflection, use of silent pauses to build drama, blending of phrases and rich menu of simple word pictures. His delivery never grated. It wore tirelessly over a long season."

Now the general manager of Westwood One sports, here is one of the letters written by Halberstam about Joe:

> Mr. David Stern
> Commissioner
> National Basketball Association
> 645 Fifth Avenue
> New York, New York 10022
>
> Dear Commissioner,
> Trust that all's well as the league prepares to launch another exciting season.
> I write you on behalf of Joe Tait, the original and longtime voice of the Cleveland Cavaliers. I've lobbied to have Joe installed in the broadcast wing of the Hall of Fame. The attached two letters, one of them to John Doleva at the Hall, are self-explanatory. As a lifelong student of broadcast sports, I can't think of anyone more deserving.
> For that matter, Marv Albert and I discussed this last week and he glowingly endorses Joe's candidacy. It's mind-blowing that Joe's not in already. No NBA or NCAA play-by-play candidate rivals Joe's credentials with respect to three critical qualifications: time in grade, influencing styles of young broadcasters and a gift for painting a picture on radio that's as accurate, colorful and spellbinding.
> A note from you to John Doleva would be absolutely invaluable.
> Thanks and regards.
> Sincerely,
> David J. Halberstam

While Joe knew Halberstam, they were not close friends. This was just something Halberstam did because he believed it was the right thing.

"I appreciate all the people who supported me," said Joe. "I enjoyed going in the year after Al McCoy did, because we both came into the league about the same time, and we both preferred to do the game on radio alone. It's great that they still let old guys like us in the Hall."

*   *   *

While Joe worked and pushed to reach a major-league market, part of him was shaped by all the years doing high school and small college games in places such as Monmouth, Terre Haute and Rockford. With the Cavs, he still drew his own scorecard on a yellow legal pad. He used a four-colored pen.

"Before each game, I'd write down the lineups, the players on each bench, the scoring averages and other key stats," said Joe. "I kept track of points, rebounds, field goals, free throws, fouls and assists. Now, they keep track of everything on computers during the game, and all the information is on a screen in front of you, but I still did my own stats. It made me concentrate more on the game and prepare better."

Joe often did a few high school radio games each season. They usually were small schools in small towns where a small station had asked him if he'd be interested in calling a game.

"One day, I met Harry Paidas from Mount Union when I was doing a high school game in Warren," said Joe. "He was at the game and wondered what I was doing. I told him that I liked high school games. He asked me if I wanted to do some Mount Union football. He said they couldn't pay me, but they had a game set for cable TV. I said I'd 'absolutely' love to do it. And I loved it. That was in 1985, and it reminded me of being back in Monmouth doing Division III football, only Monmouth lost all the time. Mount has become a powerhouse. I do a few games each season—and I love it. I'll continue to do it until they drag me out the booth."

But why Mount Union?

"Because they were the first DIII school to ask," said Joe. "On the pro level, my favorite sport to do was the Cavaliers. But if I could pick anything, it's doing the Mount games. I like the coaches, the kids, everything about DIII football. They aren't trying to get to the NFL. About all of them graduate. It's about as pure as sports comes above the high school level."

*   *   *

Joe said he was determined to retire before he came down with heart disease that required major surgery in January 2011.

"For several years, the NBA had lost its luster for me," he said. "With all the noise and the hype, it was not an environment that I cared for. There was less and less about the league that I liked, and more and more that bothered me. I really got to dislike the travel. I was getting older, and I could tell from listening to my tapes that I wasn't quite as sharp. I began to cheat."

How so?

"It's like a player, your reactions aren't quite as quick," he said. "When I was younger, I could mention every player who touched the ball, where they were on the court and put the ball through the hole just a split second after the shot was made. But now, I couldn't do it. I'll say the ball was 'passed to the left side' and not go into great detail. The eye-mouth reactions were not what they used to be for me. I didn't want to hang on too long and become an embarrassment. Chick Hearn did the Lakers for too long, and it was embarrassing for him at the end. But he had been around for so long and been so popular, people forgave him."

Joe didn't want fans to have to do the same for him.

"In Boston, Johnny Most was a cartoon character near the end," Joe said. "I didn't want to be that."

Joe said he "worked harder" at the broadcast after his love affair with the NBA withered. He felt a duty to the fans to reflect the game, and he still loved the actual radio broadcast—even when things on the court and in the arena offended him.

"I once saw an interview with Sir Lawrence Olivier where he

said that some of his best work was in vehicles that he didn't care for," said Joe. "He said he had to reach deep and put more of himself into it—so he would avoid going through the motions. I felt like that at times in the last 10 to 15 years. I wanted the broadcast to be good. I wanted the fans to feel and see the game."

The Cavs asked Joe to return for the 2011–12 season on any terms. He could do all the games, home games or even "selected" games. But he declined.

"I think you either do them all or you don't do it," he said. "And it wouldn't be fair to the new broadcaster if I were hanging around. I was 73 when I started my final season. I had heart surgery. I had doctors looking me in the eye and telling me that I dodged a bullet. Down deep, I knew it was over."

Joe paused.

"I don't have a lot of talent in other areas," he said. "But I was blessed to be able to do something that I was good at and do it for a long time. I found a place where I felt comfortable and where the fans accepted me. Not many people are that lucky, especially to last as long as I did. I'll always be grateful for that."

Joe's banner hangs alongside two of the greats from the early days of the Cavaliers. *(NBA Photos courtesy Cleveland Cavaliers)*

Acknowledgments

The authors would like to thank the following for their interviews: Gordon Gund, Burt Graeff, Bill Fitch, Austin Carr, Jim Chones, Harry Weltman, Nancy Score and Bruce Drennan. Special thanks to Roberta Pluto for transcribing all of Joe Tait's interviews.

Thanks also to Tad Carper, Garin Narain, and Jaime Diewald of the Cleveland Cavaliers for their generous help with the photos.

*   *   *

Joe would like to thank Scott Zurilla, Dave Dombrowski, Joe Frietchen, John Cuiska and Harry Paidas for all their help over the decades with his broadcasts.

*   *   *

The authors are also grateful to David Gray, Butch Maier, Rob Lucas, Chris Andrikanich, Jane Lassar, Frank Lavallo and Faith Hamlin for making this project work.

For more information and samples from
other Terry Pluto books, visit:

www.TerryPluto.com